CLINT EASTWOOD

CLINT EASTWOOD

Gerald Cole and Peter Williams

W.H. ALLEN · LONDON
A Howard & Wyndham Company

Printed and bound in Great Britain by
Hazell Watson & Viney Ltd, Aylesbury
for the publishers, W. H. Allen & Co. Ltd,
44 Hill Street, London W1X 8LB

ISBN 0 491 03241 2 (W. H. Allen hardcover edition)
ISBN 0 86379 090 9 (Comet Books softcover edition)

For Ellen Soeters

Contents

The Making of a Loner 1

Debating whether genetics or environment has the greater effect on temperament is generally a fruitless endeavour, but the circumstances of Clint Eastwood Junior's early life quickly taught him the values of self-reliance and determination. He was born to Clinton and Ruth Eastwood on 31 May 1930 in San Francisco, the first of two children. The family was middle class – Clinton Senior had trained as a cost accountant – but America was deep in the Depression and work came from wherever it could be found, even if it meant pumping gas at a petrol station. The constant search for employment took the Eastwood family all over northern California, and until his teens the only permanent home Clinton Junior knew was his grandmother's chicken farm at Sunol, some hundred miles south-east of San Francisco. The grandmother lived alone – another lesson in self-sufficiency for Clinton Junior – and, conveniently for the future, she taught her grandson to ride.

The opportunity to establish roots only came when Clinton Senior got a perma-nent job with the Container Corporation of America and the family settled in Oakland, across the bay from San Francisco. Clinton Junior found himself at Oakland Technical High School with the first real chance of his life to form lasting friendships. It wasn't an ideal time. Long years of uncertainty had thrown him back on himself; he was introverted and intensely shy and as if the normal agonies of adolescence weren't enough he was conspicuously, embarrassingly tall. At the age of fifteen he had reached his present six feet four inches. 'I was the original hang-up man,' he was to recall later. 'I was so much a loner, so introverted in those days that I simply couldn't express myself. I just drew a sort of invisible coat of armour around myself. I used to pray I'd get to be an extrovert – it seemed to be an answer to most of my personal problems.'

That desire may have prompted an English teacher to give him the first acting role of his life – in the class play. Eastwood himself rather doubts it. The role was that of an introverted teenager and it smacked

STANDARD CERTIFICATE OF BIRTH — STATE OF CALIFORNIA, DEPARTMENT OF PUBLIC HEALTH, VITAL STATISTICS

PLACE OF BIRTH. Dist. No. 3801 — City and County of SAN FRANCISCO — No. 8419

(No. Saint Francis Hospital)

FULL NAME OF CHILD: Clinton Eastwood, Jr.

PERSONAL AND STATISTICAL PARTICULARS

SEX OF CHILD: Male

DATE OF BIRTH: May 31st 1930

FATHER — FULL NAME: Clinton Eastwood — RESIDENCE: 637-Beacon Street, Oakland, Calif. — COLOR OR RACE: White — AGE AT LAST BIRTHDAY: 23 — BIRTHPLACE: California — OCCUPATION: Bond Salesman

MOTHER — FULL MAIDEN NAME: Margaret Ruth Runner — RESIDENCE: 637-Beacon Street, Oakland, Calif. — COLOR OR RACE: White — AGE AT LAST BIRTHDAY: 21 — BIRTHPLACE: California — OCCUPATION: Housewife

Was a prophylactic for Ophthalmia Neonatorum used? Yes — If so, what? Agno 3 Sol. 1%

Number of children born to this mother, including present birth: 1
Number of children of this mother now living: 1

CERTIFICATE OF ATTENDING PHYSICIAN OR MIDWIFE

Dated June 3 1930 — Address 384 Post St, City — Filed JUN 4 1930

of type casting. Whatever the teacher's motive, it was no favour to Clinton Junior. The experience caused him agonies of embarrassment and fear, etching itself deep into his memory. Ironically – and to his surprise– he actually enjoyed the time he spent on stage, but the cost of that pleasure was much too high. He vowed on the spot never to have anything to do with acting again.

Unfortunately he had no clear idea of what else he might like to do. His academic record was on the better side of average and his athletic ability – especially in basketball – excellent. But the closest he came to choosing a clear path in life was to admire those who seemed capable of doing so. Even his father's middle class background provided no pointer; an extended education hadn't prevented all those years of insecurity and worry. Clinton Senior did, however, have one piece of advice to give which his son never forgot – 'You don't get anything for nothing.'

'Although I rebelled,' Eastwood was to comment later, 'I never rebelled against that.'

When he graduated from school in the

8

summer of 1948 his first instinct was to assert his independence, despite an offer from his family to keep supporting him. Physical activity has always appealed to him – vacation jobs at school had included baling hay in Yreka, close to the Oregon border in northern California, and fire-fighting in the forests around Paradise, also in northern California – the beauty and solitude of the woods attracted him deeply. It seemed logical to renew that acquaintance and combine it with work in the open air.

Accordingly Eastwood retraced his vacation trail northward, arriving finally in the small town of Springfield in eastern Oregon, America's timber state. His earlier forestry experience quickly earned him a job in a local lumber camp. The pay was good for the time – one dollar eighty an hour – but that was mainly because the work was seasonal, and very hard. The working day lasted from sunrise to sunset, leaving Eastwood and his fellow loggers only enough energy to drop into their bunks as night fell. The one exception was Saturday night, marked by a ritual visit to the nearest town – Springfield itself, or Eugene beyond – and an obligation to get drunk as quickly as possible. 'I thought those movies about rough-and-ready lumberjacks were exaggerated,' Eastwood recalls. 'Maybe they were, but not much. One night I was standing at the bar of a saloon in Springfield when another logger punched me in the face without warning. Before you knew it, the whole place was in the damnedest fight I ever saw.'

It could have been a scene from *Every Which Way But Loose* – Eastwood's comic paean of praise to the bar brawling fraternity. Equally the all-male environment, the rugged surroundings and the tough and dangerous conditions of the job were an almost perfect match for the trail-driving world of *Rawhide*. However macho Eastwood's screen image was to become he could always back it up with direct experience.

At the time, though, the job served a more nebulous but no less important function as a kind of youthful self-testing. Physically Eastwood passed and he seemed to have no obvious problems with his work-mates but when the camp broke up for winter he alone elected to stay on. He took a job in the logging company's pulp mill – work only marginally less arduous and just as dangerous as logging itself – and lived on his own in a small cabin. Self-reliance and introversion were combining in a need for privacy and solitude – a need that was to become a key part of Eastwood's personality.

The appeal of Oregon's mountain scenery waned in the winter when skies can be clouded for months at a time and, a year after leaving home, Eastwood moved on. His family, meanwhile, had followed a new job to Seattle, Washington where Eastwood joined them. His first employment was again notable for its toughness – and the size of the wage: the value of business acumen was another early lesson – careful savings had bought him his first car at the age of fifteen and for exactly fifteen dollars. He stoked blast furnaces on the graveyard shift at the Bethlehem Steel Plant – the hours were from midnight to nine in the morning. Part of its limited appeal was that it left the days free – but it also left Eastwood exhausted. He was soon on the move again.

A succession of temporary jobs followed: truck-driving, lifeguard on a public beach at the small town of Renton on the outskirts of Seattle, filing invoices in the parts department of the Boeing Aircraft Corporation, also in Renton. Over a number of interviews Eastwood has made much of the aimlessness of his lifestyle at this time, describing himself variously as 'a drifter', 'a loner', 'a bum'. But the rootlessness of those years did not imply a lack of responsibility. Paying his own way was as important as independence; he was never a rebel in the accepted sense. His personal life was, if anything, abstemious: he didn't smoke, he drank only occasionally and then only beer, and his shyness kept women at bay – up to a point. As physical labour filled out his lanky frame, he found his good looks attracting a more than fair share of female attention. He also discovered that he had a great deal of personal charm.

Yet the very moderation of his drifting life – itself providing a kind of mental prototype of the nameless hero of the 'spaghetti' Westerns which would one day make him famous – suggested it was only a direction he lacked; determination, application, strength of character – all existed in embryo. That, and the approach of his twenty-first birthday, persuaded Eastwood that he could put off a serious choice of career no longer. The decision he made prefigured the future in an unexpected way. He would go back to full-time education, majoring in music.

In fact the choice wasn't entirely arbitrary. Eastwood had displayed some talent at school as a pianist and trumpet player, though the athletic field had been more of an attraction at the time. With the horizon still an unpromising blank, it must have looked as likely an option as any other. Unfortunately that blank was about to be filled.

The news reached him in a telegram which arrived at his parents' home. 'Greetings,' it read, 'from the President of the United States.' It was the American Services' uniquely personal method of informing the country's young men that they were about to give up two years of their lives.

Eastwood was ordered to report to Fort Ord near Carmel on the Monterey peninsular, only a few miles south of his birthplace. The abrupt change of circumstances wasn't as traumatic to him as it was to many of his contemporaries. His basic fitness allowed him to survive the sixteen weeks' initial army training with energy to spare and there was a bonus. Monterey and the Carmel valley might not boast the magnificent forest scenery of Oregon, but it was bordered by one of the most spectacular coastlines in the world. That – and the small town of Carmel itself, an artists' colony since the turn of the century with an air of well-heeled charm – attracted Eastwood immediately. He promised himself that if financial success ever did come his way one of his first moves would be to buy a house in the area. It was a promise he kept.

For the moment, however, most of his attention was focussed on a bleak landscape some seven thousand miles to the west. The outbreak of the Korean War had coincided with Eastwood's drafting and he fully expected to be posted for active duty. Rather to his surprise, although most of his fellow trainees were shipped overseas straight after induction,

A young Eastwood as Rowdy Yates in Rawhide

10

he wasn't, and he wasted no time in building on his apparent good luck.

Hearing a rumour that swimming instructors were needed at the camp's pool, he sold his abilities to the captain in charge, going into 'my act as a Johnny Weismuller type. I told them I was absolutely the greatest swimmer going.' It worked and for the next two years he gave swimming classes to the new recruits, initially in a junior capacity and then in full charge when his superiors were despatched to Korea. The arrangement suited his captain – a non-swimmer – perfectly; a sweat shirt conveniently disguised Eastwood's humble rank.

For the first time in his life Eastwood found himself with a decidedly soft option. His army pay might only amount to seventy-six dollars a month but the work was enjoyable and undemanding with plenty of free time – he was even allowed to sleep in his own poolside accommodation, even if it did only consist of a hut. But the unprecedented ease of his new existence rankled with Eastwood – as did his earnings. He was starting to cash in on his gook looks and a couple of nights out with members of the local female population could easily dispose of a month's money. Within a short while he was supplementing his income with evening work at the Spreckles Sugar Refinery in the nearby Salinas valley. The work was hard – shifting fifty-pound sacks of sugar – well-paid and not at all according to army regulations. But it was four months before the authorities found out and the work came to an abrupt end.

The setback proved only temporary. He was soon rehired as a bartender in the camp's Non-Commissioned Officers' club – for less money but less effort, with the

additional perk of five or six free bottles of his favourite Olympia beer every night. Eastwood's service career resumed its unruffled tenor.

Three important events were to disturb it before he was eventually discharged. Two were to change the course of his life dramatically. The third – and most dramatic of all – almost ended it. It occurred at the end of a visit Eastwood made to Seattle on a weekend pass to see his parents. While in his studio biographies he would always be careful to stress his good relationship with his family, there seem to have been signs of strain up to the time he joined the army. With a personality so introverted and so keen to establish independence – he didn't remain at home after his return from Oregon – some awkwardness is understandable. But the distance that the army put between them – and possibly the regularity of a settled existence – appears to have drawn family and son closer together, and Eastwood made the trip north with relative frequency.

On this occasion, however, he had overstayed his welcome, at least as far as the army was concerned. His weekend pass was within hours of expiring and he had left himself no means of getting back to Fort Ord in time.

His last hope lay in hitching a ride with a military air transport and he tried his luck at the local navy air base. No one was heading for Monterey, but a torpedo bomber was about to leave for San Francisco. It was a single-seater and the pilot wasn't inclined to break the regulations to crowd a six feet four inch army private into the cockpit with him. It took all of Eastwood's powers of persuasion to make him change his mind. The pilot still wouldn't allow his passenger in the cockpit but Eastwood could take his chances in a small maintenance compartment at the rear of the aircraft. If he had known how slim those chances were to turn out he would gladly have accepted a charge of being absent without leave. Minutes after the bomber had taken off, the door of the compartment into which Eastwood had squeezed himself flew open. Struggling to prevent himself being sucked out, he tried to call the pilot over the intercom but it only appeared to be working one way; he was unable to make himself heard. In desperation he grabbed at a length of cable and managed to loop it round the door handle, pulling the door shut. The catch was broken but by hanging onto the cable he could keep the door closed. It was scary and even more uncomfortable than before but he would be safe.

Events now took on the character of a well-crafted suspense thriller – one, ironically, that only a character with Eastwood's screen persona might be expected to survive.

Over the one-way intercom he heard the pilot announce that they were starting to climb and it was time to put on an oxygen mask. There was a mask in Eastwood's compartment but when he put it on nothing seemed to happen. The aircraft tilted upward, the engine note changed and the temperature began to drop. Eastwood was still shouting for help through the defective intercom when loss of oxygen caused him to black out. Here only good luck saved him. The pilot also began to have problems with his oxygen supply and was forced to lower his height. Eastwood regained consciousness only to become aware of another, equally serious problem.

Fog had closed in over the bomber's destination, and the pilot seemed none too certain of his position. Worse than that, the fuel supply was low. As darkness fell, the aircraft skimmed over the sea, searching for a familiar landmark or even a light. The pilot was still looking when the engines skipped a beat, coughed and finally died.

The crashlanding, when it came, proved to be relatively smooth, though Eastwood had only a few seconds to extricate himself from his cramped compartment. He met the pilot – who was wearing the aircraft's only lifejacket – on the wing. Neither had any clear idea where the coast was but the rapidly sinking bomber forced a swift decision and they set off together in what they hoped was the right direction. In fact they had come down some three miles off Point Reyes, a stretch of national seashore about twenty miles north of San Francisco and not the most densely populated of coastlines.

In the darkness the two men soon lost each other. Eastwood had no choice but to swim on alone and after an hour was rewarded with the faint outline of a rocky shore. But even at this late stage fate had another hand to deal – in the shape of a swarm of highly dangerous jelly fish.

'I thought I might die,' he recalls. 'But then I thought, "Other people have made it through these things before." I kept my eyes on the lights on shore and kept swimming.' Nevertheless it took all his remaining strength to negotiate a safe path and so exhausted was he that he has no clear memory of reaching the beach. All he remembers is waking up and finding himself sprawled on some rocks.

The coast seemed deserted and there was no sign of the bomber pilot, who actually landed safely some five hundred yards further along the shore. Eastwood took his bearings from the lights of a radio relay station he could just see and began walking. 'I didn't mind the swim,' he was later to joke, 'but that five-mile hike before I found a highway really bothered me.'

The whole hair-raising incident had been the strongest test yet, and the clearest vindication of Eastwood's qualities of self-reliance. Luck had certainly been with him but even a moment's faltering would have cost him his life. It was a lesson he would not forget.

One of the first people to hear the story was a young student at the University of California at Berkeley, over the bay from San Francisco. Her name was Maggie Johnson; she was blonde, attractive and intelligent and she had made a strong impression on the young Eastwood. He had met her through an old schoolfriend, Don Kincaid – a contemporary whom Eastwood had admired for his clarity of purpose: Kincaid had always wanted to be a dentist and worked hard until he had achieved his ambition. At the time he was going out with a girl at Berkeley and she had a room-mate who might be Eastwood's type. That at least was Kincaid's argument and it seems to have been persuasive: Eastwood gave up two local engagements – a clear sign of his growing popularity with the opposite sex – to join his friend on a weekend visit to Berkeley.

His sacrifice – and Kincaid's arguments – proved to be correct. Eastwood and Maggie got on well from the first moment they met. He liked her good looks, and her height – she was five feet seven – not a negligible consideration for a self-conscious young man who usually towered over his partners. They shared a similar sense of humour and a love of the outdoors. Most importantly, Eastwood commented later, 'there was nothing phony about her'. Seeing through to the heart of things, spotting the essentials of any situation and acting on that observation, would become one of the mainstays of Eastwood's success, allowing him to make artistic and business decisions that seemed to militate against every conventional piece of wisdom or advice but which usually turned our right. That quality already existed in him in his constant desire to be true to himself, to measure himself against his own criteria, largely regardless of what others thought. Meeting a girl – and an attractive one – who seemed capable of the same clarity of mind was a jolt, but a distinctly pleasurable one. Eastwood's previous relationships with women had been conducted on a much more basic level. The 'few brews' and quiet conversation he enjoyed on his first date with Maggie was something quite new.

'It was no such thing as love at first sight,' he remembers, 'but we liked one another right away.' While each of them continued to go out with others, a chord had been struck and Eastwood began to spend more and more weekends at Berkeley.

It was during this time that an equally important meeting took place at Fort Ord. A film unit from Universal Studios used the camp for some location shooting and a curious Eastwood watched them at work. Over a lunch break an assistant director introduced himself and suggested that Eastwood's looks might bring him some film work. The unit's director agreed and

An early studio portrait

14

told the young conscript to look him up at Universal when his service was over and see if a screen test could be arranged.

If Eastwood's views on acting had remained as they were after his traumatic experience on the school stage he might have been inclined to dismiss the entire incident – but they had not. His service career had brought him into contact with two professionals, the late David Janssen – later to star in *The Fugitive* and *Harry O* – and Martin Milner – who was to achieve popularity in *Route 66*. Both had been on the stage since childhood and encouraged Eastwood to try his hand. Though he was still unconvinced he had to admit 'they seemed to enjoy themselves'.

When his discharge came in February 1953, however, he felt he owed it to himself to take up the visiting director's offer, and he travelled down the coast to Hollywood. Whatever hopes he might have harboured were quickly dashed – the director had moved on from Universal.

But he still had his ambition to resume his education and, under the GI bill, he now had the money to do it. His plan to major in music hadn't survived his service career; instead he enrolled in the Los Angeles City College for a course in business administration. 'That,' he was to comment later, 'is what every student does who hasn't the faintest idea of what he wants to do when he graduates.'

Once more his monthly allotment – of $110 – proved insufficient. He took a part-time job as a petrol attendant in a Signal Oil gas station on Santa Monica Boulevard – convenient both for the beach and the unemployment office, which happened to be opposite. He found himself a small apartment in Beverly Hills and paid for it by supervising the apartment building for

its owners. Other part-time employment followed: as a lifeguard again and digging the foundations of swimming pools for the United Pool Company.

He took this last job with a friend, George Fargo, and an incident that occurred there reveals another side of Eastwood's personality. The two young men got into an argument with a foreman who eventually fired Fargo. Immediately Eastwood began peeling off his work clothes. The foreman asked what was up. 'Well,' Eastwood replied, 'George is my friend and he hasn't got a ride home.' And the job was over. Eastwood's friendship is not granted easily, but once given his loyalty is fierce. Most of his closest friends pre-date his success and as a director and producer of films he prefers to work with a close-knit technical team of familiar faces.

Eastwood's abrupt departure from the United Pool Company, however, wasn't entirely altruistic. Life in his first year in Los Angeles was hard and not particularly rewarding. The business course was less a concrete decision than a sop to his own urge to make good; underneath he was as aimless as ever. Only one strand in his life seemed to hold any promise – a career in acting: he was still in touch with Janssen and Milner who continued to persuade him to give it a try. But as 1953 drew to a close something happened to bring all of Eastwood's hopes and ambitions into sharp focus. On 19 December he married Maggie Johnson.

Maggie had come to Los Angeles after graduating from Berkeley and taken a job as a secretary with Industria Americana, a firm which exported car spares. Despite Eastwood's work commitments they had seen a lot of each other, soon reaching a point where marriage seemed both inevit-

16

able and desirable. After a quiet wedding they honeymooned in Carmel but the circumstances of their lives did not change markedly; within a short while Maggie was adding to their joint income by modelling part-time for the swimsuit manufacturers, Caltex and Catalina.

Eastwood had reached a point where, whatever his misgivings, he felt he should give Hollywood another try. Gathering together some photographs Irving Lasper – a still photographer and close friend – had taken of him, he went back to Universal Studios. This time his persistence paid off. A staff director called Arthur Lubin – he had been responsible for a number of Abbott and Costello comedies and, most notably, a 1943 version of *The Phantom of the Opera* starring Claude Rains – gave him a screen test. It was of a peculiar kind – generally known as a 'personality' test. There was no dialogue nor any kind of acting ability demanded; the person under test was simply encouraged to chat about themselves in front of a lens, the object being to judge their photogenic quality, if any – to see if the camera 'liked' them.

The result didn't impress Eastwood. 'I thought I was an absolute clod,' he told *Playboy* magazine in a rare interview in 1974. 'It looked pretty good; it was photographed well, but I thought "if that's acting, I'm in trouble!"'

But it was progress and he couldn't disguise his jubilance when he rushed home to report to Maggie and to wait for the verdict. And wait, and wait.

Over the next fortnight Eastwood earned himself a crash introduction to the chronic insecurity and frustration of an actor's life. Not a word came from Universal. At last Eastwood tried to ring Lubin direct, without success. Two weeks stretched into a third and he began to believe his initial misgivings had been only too accurate. Then, early one morning, a telephone call summoned him to Universal. No news, it turned out, had been good news. The studio were willing to offer him a six-month contract at seventy-five dollars a week. Clinton Eastwood, ex-logger, ex-conscript, ex-digger of luxury swimming pools, had become an actor.

Cowboy Beginnings
From *Revenge of the Creature*
to *Rawhide*

Playing the Universal Star Game

If Eastwood began his acting career with an understandable burst of optimism it wasn't an emotion shared by Hollywood. The golden years of America's film industry – dominated by the major studios, Columbia, Fox, MGM, Paramount, RKO, United Artists and Universal – had been the thirties, when Hollywood's movies, and the stars they created, ruled the cinema-going world. Even the hiccup of the Second World War seemed a relatively minor interruption. The loss of overseas markets was more than compensated for by a massive upsurge in cinema attendance at home, and 1946 proved to be the most profitable year in the history of Hollywood. But within a few short years all that was to change.

A series of body blows began with serious labour difficulties, culminating in a 25 per cent pay increase for studio employees. At the same time anti-trust laws – applied particularly against Paramount and MGM – insisted that the major studios separate their production and distribution operations; previously they had controlled both, allowing them to maintain a stranglehold on virtually every aspect of popular cinema in the United States. Then in October 1947 the House Committee on Un-American Activities opened its 'investigation of communism in motion pictures'. Panicking, Hollywood began a self-lacerating process that lasted until 1951 and resulted in the blacklisting of some of its finest and most incisive talents. At its height the mildest social comment in a film might be denounced as rampant subversion. The 'reds-under-the-beds' scare not only vitiated Hollywood's ability to mirror and respond to the hopes and aspirations of its traditional audiences, it left the way wide open to film makers who didn't share its squeamishness. Foreign directors like Poland's Andrzej Wajda and Italy's Vittorio De Sica and Roberto Rossellini made films so grittily realistic and so powerful they seemed to come from a different universe. In its weakened state – still hidebound by the practices of the thirties – Hollywood could not hope to compete, at least in

19

terms of innovation. But its biggest threat came from home. The novel medium of television seemed to offer everything the cinema could and much more conveniently; its audience didn't even have to leave its own fireside. Furthermore its financial organisation was much more secure. Its revenue came from advertising which was paid in advance, guaranteeing the profitability of any given programme. And if the programme's popularity waned for any reason it could be chopped overnight – most television at this time was live. The studios, meanwhile, had no guarantee of anything, beyond the previous track records of their stars. Each new film demanded a heavy capital outlay. It might be weeks before its success or failure could be judged and, if it failed, the only way to recoup the loss was to spend yet more money on another film – and all this at a time of steadily increasing costs.

When Eastwood joined the industry cinema audiences were declining, from a peak of 90 million weekly attendances in 1948 to barely 35 million in 1956. Fortunately for him Universal Studios still followed the thirties pattern of signing up large numbers of hopeful young actors and actresses on the assumption that one or two might eventually attain the stature of their current contract stars, Rock Hudson, Tony Curtis and Jeff Chandler. In exchange for lessons in screen acting and general 'grooming' to fit the required model, the new recruits were used in walk-on roles and minor bit-parts. It was the closest Hollywood came to a screen apprenticeship but its success or failure depended entirely on each individual – and a large degree of luck.

But for the first time in his life Eastwood had a worthy focus for his energies and he decided to make the best of his chance. While Universal were teaching him the rudiments of performing on film – they included riding (for Westerns), sword-fighting (for swashbuckling), dancing and table manners (for more genteel productions) – he began additional evening classes in acting. His diligence paid off. At the end of six months his contract was renewed, his salary raised to a hundred dollars a month and his first screen appearance soon followed.

It was in a science-fiction B-movie called *The Revenge of the Creature*, a sequel to one of the studio's bigger successes of the previous year, *The Creature from the Black Lagoon*. Directed by Jack Arnold – a science fiction specialist who had establised his other worldly reputation with *It Came From Outer Space* in 1953 and in 1957 would make the classic *Incredible Shrinking Man* – it was shot in 3-D – one of Hollywood's numerous technical counterploys to the attractions of television. The plot concerned a prehistoric gill-man (actually a skin-diver in a rather impressive costume) who is discovered, coelacanth-fashion, in a tributary of the Amazon and brought back to Florida. There, in the manner of most movie monsters from King Kong onward, he escapes and wreaks general havoc.

Eastwood had a name part – that of Jennings, a lowly lab assistant – so lowly, in fact, that his screen appearance lasted only seconds. It involved fumbling around for a missing laboratory mouse and in Eastwood's judgement was only included because the film was running short.

But it led to a slightly more substantial part in *Francis In The Navy*, one of a comedy series starring Donald O'Connor and a talking mule whose voice was supplied by Chill Wills. Eastwood played one of

O'Connor's sailor companions – the plot involved the mule being mistakenly drafted into the services. His dialogue was as minimal as in the first film, but he was conspicuous enough to earn his first critical plaudits, even if they only amounted to single-word comments – 'engaging' and 'promising' being among them.

In the eighteen months Eastwood spent at Universal he was to make fourteen appearances in all, but only six to any visible degree. They included *Tarantula* – another Jack Arnold film where Eastwood, totally disguised by helmet, mask and goggles, played a jet pilot who deals the death blow to the movie's conventionally rampaging monster – a fifty feet high, atomically mutated spider. There was also *Lady Godiva* with Maureen O'Hara and George Nader with direction by the man who had given Eastwood his initial screen test, Arthur Lubin. In a rather dull tale, whose title promised rather more than Hollywood felt it prudent to reveal at the time, Eastwood was billed as First Saxon, though at the bottom of the credit list. But it was better than *Star In The Dust*, Eastwood's first western where he received no billing at all.

Eastwood was learning a lot but times were far from easy. There were problems at home where Maggie contracted hepatitis, having it 'about as badly as you can get it without ceasing to exist', Eastwood recalls. She was unable to work properly for a year; that, and the medical bills for her treatment, put a heavy financial burden on the young couple. Eastwood's salary might be a hundred dollars a week by now but his contract only guaranteed forty weeks' work a year.

There were growing problems at the studio too. Like many young actors before

and after him, Eastwood was becoming aware of a classic dilemma of the profession. Parts for young male actors are relatively scarce – the better roles come with maturity as they reach their thirties and forties – while the reverse applies to young women. Cinema – and theatre – are full of ingenue and femme fatale roles; at the very least, a pretty girl with promise, or only moderate talent, can find employment in a decorative role. As a result the young actresses on Universal's contract roll outnumbered the young actors by up to four to one. The pressure was on the men to make good very quickly.

Eastwood was quite prepared to work as hard as necessary. What rankled with him was the studio's persistent attempt to mould him in what they regarded as a 'star' image. He was criticised, variously, for being too tall, for walking with a slouch, for speaking too softly and without sufficient inflection. It was an assault on the sense of self-reliance and independence he had spent so long in building up, and, worse than that, it seemed to be based on false premises. Hollywood's only guideline to future success was success in the past. If a newcomer didn't somehow fit into a proven mould – as the 'new' Tony Curtis, or Clark Gable or Gary Cooper – he was an unknown quantity and therefore not worth risking where money was concerned.

But the studios were equally aware that the biggest stars were usually outsiders, newcomers who broke the existing moulds. Their way out of this Catch-22 situation was to give their young contract 'stars' as much exposure as possible in a variety of films. Hopefully a spark of fresh talent would catch the eye of studio executives – or the fans.

1795-3

FORM D-16 2M SETS 3-56 A.P.

RKO Radio Pictures
DAY PLAYER AGREEMENT

Date of Agreement	Name	
1/7/57	CLINT EASTWOOD	
Date Employment Starts	Address	Phone No.
1/8/57		POp. 22473
Weather Condition	Part	
RS	Dumbo Pilot	
Time on Set	Production Title	
9:45 am	Lubin — #812	
Wardrobe or Make-Up Call	Daily Rate	Weekly Rate
9:00 am – M 9:30 am – W	$175.00	

This agreement covers the employment of the above named Player by RKO Radio Pictures, in the production and at the rate of compensation set forth above and is subject to all of the provisions and conditions applicable to the employment of day players contained or provided for in the "Revised Basic Agreement of 1952" between the Screen Actors Guild, Inc., and RKO Radio Pictures, as such agreement may be supplemented or amended; and the Player warrants, represents and agrees that the Player is and shall be a member in good standing of Screen Actors Guild, Inc., and will remain so for the duration of this employment.

The Player hereby grants to RKO Radio Pictures, its successors and assigns forever, without limitations, all rights throughout the world in and to all results and proceeds of the Player's services rendered hereunder, including but not limited to, the rights to reproduce, use, perform, exhibit and dispose of, in any manner or through any means or medium whatsoever, any pictures, likenesses or reproductions made hereunder of the Player, his poses, acts, plays, performances and appearances, and any recordations or reproductions made hereunder of the Player's voice, and of all instrumental, musical or other sound effects produced by the Player, together with the right to use and display the Player's name and likeness for commercial and advertising purposes in connection therewith.

RKO RADIO PICTURES
A Division of
RKO Teleradio Pictures, Inc.

Clint Eastwood   By _William Hurbit_
Player   Casting Director

In those first brief appearances Eastwood did not appear to do either. When his second six-month option – and a rise of twenty-five dollars a month – became due, Universal were only prepared to renew his contract at the existing salary.

It was a blow to Eastwood's ego and for a while he was tempted to walk out – he was quite capable of breaking the mask of his taciturnity with bursts of temper at this time. But his period at Universal had taught him how little he knew of the movie business and he realised how invaluable further experience was, however frustrating at present. He was rewarded with his most substantial role yet – all four lines of it – but it was opposite one of Universal's top names, Rock Hudson.

The film was *Never Say Goodbye*, a sentimental account of divorced parents reuniting to provide a home for their child. The cast included Eastwood's ex-army colleague, David Janssen and Eastwood found himself once more in a laboratory assistant's white coat. An incident during filming gives at least some indication that he was developing an actor's eye for props. Director Jerry Hopper wanted him to wear glasses to lend a more serious look to his youthful features. Eastwood sorted through about a dozen pairs and selected a pair that seemed right. The moment Rock Hudson saw him wearing them he demanded some too. The selection process was repeated and Hudon made his choice – the pair Eastwood was wearing.

The triumph, however small, was short-lived. Universal failed to renew his con-

Top: A scene from Francis In The Navy, *1955. Eastwood, on the far left, played the part of Jonesy, the sailor. Bottom: Eastwood's first contract with RKO Radio Pictures*

tract a third time and he was back to digging swimming pools.

At the beginning this sudden blow seemed fortuitous. Arthur Lubin – director of Eastwood's first screen test – was now working with RKO Radio Pictures on a comedy to be called *The First Travelling Saleslady*. The unlikely adventures of a corset designer and her secretary who try to sell barbed wire in the Wild West, it was to star Ginger Rogers and comedienne Carol Channing, and Lubin had a part for Eastwood. He was to play a young army officer, smitten with Miss Channing, and was promised 'introducing' billing – a considerable step up from his Universal appearances.

Though Eastwood's height may have had a good deal to do with his choice – Miss Channing was, and is, by no means short – the part gave him his first close-ups and the opportunity to play romantic light comedy. He acquitted himself well but the film died a death at the box office.

Nevertheless RKO were impressed enough to cast Eastwood in a second film, *Escapade in Japan*. The story of two young boys, American and Japanese, who go in search of the former's parents in Japan after a plane crash, it was little more than an extended travelogue. Directed again by Arthur Lubin, Eastwood played Dumbo, an unconventional American pilot who gives the boys the idea for their quest.

For a while it looked as if he might build a reasonable freelance career on his RKO work, but the hope proved illusory. Affairs at the studio had been unsettled since Howard Hughes had bought a controlling interest in 1948. *Escapade in Japan* was hardly finished before Hughes decided finally to sell out. The film was released, ironically enough, through Universal, who

23

showed no inclination to renew Eastwood's contract on the strength of it. Under its new owners, RKO abandoned film making.

There followed one of the most trying periods of Eastwood's career. The usual difficulties of any young actor attempting to make his way were exacerbated by heavy cutbacks in Hollywood – between 1951 and 1959 film production dropped from around four hundred new films a year to less than two hundred. The B-movie, once a fertile source of employment for the budding screen actor, was fast disappearing.

There was only one growth area in the acting profession – television, now finding its feet as an entertainment medium. But it was still generally despised by the Hollywood fraternity, regarded as a definite backward step after the kudos of a studio contract.

Between bouts of swimming pool construction, lifeguarding and unemployment, Eastwood was inclined to take a more pragmatic view. 'TV was like a younger brother, or a second-class citizen,' he recalls. 'But to me it was a logical place to really learn the business. Most of the people in television were doing the newest things, and in TV you had to work twice as fast, twice as hard to get half the credits.'

He began to find small roles in series like *Navy Log*, *Man of Annapolis*, *West Point* and *Highway Patrol* – which gained him his first piece of fan mail. Most of these involved action of some kind and he built on that slim foundation by offering to do his own stunt work in any roles that demanded it. 'Once in a while,' he says, 'I'd get a supporting lead because I could ride a motorcycle, jump off a building or

some crazy thing.' It was the beginning of a reputation for tough roles and in 1957, a year after his last big screen appearance, it seemed to be leading back into a cinema career. Twentieth Century-Fox offered him a supporting role in *Ambush At Cimarron Pass*.

In a conventional tale of former Civil War enemies uniting to fight off marauding Apache indians, Eastwood played a contentious ex-Confederate. It was shot in just ten days and the studio hoped to give it distinction by filming it in a new colour technique known as Regalscope. Neither the film, nor the process, made much impression. It might have provided Eastwood with his largest role yet – and praise for his 'fine portrayal' from the show-business newspaper *Variety* – but he had no hesitation in dubbing it 'probably the worst movie ever made'.

He followed it with another cinema role in what promised to be his most important film yet, though he had not a word of dialogue. Warner Brothers' *Lafayette Escadrille* – a would-be epic on the volunteer American pilot unit of the French air corps in World War One – was to be directed by the veteran director William Wellman. Wellman was something of a Hollywood legend. Hard-drinking and hard-talking, he had won the industry's very first best picture Academy Award with his aviation classic *Wings* in 1927. Other notable successes included *The Public Enemy* in 1931 – which launched James Cagney – and the classic 1943 western, *The Ox-Bow Incident*.

Top: Ambush At Cimarron Pass, *1958. This was Eastwood's first major part.* Bottom: A scene from Lafayette Escadrille, *1958. Eastwood is on the far left*

24

Wellman had actually been an ace pilot in the Lafayette Escadrille and great things were expected of the film. Unfortunately the successes of his career had been matched by more than a few pedestrian efforts and this proved to be one. It was his last film and, as it happened, the last that Eastwood would make for almost seven years.

The Seven-Year Hitch

By the end of the 1950s the B-movie might have gone into serious decline on America's cinema screens, but it enjoyed a highly successful renaissance elsewhere – in the television series.

Television companies found an irresistible audience winner in weekly dramas featuring the same character or characters in broadly similar plot situations. Understandably, if ironically, most of those dramas were derived from Hollywood originals and in 1958 none was more popular than that B-movie staple, the Western. Over thirty Western series flashed across America's television screens at this time, with only the most popular reaching British shores – *Wagon Train, Maverick, Wyatt Earp, Cheyenne, Bronco, Laramie, Have Gun Will Travel*, and so on.

Top of the league was indisputably *Gunsmoke*, which was to run a record-breaking twenty years. Created by producer Charles Marquis Warren for CBS television, it opened in 1955 as a half-hour weekly series. Three years later NBC's hour-length *Wagon Train* was rivalling it in the ratings and Warren was keen to match the newcomer's success with a sixty-minute Western series for CBS.

Like *Wagon Train*, it was to be a travelling series built around a group of familiar characters but with more realism and more emphasis on the working life of the nineteenth-century professional cowboy. The historical model was the massive cattle drives from Texas to the railheads of the Mid-West in the 1860s with background details culled from contemporary accounts – chiefly George C. Duffield's *Traildrover's Diary*. The Hollywood model was Howard Hawks' 1948 Western classic *Red River* – an account of the first such drive along the legendary Chisholm Trail. The film featured two principal characters – John Wayne, the elder, more experienced would-be cattle baron and Montgomery Clift as his youthful, more impetuous antagonist.

When Eastwood's agent got wind of the project and rang CBS to see if his client might suit the lead role, Warren was still thinking in terms of a single hero for the series, the trail boss of the herd. He would have to be in his late thirties and, as Eastwood himself pointed out, 'I don't photograph old at all.' CBS agreed. Eastwood was now twenty-eight with some four years in the acting profession behind him and a fair number of credits to his name, though none he felt particularly happy about. His chief interest still lay in the cinema, but a role in a successful television series was a worthy goal. The financial security and the opportunity to gain experience it offered had as much appeal to Eastwood's habitually cautious nature as the fame.

But the new western series – to be called *Rawhide* – was far from the forefront of his mind when he called in at CBS to see an old friend of his and Maggie's. Sonia Chernus was then working in the script department and had a good deal of inside knowledge on the network's new projects. That included *Rawhide* and when Eastwood described what his agent had discovered she thought it would do no harm to try a personal approach. She took Eastwood along to the office of Robert Sparks, the executive producer of the series. Rather to Eastwood's surprise he expressed an immediate interest and called in Charles Marquis Warren for a second opinion.

It emerged that the network were now looking for two leads for the new series. Most of the top-rated Westerns boasted twosomes: wagonmaster Ward Bond and scout Robert Horton in *Wagon Train*, Marshall James Arness and deputy Dennis Weaver in *Gunsmoke*, gambler James Garner and rascally brother Jack Kelly in *Maverick*. Warren was moving closer to the *Red River* model. He had already cast the role of the trail boss and was searching for a suitable foil.

Eastwood went through his credits – 'always increasing the importance of the roles by about fifty per cent, praying to God they would never ask to see *Ambush At Cimarron Pass*. Which of course they did.' Depressed at the thought of the executives' reaction when they saw 'the worst movie ever made', he went home – only to receive a phone call that afternoon. Despite Eastwood's misgivings they were impressed; they wanted him to do a screen test.

It was the start of an emotional rollercoaster – as if ill fortune were determined to have its final fling before yielding, at long last, to good.

The screen test did not go well. Eastwood had difficulties with the lines he was given and improvised in places – not a wise move when it turned out that the director had written them. A week of silence followed in which he became con-vinced he had thrown away his opportunity. Again a telephone call reassured him. He was to play the second lead, the ramrod Rowdy Yates. A jubilant Eastwood signed a contract only to learn that CBS were uncertain whether to shoot a pilot film and judge the audience response first – the common practice today – or commit themselves immediately to a full thirteen-episode series. To Eastwood's relief they chose the latter. He found himself en route for Arizona and two months of location filming. They had completed shooting for ten of the first thirteen episodes when the rollercoaster took another dip. CBS were worried about the current abundance of television westerns. A new one was too much of a gamble. They had decided to scrap it. It was the lowest point in Eastwood's acting career and only leavened by the fact that he knew he had given his best to the part – though that knowledge would have to remain private: when Eastwood went for a part in a feature film, CBS refused to let the producer view the *Rawhide* footage. 'Here my career was, lying in the basement of CBS,' he says. 'I was the star nobody had ever seen. I wasn't even the actor on the cutting room floor. I was the player who was locked up in a vault.' It was now close to Christmas 1958. Clint and Maggie took the train home to Eastwood's parents, who had since moved back to Oakland from Seattle. But the switchback had finally run its course. Almost immediately a telegram arrived from Eastwood's agent. Another series had apparently slumped in the ratings, leaving a gap for *Rawhide*. It was going ahead after all as a mid-season replacement. 'Mag and I did a little champagne trick and yelled a lot,' Eastwood recalls. 'I stuck my head out the window and shouted some profane things.' If any-one deserved to, he did.

The first episode of *Rawhide* was transmitted at 8.00 pm on Friday, 9 January 1959. Eric Fleming's taciturn trail boss, Gil Favor, straightened in the saddle, ordered 'Head 'em up, move 'em out!' through teeth that were to seem permanently gritted, and dust clouds, hooves and horns filled the screen. As the title credits filed past, singer Frankie Laine thundered out the series' evocative theme song: 'Rollin', rollin', rollin', keep them dogies rollin' – Rawhide . . .'

The opening story – *Incident of the Tumbleweed Wagon* (each episode was an 'incident' of some kind, another reference back to genuine nineteenth-century trail diaries) – was in fact the ninth filmed. It fulfilled Charles Marquis Warren's intentions of greater realism by being almost entirely shot on location, though it rendered both Eastwood and Fleming less than conspicuous. 'The average viewer, without benefit of a credit sheet, might well say, "Who stars in this series?"' commented reviewer Hank Grant in the *Hollywood Reporter*, though he did find the series promising.

Warren's choice could well have been dictated by a general television practice which saves the best of a series until the end of an initial run – as the best guarantee for a continuation – but he could equally well have been hedging his bets on his two stars. Both Eastwood and Fleming were virtual unknowns and only Warren's reputation as the leading light in television Westerns had got the show this far.

He needn't have worried. Despite an unspectacular beginning, *Rawhide's* popularity rose steadily until in its second year it was among America's top ten television shows. That proved to be its peak but it was destined to become the fourth longest-running television western – 217 episodes over seven years – only beaten by the eight years of *The Virginian*, *Bonanza's* fourteen and *Gunsmoke's* astonishing twenty.

Despite the exclusively male environment, the show corresponded to the popular 'family' formula, as exemplified by *Wagon Train*, *Bonanza* and others. Gil Favor, the honorable ex-Confederate war veteran, tight-lipped, authoritarian and experienced, represented the father figure. Eastwood's Rowdy Yates was his more impetuous and naive 'son' – his frequent urge to kick over the traces tempered by an unshakeable faith in his trail boss.

Domesticity, the older generation and humour were provided by Paul Brinegar's grizzled and cantankerous cook Wishbone, and Mushy (James Murdock), his slow-witted assistant – a running joke with Yates depended on the abysmal quality of the chuck wagon's menu. Incidental figures were Pete Nolan (the scout, played by Sheb Wooley) and Jesus – pronounced 'Hey soos' – the Mexican wrangler, played by Robert Cabal. The long drive from San Antonio, Texas to Sedalia, Missouri never actually ended but guest stars, natural hazards and Rowdy's inclination to get himself into trouble supplied plentiful grist to the scriptwriters' mill. Otherwise the series was very much a child of its times. The drovers and the pioneers they met in their travels were bringing the undisputed benefits of civilisation to an untamed

Eastwood appeared in Rawhide *for over seven years*

West. Morality might be debated but right and wrong were never seriously in doubt. Villains were easily identifiable by their clothes and the fact that they always drew first. When shooting occurred, bullet wounds hardly bled at all – if they weren't completely invisible. Women supplied the romantic interest, but no sex, and however deep the attachment formed with any regular cast member it was destined for a regrettable but inevitable failure within the next fifty minutes. In fact the deeper the attachment the more dire the consequences for the offending female.

Though Rowdy Yates was far from an original creation, the role was a pivotal one and very much everything Eastwood could have wished for at the time. It was a character he understood well; it was an action role and it was filmed largely in the outdoors, which Eastwood had always preferred. He also respected Warren's intentions for the series. 'We're doing stories as they pretty much happened,' he opined. 'Occasionally I guess we hoke one up for dramatic purposes, but generally speaking we're doing the things that guys on the cattle drives really did.' And on top of all that he was a star. Fan mail began to flood into CBS. The publicity machine ground into action and the press jostled for interviews. It would have been a heady experience for any young actor but Eastwood's innate caution kept it well in perspective. It was a year before he and Maggie moved out of their small apartment to a small ranch house in the more exclusive

With Paul Brinegar (centre) and Eric Fleming in Rawhide

Sherman Oaks area of Los Angeles. The interviews he gave established the contented nature of his private life but characteristically gave away little. Otherwise he stressed his positive approach to his work and to life in general with a strong emphasis on physical well-being.

'Try to be optimistic,' he told *TV Guide*, still one of America's widest read and most anodyne magazines, 'a bright outlook helps in everything. A discouraged attitude is a physical hindrance . . . Eat fruits and raw vegetables . . . The worst exercise you can get is with a knife and fork . . . Avoid alcohol in excess. A lot of actors don't condition themselves to long periods of hard physical effort,' he added. 'Toward the end of the day it shows in their performances.'

The homilies had much of the parodic edge of *Bronco Billy's* advice to his 'little pards' – though, one presumes, unintentionally so. Everything Eastwood said he did actually believe, and if the CBS handouts tended to skate over his drifting days and saddle him with a lifelong love of acting it was a compromise he could live with. On the *Rawhide* set he won a reputation for reliability and solid professionalism. He knew he had been lucky and his army experience had taught him not to look a gift horse in the mouth. But that didn't mean he could afford to neglect opportunities. Eastwood's fascination with the cinema now extended to the whole of the film-making process. 'As soon as a lot of people get into a series that's a success they can't wait to get out of it,' he said later. 'They think they're going on to bigger and better things and maybe that might be the case. But I wanted to learn just as much as I could about film and when you've done a couple of hundred

shows in seven or eight years you can pick up a lot.'

When he wasn't on camera himself he spent an increasing amount of time with the technical crew, watching how they did their jobs, discovering what helped and what hindered. Most particularly he studied the show's numerous directors – who included Jack Arnold from *Revenge of the Creature* and *Tarantula*. Some, like Ted Post – later to direct Eastwood's success *Hang 'Em High* and *Magnum Force* – impressed the young actor with their efficiency and flair. Others less organised were guided by the regular members of the cast and the unit.

This, more than anything else, came to persuade Eastwood that he would like to try directing himself. He began by suggesting the kind of personal stunt work he had done in his first days in television and found, rather to his surprise, that he was now too valuable for risks of that kind. He suggested odd shots to liven the action – once offering to take a camera on horseback among stampeding cattle, only to be told it was against union rules, which it wasn't. Eventually, after clearing it with Eric Fleming, he asked the producer if he could direct an entire episode. The response was favourable – on condition he first tried his hand with some trailers for the next season.

An enthusiastic Eastwood went ahead, working for nothing. But when the time came for the full episode, CBS – who had apparently had difficulties with another series' actor doing the same – ruled against it.

As the series stretched into its second and third years Eastwood's frustrations began to grow on the acting side too. Rowdy Yates, despite his limitations, still

32

offered a challenge – 'In a series you know you are going to work every week,' he commented. 'And if you try something one week and it doesn't work, you're going to be employed the next, so it doesn't matter. You can try anything you want and file all the things that work for you in your brain and discard what doesn't. It's a great training ground.' But he had not given up his ambition of moving on to feature films – *Maverick's* James Garner was already making the transition and Steve McQueen of *Wanted: Dead or Alive*, another Western series, was soon to achieve superstar status on the big screen with *The Great Escape*. While *Rawhide's* producer was happy to ensure that Eastwood got equal exposure with Fleming in the series, CBS kept a tight rein on his extracurricular activities.

The situation came to a head in July 1961 when in an uncharacteristic outburst he told the *Hollywood Reporter's* Hank Grant: 'I haven't been allowed a single feature or TV guesting offer since I started the series. Maybe they figure me as the sheepish nice guy I portray in the series, but even a worm has to turn sometime. Believe me, I'm not bluffing – I'm prepared to go on suspension if necessary, which means I can't work here, but I've open features in London and Rome that'll bring me more money in a year than the series has given me in three.'

There was very little substance behind the threat but enough to make CBS sit up. They agreed to let him pursue an independent career during his summer breaks from the series. Two years would go by before a feature offer did appear – and, oddly enough, from Rome. But it would change his life dramatically and permanently.

Spaghetti Junction 3
A Fistful of Dollars
For a Few Dollars More
Le Streghe
The Good, the Bad and the Ugly

A Holiday in Spain

Early in 1964 a plump, bespectacled, spaghetti-loving Italian film director – who happened to have an obsession with America's Wild West – had a problem. He had just spent all of the previous year persuading three European production companies – Jolly Film of Rome, Ocean Film of Madrid and Constantin Film of Munich – to put up a total of $200,000 in order to make a Western – in Spain. It would be a remake of a classic Japanese samurai movie, *Yojimbo*, made with an Italian crew and an Italian, German and Spanish cast. All it needed was a leading actor who, for reasons of box office, had to be an American.

Such an unlikely pot pourri was not that uncommon for Italy's frenetic film industry – of which the director, Sergio Leone, was something of an ideal son. The actual offspring of an Italian pioneer director, Leone had begun his career auspiciously, working for leading Italian directors, including Vittorio De Sica whose neo-realistic films had so startled post-war Hollywood. During the fifties he had been an assistant to numerous Hollywood directors who had come to Rome's Cinecittà Studios largely for tax reasons to make a series of telly-bashing 'sword and sandal' spectaculars – notably *Quo Vadis* (1952), *Helen of Troy* (1955), *Ben-Hur* (1959) and *Sodom and Gomorrah* (1961); Leone, a keen student of American cinema, worked on all four.

But if Hollywood epics provided publicity and cash for Cinecittà, they also prompted an astonishing amount of bread-and-butter film-making, designed for local consumption. America's B movies might have found a home in television, but Italy's were alive and well and filling Italian cinemas.

Usually shot in five or six weeks for under $200,000, with stock footage used over and over again, they were relentless and ruthless scavengers of existing cinema culture. In a frantic search for new audience attractions, a succession of familiar genres was seized upon and presented in a characteristically Latin way, only to be discarded instantly as a fresh craze made

35

itself obvious. Sentimental tearjerkers gave way to muscleman epics like *Hercules, Hercules Unchained, Hercules Versus Samson* and so on, to lurid, semi-documentary exposées of bizarre and titillating aspects of the world (based on the success of films like Gualtiero Jacopetti's *Mondo Cane*) to countless James Bond imitations. They were designed to be as sensational, as eye-catching and as instantly forgettable as the most basic popular journalism. That did not mean, however, that they could not occasionally be startlingly innovative. Leone underwent his own directorial apprenticeship with two muscleman epics – *The Last Days of Pompeii*, (1959) which he took over when the credited director, Mario Bonnard, fell ill, and *The Colossus of Rhodes* (1961). But in spite of the success of both, his heart was set firmly on the Western.

He got his chance to make one with the sudden collapse of the 'sword and sandal' epic in 1962, and the simultaneous and unexpected success of a series of German-made westerns. Starring ex-patriate, ex-Tarzan Lex Barker as a Teutonic pioneer in the Old West, they were filmed in large part in Yugoslavia. Munich's Constantin Films were one of the co-producers.

Leone's choice of a Japanese source for his story wasn't as strange as it might sound. *The Magnificent Seven* – John Sturges's Western version of Akira Kurosawa's *Seven Samurai* – had proved a Hollywood success in 1960. Kurosawa's *Yojimbo* appeared the following year and Leone could be forgiven for hoping that lightning might strike in the same place twice.

But he still needed an American name to head the credits. There was a strong tradition of so doing in Cinecittà. To its audiences an American name was an indication, however slight, of Hollywood quality, and a colony of highly paid expatriate American actors had grown up in Rome to cater for that demand. There was also a hope that the Italian version might be mistaken for a Hollywood original – both were invariably screened with dubbed dialogue so that differentiation wasn't always obvious. Cinecittà's 'quickies' were normally shot with post-synchronised sound; the practice saved money and time since foreign language versions were also usual.

Leone's sights were set commendably high – he wanted Henry Fonda to play his hero, but predictably the Hollywood star was a little beyond Leone's financial league. Next he tried Rome's expatriates. Again the topliners – like Steve Reeves whom Leone knew from *The Last Days of Pompeii* – were either too expensive or already lined up for the required period. One however – a star of the muscleman epics called Richard Harrison – suggested Clint Eastwood. *Rawhide* was enjoying healthy international sales at the time, but Leone had never seen it. Instead he approached James Coburn – one of *The Magnificent Seven*. Coburn was interested but wanted $25,000 – much too large a slice of Leone's already minimal budget. Eastwood – the name Leone had never heard before – began to seem a more attractive prospect.

The director watched an episode of *Rawhide – Incident of the Black Sheep*. 'Clint Eastwood,' he recalled later, 'hardly said a word, but he was good at getting on a horse, and he had a way of walking with a tired, resigned air.' The actor was younger than the character he had originally pictured but Leone decided there was a framework he could build on – especially

36

as the rising TV star was willing to accept a salary of $15,000. It seemed a gamble worth taking, and it was to prove the most momentous and rewarding in the lives of both men.

It had seemed far from that when news of the offer first reached Eastwood in a telephone call from his agent. 'He asked me if I would like to go to Europe and make an Italian-German-Spanish co-production of a remake of a Japanese film in the plains of Spain and I said "Not particularly."'

He was now in his thirty-fourth year, his sixth in *Rawhide* – whose appeal was beginning to slacken both personally and in the ratings. But the world of Cinecittà was eight thousand miles and a whole film-making style away – if Hollywood was prepared to look askance at television acting an appearance in Italian B movies was no more than an easy laugh. Nevertheless he agreed to read the script.

Leone had written it in three weeks with the occasional help of two collaborators. It was long-winded and somewhat bizarre in its attempt to reproduce Western slang (Leone's command of English was still rudimentary). Eastwood also recognised the plot of *Yojimbo* which he had seen. In Kurosawa's film, Toshiro Mifune plays a nameless samurai who wanders into an isolated community which is terrorised by two rival factions. He hires himself out as a yojimbo or bodyguard to each in turn, playing one side against the other and observing the murderous results with cynical detachment. Finally tiring of his games he provokes a general slaughter which he climaxes by tackling the most formidable of the local villains, and then moves on. His motives are boredom and a genial contempt for his opponents – none of whom survives his apparently casual but lightning fast dexterity with his sword. Eastwood was aware of the success of the earlier 'Westernisation' of Kurosawa's *Seven Samurai* (and if he had forgotten, Leone's working title for his film – *The Magnificent Stranger* – would have instantly reminded him) and he had noted that elements of *Yojimbo* were reminiscent of the Western, though he considered the film 'too stylised' to be easily adapted – 'at least by the old standards'.

But Leone was manifestly not working by the 'old standards' and that aspect appealed to an actor who was over-saturated with the traditionally heroic view of the West. In later interviews Eastwood would recall being intrigued at the way the script toyed with audience expectations of an over-familiar genre. 'The typical Western done for many years was: hero rides into town, sees school marm on porch of school, sees man beating horse, he interferes, hits man who's beating horse while the school marm looks on. You know that two people are going to get together and it isn't the guy and the horse. In this one: man rides in on an ancient horse, very shabby looking, sees man kicking kid, sees woman obviously in a distraught position at the house, obviously a prisoner of sorts and he turns and rides off . . . Right away you say: "This can't be the hero. He doesn't have a white hat and he isn't doing the normal thing." . . . You couldn't predict the end of the film.'

Finding things to like in the script and accepting Leone's offer were, however, two different things. Eastwood's agent and his business manager – he was now well heeled enough to have both – advised against it; Maggie Eastwood – whose opinion Eastwood valued – liked it. And it was domestic reasons as much as professional ones that finally made up Eastwood's mind. Though the fee on offer was low, he and Maggie would get an expenses-paid trip to Europe which they both wanted to visit. If the film turned out to be a disaster, which seemed all too possible, Eastwood decided that it was unlikely to harm his reputation in America, since no audience outside Europe would ever see it. Furthermore he had nothing much else to do during his summer break from *Rawhide*.

The gamble was a small one compared to Sergio Leone's but Eastwood – cautious as ever – insisted on being able to make dialogue changes before he signed any agreement. He also began to work on the character he was to play: Leone's Man With No Name was as mysterious and ruthless as Kurosawa's hero and as lethally proficient with his chosen weapon, the six gun. Eastwood even began to think about the character's costume. He chose some black Levis from a western clothes shop on Hollywood's Santa Monica Boulevard, adding a hat, a sheepskin vest and a poncho. His boots and gunbelt were an unwitting donation from the *Rawhide* props department. And in a Beverley Hills store he bought some cheap thin black cigars.

Later Leone would go to great pains to state it was he rather than Eastwood who had created the image which would transform the actor into an international star. Leone originally considered him 'a little sophisticated, a little "light", and I wanted to make him look more virile, to harden him, to "age" him for the part as

'The Man With No Name' in A Fistful of Dollars, 1964

well – with that beard, that poncho which made him look broader, those cigars. When I went to find him, in order to offer him the part, he had never smoked in his life; this posed problems for him, to have a cigar constantly in one's mouth when one does not know how to smoke . . .'

Eastwood has always agreed about the 'problems' of the cigars, which were to become a trademark of the Man With No Name. 'I didn't really like them,' he says, 'but they kept me in the right kind of humour. Kind of a fog. They just put you in a sour frame of mind.' Whatever the exact details, it is indisputable that the Man With No Name was very much a collaborative effort between director and star – though a fairly bizarre one; at the time of their first meeting neither knew more than a few words of the other's language.

Leone provided the vision – based as much on an urge to parody the traditional Western as a genuine love of it – and the driving force, although his organisational abilities caused the methodical Eastwood to blanch a little; when he first arrived on location the crew were missing: they had gone on strike because they hadn't been paid for a fortnight. Eastwood began by acting as a script doctor. He was very different now from the budding TV star of 1958. Six years of *Rawhide* had given him the equivalent experience of appearing in well over a hundred separate films and he had learned lessons from each one. Leone's dialogue needed drastic trimming – as much to disguise the quality of the English as to improve the pace. This process went on throughout shooting. The

With Jose Calvo in A Fistful of Dollars

40

FD-(25)-3

effect was to make the hero more mysterious and more laconic – which in turn acted as a counterpoint to the macabre humour which Eastwood had always liked in the script.

The economy of the dialogue was matched by the economy of Eastwood's performance. Quite apart from his understandable urge to get as far away as he could from the Rowdy Yates' image of the likeable, impetuous all-American boy, Eastwood had an obvious model for a terse, impassive, possibly dangerous figure in his *Rawhide* co-star, Eric Fleming. Gil Favor, trail boss, was always as upright and noble-minded as the finest conventional Western hero, but there was never any doubt of his total professionalism – or the innate ruthlessness which that implied. And he achieved that effect with a minimal display of emotion.

A Mr Favor whose professionalism was devoted exclusively to the acquisition of dollars was an excellent starting point for Eastwood. Another was the flamboyant acting style of his fellow performers. 'Italian actors,' he was to comment, 'come from the Hellzapoppin' school of drama. To get my effect I stayed impassive and I guess they thought I wasn't acting. All except Leone who knew what I was doing.'

Leone had noted this economy of effort in Eastwood's own personality: 'In real life, Clint is slow, calm, rather like a cat. During a shooting he does what he has to do, then sits down in a corner and goes to sleep immediately, until he is needed again. It was seeing him behave like this on the first day that helped me model the character.'

With that strange inevitability that oftens marks success, the apparently random strains of Eastwood's life were coming together to create the Man With No Name – his self-reliance, his valued independence, his unwillingness to get involved, unless on his own well-considered terms, his need to do well in whatever he set his mind on; even the rootlessness of his late teens had its correlative in the squinting, enigmatic, coolly confident figure on the big screen.

The seven-week shooting schedule began in May. The interiors were filmed at Cinecittà, the exteriors at a small village called Colmenar outside Madrid where a Western set had been built some years previously and was now in a state of disrepair, giving it the appearance of a ghost town – an effect Leone wanted. Equally important was the arid landscape of Almeria in southern Spain whose rocky hills and impoverished villages were pressed into service as a European equivalent of the Old West; the specific area depicted would be the Mexican-American border – to account for the scalding sunlight and the swarthy complexions of the cast. Although the phenomenal success of *A Fistful of Dollars* – as Leone's film would eventually be called – was to make this area of Spain world famous and, because of the unspoilt views and the cheapness of local labour, transform it into something of a film maker's Mecca during the sixties, Italian Westerns were by no means unknown there. Twenty-five Italian Westerns had been made before Leone's, though none had attracted enough attention to begin a craze of muscleman epic proportions. The triumvirate of production companies back-

Top and bottom: *Two scenes from* A Fistful of Dollars

ing Leone was currently making *Las Pistoles No Discuten* (*Pistols Don't Argue*), using exactly the same locations and a much bigger budget. The star was another expatriate American, Rod Cameron, and his film was expected to be the success. Like Eastwood, Leone was very much a second thought, the chief advantage of that being that he was left more or less to his own devices.

Despite the communication difficulties and his director's freewheeling working methods, Eastwood enjoyed himself. He had more influence on what was happening than was possible with the rigid formula of *Rawhide* and there was none of the pressure of a full-scale Hollywood production – at least in terms of his future career. And he knew that he and Leone were doing something different. If the production did have the overtones of a comic opera (Leone wore western clothes on the set, including toy pistols, and flamboyantly acted out each part in advance) then it was a worthy experiment.

By the end of shooting director and star had developed a healthy respect for each other; in the Italian trade press where the production was first announced Eastwood was credited as 'Western consultant' as well as star, and Eastwood would later describe Leone as one of his main influences as a director in his own right. But when Eastwood said goodbye and flew back home to begin the next *Rawhide* season, he fully expected never to see the tubby Western enthusiast again.

The first news he had of Leone's film – though he didn't realise it at the time – was a report in *Variety* about a sudden craze for making Westerns in Italy after the remarkable success of *A Fistful of Dollars*. That meant nothing. As far as Eastwood was concerned he'd been starring in *The Magnificent Stranger* when he left.

Two days later he read how *Fistful* 'starring Clint Eastwood' was doing roaring business in Rome. 'Then I got a letter from the producer, who hadn't bothered to write me since I left even to say thank you or go screw yourself or whatever, asking about making another picture.' The backers' reticence was understandable; they had regarded Eastwood's laconic acting style as evidence of a complete lack of talent and made few bones about expressing their opinion. This ungainly reversal amused Eastwood.

His amusement, tempered as it was by the perspective of Hollywood, was to turn to incredulity when he flew back across the Atlantic to attend the film's premiere in Paris. His reception was little short of hysterical. Whatever Hollywood thought, Clint Eastwood was a superstar in Europe.

Genesis of a New Myth

Per un Pugno di Dollari directed by 'Bob Robertson' (the makers hoped to disguise its provenance by giving the crew and cast American pseudonyms) had been almost literally an overnight success. After sneak previews in Naples and Rome, where cinema-owners and critics both declared the film to be worthless, it opened in a back street cinema in Florence in August 1964. Despite minimal publicity the theatre was soon packed every night. Within a week queues stretched along the pavement. The film's Rome premiere followed in November and by the end of the year *A Fistful of Dollars* had become the most commercially successful Italian film to that date.

It was a near perfect example of a 'sleeper' – that odd phenomenon which simultaneously delights and infuriates the film industry: the 'ugly duckling' product, made on a shoestring budget, which miraculously transforms itself into a highly profitable 'swan' and knocks for six costly rival films which previously seemed cast-iron certainties.

But why did *Fistful* become such an immediate cult? Its plotline was hardly original, matching that of *Yojimbo* virtually incident by incident, and Kurosawa's film had only made an impression on the art house circuit.

The difference lay in the manner of Leone's extrapolation of its themes into a Western context, and Eastwood's charismatic embodiment of his director's new vision.

The films begins, like so many traditional Hollywood Westerns, with a stranger riding into town. But there are no lush prairies behind him, or even the desolate grandeur of John Ford's Monument Valley with its towering buttes and giant cacti. The landscape is flat and arid, featureless beneath a pitiless sun.

The town the stranger enters – San Miguel – is barely an improvement on it. Wind-blown and fly-blown, it seems to maintain only a tenuous hold on existence, its signpost a noose on the branch of a dead tree under which the stranger rides. It hardly displays the bustling optimism of a newly created frontier town, nor its alter ego, the ghost town, but something in between, where the ghosts still somehow cling to life. The stranger is an odd mixture too. He has the tall, lean, good looks of a Western hero, but his even features are masked by a ragged beard that has only just emerged from stubble. His clothes are dusty and threadbare – more appropriate to a conventional Western villain; his poncho is the kind of garment normally reserved for Mexican extras. Is he some form of *gringo* bandit? And then there is his mount – not a horse but a patiently plodding mule. Is it meant to be a joke?

In fact all these appurtenances have one thing in common: they are eminently practical in the context of this landscape. This is how someone might well have dressed and travelled in the American South West in the last quarter of the nineteenth century. Leone's oblique realism has become a sly criticism of the traditional Western's way of presenting the West and its heroes. But his main intention has little to do with setting the social history record right. Something is clearly very wrong in San Miguel.

The harshness and danger of the surrounding landscape are more than matched by human perils within. Black dressed widows scuttle about the dusty street. A beautiful woman appears at a doorway in obvious distress, glances appealingly toward the newcomer and is dragged back inside, her young child earning a kick in the process. A dead man, strapped upright to a horse with the words '*Adios amigo*' scrawled across a card pinned to his chest, moves past.

The stranger's squinting gaze takes it all in. He's watchful, aloof, deliberately uninvolved. Only the gently ironic way he tips his hat toward the dead man betrays his awareness that things are amiss, that this moral universe isn't necessarily his. But neither is it the universe of the conventional hero. He's apparently unaffected by damsels in distress – or by the attentions of vicious bullies. As he passes a group of jeering heavies they loose off some shots, deliberately spooking his mule. The stranger is forced to clutch at a wooden beam outside the saloon to avoid being thrown into the dust. But teaching loudmouthed bullies to behave – another typically heroic function – doesn't appeal to him. His concerns are elsewhere and in the saloon we learn where.

San Miguel, he is told, is divided between two rival gangs: the Baxters, led by the sheriff, and the Rojos, led by Don Miguel Rojo. Their rivalry is intense and murderous, and Don Miguel is currently hiring gun men. The stranger moves down the street to the Rojos' headquarters and informs the Don that he 'might just be available'. He adds, casually spitting out a fragment of tobacco from the half smoked cigar in his mouth: 'I got to tell you before you hire me. I don't work cheap.'

His style is laconic, coolly confident and, with his air of total self-sufficiency, giving away nothing. Without waiting for a reply, he turns and walks slowly back toward the heavies who spooked his mule. By now he has attracted the nervous attention of several of the townsfolk, including an undertaker working on a coffin at the roadside. 'Get three coffins ready,' the stranger tells him as he passes.

The heavies greet him ominously with the words scrawled on the dead man he saw earlier: 'Adios, amigo,' and jeeringly warn him off. Replying in disturbingly reasonable terms, the stranger informs them that he understands their mule-spooking joke perfectly but the animal sees it differently. 'You see my mule don't like people laughing. Gets the crazy idea you're laughing at him. Now if you'll apologise, like I know you're going to – I might convince him that you really didn't mean it.'

The reasonable tenor of his remarks disturbs because his eyes – rising slowly to the men as he talks – suggest a quite different meaning. But his incongruous and humorous approach to what can only end in a gunfight also reveals his superior intelligence – 'Huh?' grunts one of the heavies as he begins. The stranger has the hero's ability to out-think his villainous opponents.

Now he displays the skill no traditional Western hero can do without and still deserve the name – expertise with the gun. Here he is almost superhumanly pre-eminent. He draws and fires five times before some of the heavies have even cleared their holsters. All four tumble into the dust.

Their employer – Sheriff Baxter – appears, threatening all manner of retribution. For the first time the stranger registers a positive emotion – a contemptuous and intimidating snarl. Instantly demoralised, the Sheriff fumbles in his pocket for his badge of office. 'Well, if you're the Sheriff,' snaps the stranger, unimpressed, 'you'd better get these men underground.' And he walks off. Whatever his moral values – and the evidence at this point is that they are largely monetary – he plainly shows that most ancient of heroic virtues: ruthless and unbending determination. Nobody, if he so chooses, stands in *his* way.

The scene ends as the stranger re-passes the undertaker, now gaping at him with understandable awe. 'My mistake,' observes the Man With No Name drily. '*Four* coffins.'

There is no hint of remorse, no hesitancy, merely the laconic humour of a dedicated professional after a job well done – a professional in the art of survival in a vicious and anarchic world.

As his shabby clothes and the grimy environment in which he moves indicate a pitiless realism, so the Man With No Name is the supreme realist. The cosy morality of the Hollywood Western would earn an instant bullet here – and probably in the back. It's a lesson the stranger learnt long before this film began.

But the hero's brutal realism is only one element in Leone's dissection of the Western. The dialogue – pruned as it was by Eastwood who had understood its 'satiric undertones' from the beginning – is a parody of traditional western tough-talk. The direction – languid and staccato by turns, using rapid cutting and extreme close-ups, especially in scenes of tension like the above gunfight – mocks Hollywood's unobtrusive style: Leone's technique is constantly on view, teasing, intriguing, startling and occasionally blasting the audience out of their seats, especially with the speed and violence of the gunplay. No Western hero has drawn faster than Eastwood (once timed at 0.45 of a second, to draw, cock and fire) until Gene Wilder's Ringo Kid in *Blazin' Saddles* who drew, fired and re-holstered so swiftly – or so director Mel Brooks would have us believe – that no movement was discernible. Here the amplified sounds of the gunshots play their part – as does the soundtrack generally, where natural sounds are used to heighten dramatic tension or even suggest an ironic comment on the action (in *The Good, the Bad and the Ugly* – the last and most elaborate of Eastwood's Italian Westerns – a cock crows as one of the characters is betrayed). But nowhere is the use of sound more important than in the film's music, by Ennio Morricone.

Until *Fistful* most Western film music had tended to consist of variations of traditional saddle ballads – often emulating the rhythms of riding – or fairly anonymous musical 'wallpaper' underlining the mood of the moment; rare exceptions were impressive, large orchestral scores, like Jerome Moross's for *The Big Country* or Elmer Bernstein's for *The Magnificent Seven*.

In a unique collaboration with Sergio Leone, Morricone set out to create something completely different. His starting point – as Leone's and Eastwood's had been with the anti-heroic stranger – was a grounding in reality. Not the traditional reality of rhythms that echoed the hoof beats of a cowboy's mount or the jingling of a bridle, but the actual sounds of a genuine Western environment: the cracking of a whip, the vibrant twanging of a jew's harp, gunshots, church bells and indeterminate cries of animals and humans: whistles, grunts, groans and the occasional heavenly choir. Distorted electronically and combined with a powerful main theme on electric guitar, they both parodied and redefined every Western theme ever heard before. 'It was,' as critic Chris Frayling has described it graphically, 'as if Duane Eddy had bumped into Rodrigo, in the middle of a crowded Via Veneto.'

Morricone's music for *Fistful*, and its two sequels, was operatic in its intensity, and its effect. Its dissonances and unexpected chords echoed the bleak, unpredictable and violent world of the films and it underlined and even defined the emotions of the characters: in *Fistful* a note on a jew's harp or a brief trill – as in the initial gunfight with Baxter's heavies – signals that the stranger means business, sometimes in apparent contradiction to his present activity. At one point he appears to be drunk – the soundtrack tells us otherwise.

In later films the main characters are associated with specific musical effects, so that their presence or imminent arrival in a scene can be announced by a repetition of those sounds.

Certainly Morricone's use of music – revolutionary as it was in a Western – would have been familiar to an Italian audience with its strong operatic tradition, but the effect would have remained little more than a curiosity if the music itself hadn't been so memorable. The twanging guitars, flaring trumpets and bizarrely inarticulate grunts, cries and whistles of Morricone's scores gave Leone's Westerns an unmistakable musical signature and were a major part of their success.

But it was 'El Cigarillo' – as Eastwood was dubbed – who provided the prime attraction. To a Latin audience – and *Fistful's* success quickly spread to South America – the Man With No Name was the ultimate in *machismo*: cool, confident, wholly masculine yet apparently indifferent to women (his only contact with the traditional damsel in distress in *Fistful* is when – rather uncharacteristically – he frees her and her child from captivity and allows them to escape from town).

Yet that potentially wooden quality was constantly mitigated by a dry humour and a devious intelligence: whenever the Baxter–Rojo conflict is in danger of cooling down, the stranger arranges – *Yojimbo*-style – for it to flare up all over again. In his final confrontation with the sadistic arch-villain Ramon Rojo (played by 'John Wells', in fact Gian Maria Volonté, then a successful Italian stage actor), he guys his own apparent invincibility by striding openly toward his better-armed opponent, inviting a succession of bullets from the other's rifle – 'the heart, Ramon . . . aim

for the heart or you'll never stop me'. Only when he comes within revolver range does he throw back his poncho to reveal a makeshift iron shield – which is of course the last thing Ramon sees.

To Leone's mind the supernatural suggestion of that scene – however practically explained – together with the stranger's general air of invincibility and mystery lend the character an allegorical dimension; he is specifically 'the incarnation of the archangel Gabriel – in his role as angel of death. That kind of pretension is debatable at the very least but it does underline Eastwood's personal success in the part. As with Morricone's music, tampering with an established genre would have meant very little without a high degree of personal talent. On screen, in his first solo leading role, Eastwood had undeniable charisma, the 'watchability' of a young Gary Cooper, to whom he was swiftly compared by Vittorio De Sica. It was his good fortune that the screen persona which first enabled him to display this quality struck such a remarkable chord with his times.

As with the most successful of the world's cinema stars, Eastwood did not so much act in the accepted sense as create a myth – a myth that audiences could universally recognise. Eastwood himself was well aware of this: 'Any actor going into pictures has to have something special. That's what makes a star while a lot of damn good actors are passed by. The public recognises their work as good but they don't run out to see them with their three dollars for a ticket. The public goes to see

For a Few Dollars More, *1965*

48

the stars.' The decade that saw the first of Leone's 'spaghetti' Westerns, as they were – perjoratively – called, was a period of social revolution, and its mirror image, disillusionment. There was an explosion of creativity and experiment after the press-ure-cooker atmosphere of the fifties, when post-war austerity and an awareness of the atomic bomb had cultivated drabness and uniformity. Then the need had been to rebuild a war-shattered world, to make good. By the sixties much of the world had made good; now it was time to have fun.

Traditional values tottered under a wave of experimentation – in living styles, in sexual mores, in all forms of the arts and even in human perception, under the influence of mind-expanding drugs. Fuelled by affluence and a spiralling economic growth rate, the world seemed turned upside down – or about to be. But there was a reverse side to this outburst of self-expression. Rapid advances in science and technology – symbolised by the first manned space launch at the beginning of the decade and the moon landing at its end – tended to dehumanise the individual, to convert him or her into a succession of dots on a computer punch card, a cog in a corporate machine. And not everyone saw the desirability of so much self-expression – especially when it revealed itself in revolutionary violence. Not everyone was of an age, either, to appreciate a decade that worshipped youth. Whatever new freedom was won at this time, it was more than matched by a sense of confusion and uncertainty.

Eastwood's Man With No Name persona had a unique appeal to all of these disparate elements. To the young, busy experimenting with psychedelia, his Italian Westerns had the vigour and humour of comic books; their incongruity, their iconoclastic attitudes, their relishing of technique and style for their own sake were characteristic attributes of sixties' pop culture. To the confused, to the uncertain, to those who hankered after the stability of older values, he represented a figure of cast-iron certainty. To the oppressed, he was a man who refused to accept interference or bother from any source. To the repressed and the lonely, his supreme and plainly untroubled self-sufficiency was a justification of their own isolation. In *A Fistful of Dollars* Sergio Leone had provided Eastwood with a near-perfect embodiment of the actor's own adolescent fantasies of inviolable self-reliance.

An Italian Horse Opera

Copyright problems with *Yojimbo*, and a certain degree of scorn by American distributors, were to keep *Fistful* out of the United States until 1967. There Eastwood was known purely as the co-star of a waning TV Western series. But his appreciation and respect for his enthusiastic European audience was growing – especially when he was able to negotiate a fee of $50,000 to star in a sequel, plus fringe benefits that included a new Ferrari.

Leone, too, found the financial restraints lessening. His budget for the new film, appropriately entitled *For a Few Dollars More*, rose to $600,000. This time he avoided copyright problems by co-writing his own script with Luciano Vincenzoni.

The story re-introduced the Man With No Name virtually intact, though now with a stated profession – that of bounty hunter. The world in which he operates is as unscrupulous, anarchic and brutal as ever – only more so. This time, however, he is forced to compromise his independence by entering an uneasy alliance with a fellow professional, Colonel Douglas Mortimer. Both are in pursuit of El Indio, a ruthless bandit whose sadistic relish of killing verges on psychosis – only the calming effect of cannabis apparently keeps him from toppling over the edge.

El Indio has newly escaped from gaol and the two bounty hunters deduce that he can only regain the prestige he lost at his capture by robbing the bank at El Paso, the most impregnable bank in the territory. When they spot Indio's men 'casing' the bank they realise they are correct. They decide to divide their efforts, tackling the gang from both inside and out. The Man With No Name gains admittance by breaking one of El Indio's most trusted lieutenants out of gaol. When the time comes for the robbery, No Name is despatched with three other gang members to a nearby town to create a diversion that will clear El Paso of lawmen. En route he disposes of his three companions, but arrives back too late to prevent the robbery. Mortimer now suggests that No Name persuade Indio to take the stolen money – still contained in a locked safe – to a point where the Colonel will arrange an ambush. No Name agrees to the plan and promptly tells Indio to go in the opposite direction. Indio, however, chooses a third direction – the town of Agua Caliente. There, as a result of a peculiar course of deduction, Mortimer is waiting.

He persuades Indio that he alone can open the locked safe – using a metal drill and acid – which he does and the money is placed in a locked chest. That night Mortimer and No Name try to steal it but are discovered by the gang and savagely beaten, though not before they have concealed the money.

Indio then allows them to escape and sends his men after him, knowing there will be few survivors from the battle. His plan is to take the opportunity to escape with all the money for himself. It is now that he finds the money chest empty but for his own reward poster.

Mortimer and No Name, meanwhile, have wiped out the rest of the gang and return to confront Indio. Mortimer makes the first approach, revealing that his motive for going after the bandit is revenge: Indio raped the Colonel's sister and killed her young husband, driving the girl to suicide. Indio succeeds in disarming Mortimer, but No Name steps in to ensure the odds are even in the climactic gun duel, which the Colonel wins.

His thirst for vengeance slaked, Mortimer donates his share of the reward to No Name. No Name piles a wagon high with the bodies of the bandits and drives off into the distance, calculating his profit as he goes.

For a Few Dollars More represented a considerable advance on its predecessor, in almost every field. For all its revolutionary approach, *Fistful* did not conceal its low-budget origins; even for a semi-ghost town San Miguel was remarkably underpopulated and its interiors very sparsely furnished; technically the film had many rough edges. In retrospect it is very much a blueprint for the future.

A bigger budget allowed Leone to spread his directorial wings. Not only was the new film almost a third longer in running time, and embellished with another imported American 'star' (Lee Van Cleef, formerly a Hollywood 'heavy', played

Mortimer) and with a host of special effects adding to the violence and ingenuity of the action, but it also greatly expanded the themes and techniques of *Fistful*.

Hollywood Westerns had often been described – disparagingly – as 'horse operas'; the situations, the characters, the action were that formalised. In *For a Few Dollars More* Leone came closer than any previous director of Westerns to making the genre genuinely operatic.

The opening shot immediately establishes the mood of what is to come. A lone rider canters across a desolate landscape. Distance and the immensity of his surroundings combine to make him anonymous, insect-like, almost an after-thought in this context – a suggestion quickly reinforced by the crash of an unseen rifle. The rider falls and a title flashes onto the screen: 'Where life had no values, death sometimes had its price.' The first twenty minutes of the film are devoted to three separate and self-contained episodes. Unrelated to the main plot, they introduce each of the chief characters. It's an indulgence in plot terms, but it allows each character to demonstrate his highly individual style, aria-like, and style in a Leone Western is at least as important as plot.

The Man With No Name, dressed as in *Fistful* and again disconcerting a sheriff as he asks for details of a wanted criminal. Tracking the man down to a nearby town, he interrupts his poker game, dealing each of them a hand. No Name's hand wins and the loser, rather belatedly, asks what they

Eastwood played the part of 'No Name' again in For a Few Dollars More

52

have been betting on. 'Your life,' replies No Name. A brawl develops into a gunfight as three companions come to the wanted man's aid. No Name despatches all four with characteristic economy.

He picks up his reward from the local sheriff and again comes that hint of a different morality; clearly the lawman has made no attempt to apprehend the criminal himself. 'Tell me,' asks No Name, 'isn't a sheriff supposed to be courageous, loyal and above all – honest?' As the man stutters a reply, No Name plucks the tin star from his shirt and tosses it towards a crowd of onlookers on the porch. 'You people need a new sheriff,' he tells them.

Elsewhere Colonel Mortimer is travelling by train to the town of Tucumcari for a similar purpose. Hawk-nosed and hard-eyed, he reads a large Bible, prompting a talkative fellow traveller to address him as 'Reverend' – a view that changes swiftly as he spots the Colonel's unusual, long-barrelled pistol. Informed that the train does not stop at Tucumcari, Mortimer promptly pulls the communication cord. A hard look and a fresh view of his remarkable gun persuades the outraged conductor that this illegal act might in this case be excused. Snatching a reward poster from the local railway depot, Mortimer rides into town, intimidates a saloon barman into revealing the whereabouts of the man in the poster – he's upstairs – and goes in search of him. Mortimer's methods are as economical as No Name's and perhaps even more measured.

He announces his presence by sliding the reward poster under his quarry's door and then stepping quickly to one side. A rain of bullets from inside vindicates his foresight. Kicking open the shattered door, he enters in time to see the man escaping into the street below. Pausing only to beg the pardon of the criminal's naked and, by now, hysterical woman companion, he moves unhurriedly downstairs again.

Outside he unwraps what appears to be a bedroll tied to his horse's saddle. Neatly arranged in clips are four specialist firearms, ranging from a buffalo gun to a shotgun. Selecting a rifle, he takes aim at the criminal, now mounted and galloping into the distance, and fires. The man's horse crumples. A second shot wounds the rider. Mortimer replaces the rifle as the enraged criminal opens fire with a hand-gun. But the range is too great and the bullets merely kick up the dust several feet away. As the man stumbles closer, Mortimer draws his long-barrelled pistol and calmly attaches a rifle stock to its butt. The criminal's bullets are chewing the ground between his boots when the Colonel fires once, drilling a neat hole in his quarry's forehead.

By existing Hollywood standards Mortimer would be a thorough-going, if attractively stylish, villain. But his ruthlessness shrinks into insignificance as we meet this film's villain, El Indio, played once more by Gian Maria Volonté. He is languishing in gaol when his gang stage a sneak attack to release him. His first request is for a gun, his first act of freedom to bid his elderly cellmate 'Adios, amigo!' – something

of a catchphrase for Leone heavies – and shoot him dead at pointblank range. After massacring the gaol's warders, the gang rides to the home of the man whose evidence put Indio inside. Here the bandit relishes the man's terror and pleas for mercy as his wife and eighteen-month-old baby are dragged away and shot, off screen. He then allows his victim the opportunity to revenge himself in a gun duel, choreographed by the tinkling of a musical watch Indio owns. When the music stops, the shooting starts, and naturally Indio wins. This climax to an orgy of killing leaves the bandit shaking uncontrollably, teetering on the verge of madness. His lieutenant hands him a joint and he retreats into a state of fugue.

The musical set-piece of Indio's gun duel marked a new level in Leone's collaboration with Morricone. Lingering close-ups as the watch's tinkling tune winds to its finish milk the scene for every drop of tension. In the film's final confrontation – in a neat reversal which puts Indio in an identical hot-seat – it is Mortimer's musical timepiece that sets the pace. The same tinkling tune swells into a full orchestral arrangement while the tension rises and rises. Every narrowing look, every bead of sweat, every slight movement of a trigger finger is savoured in the process, but the device of the watch has a thematic relevance too. Indio's watch – a companion to Mortimer's – is one the Colonel gave originally to his sister as a wedding present; its tune is Indio's death song.

Leone's growing self-assurance was matched by Eastwood's. His pairing with Van Cleef in a kind of grotesque parody of the Rowdy Yates–Gil Favor relationship added an extra dimension to No Name's enigmatic character. They address each other as 'old man' and 'boy' respectively; Mortimer describes himself specifically as an older version of No Name: 'Were you ever young?' No Name asks him. 'Yes, boy, as young as you and every bit as reckless,' the Colonel replies. 'And then one day something happened – something that suddenly made life very precious to me.' The event is, of course, Indio's destruction of his sister. Appropriately enough in this vicious world the only emotion a survivor can allow himself is a violent one: a desire for vengeance.

But the relationship does not work entirely to Eastwood's benefit. It's Mortimer who has the more relaxed style (he doesn't get into a brawl when he takes *his* wanted man) and the better weaponry, and it's Mortimer who comes up with the ideas for trapping Indio, even though No Name is happy to twist them to his own advantage. Eastwood moves closer to fulfilling the promise of *Fistful* when No Name acts alone – talking his way into Indio's gang by telling the exact truth (that he decided the best way to pick up the bounty on all of them was to join the gang and turn them all in at the first opportunity) and calming asking for a match when an outraged gang member shoots the cigar from his mouth. Or when he breaks Indio's lieutenant out of gaol by appearing unannounced at the man's cell window, tying dynamite to the bars, igniting the fuse with his cigar then vanishing with a broad smile before an explosion demolishes the cell wall.

As critics David Downing and Gary Herman have pointed out 'there is a whole world view in that smile. It is the smile Newman and McQueen have perfected, a smile of awareness and the self-control it brings.'

58

The leading male cinema stars of the sixties and seventies were to combine that cool self-assurance with breath-taking audacity – the audacity of Sean Connery's James Bond demolishing an adversary or Steve McQueen's mad career across the landscape on a stolen motorcycle in *The Great Escape*. No other actor would embody those qualities so purely, so forcefully and so resonantly as Eastwood, but context would always be vitally important. It was something he fully realised when he first read the *Fistful* script. 'The hero was an enigmatic figure, and that worked within the context of this picture. In some films he would be ludicrous. You can't have a cartoon in the middle of a Renoir.'

There are hints of that incongruity in *For a Few Dollars More* when No Name talks vaguely of buying a spread upcountry with his bounty money. It simply doesn't ring true and Mortimer – the No Name of the previous generation – is living proof of it.

'When you have to shoot, shoot. Don't talk!'

Like *Fistful*, the exteriors of *For a Few Dollars More* were filmed in Almeria and the interiors at Cinecittà. Between shooting on the twelve-week schedule Clint and Maggie received the full force of Italian adulation. Fans pursued them everywhere, *papparazzi* recorded every public appearance. Even for a man of Eastwood's disposition the atmosphere was heady, and it became even more gratifying when Vittorio De Sica asked him to appear in a film he was making.

De Sica had made his reputation with *Bicycle Thieves*, one of a series of starkly realistic Italian films of the late forties which had earned him an Oscar for the best foreign film, and remains a classic to this day. His career as a director had waned in the fifties and he had turned to acting with great success, even appearing in a British television series *The Four Just Men* in 1959.

In the sixties, however, commercial success with two comedies, *Marriage, Italian Style* and *Yesterday, Today and Tomorrow*, revived his directorial fortunes and when Eastwood came on the Italian scene he was one of Italy's most successful and respected film-makers.

The new film, *Le Streghe* – 'The Witches' – was a five-part compilation with a different director for each section. It was designed as a showcase for the talents of Silvana Mangano, a leading Italian actress whose career had gone into temporary decline. Dino De Laurentiis, the film's producer and Miss Mangano's husband, hoped it would boost her fortunes. De Sica directed the last episode, entitled 'A Night Like Any Other', a modern fantasy in which Eastwood played Miss Mangano's conservative-minded husband.

Despite a brief interlude where he appeared as an idealised cowboy dressed in black, Eastwood made no great impression. Neither did the film in Italy, or America which it did not reach until some years later. United Artists gave it a limited art-house distribution before shelving it, a decision with which Eastwood seems to have concurred. 'It was a drawing room thing, half reality, half fantasy,' he told an interviewer. 'It was good to get out of my boots, though.' A review in *Variety* was more specific, dubbing the film 'dismal' and 'pointless'.

Eastwood's ego could survive the blow.

Before leaving Rome he negotiated a deal for a third Western to be made during his next *Rawhide* break. The fee was $250,000 plus ten per cent of the western hemisphere profits. The waning TV Western series was beginning to look like very small beer.

When Eastwood returned to Hollywood he was no longer inclined to be bashful about his Italian connection. 'I'm probably the highest paid American actor who ever worked in Italian pictures,' he told columnist Sheilah Graham. 'Only Mastroianni gets more in Italy. I don't want to make all my Westerns in Italy and Spain, but in Europe I'm in a better position to get the films I want and to work with people like De Sica . . . For the first time in my life, I can pick the parts I want to play.'

Even his *Rawhide* career was showing an improvement, albeit temporarily. Eric Fleming had been having difficulties with CBS, culminating in his acceptance of a big screen role with Doris Day in *The Glass Bottom Boat*. As a result the network had fired him. The series' ratings were now faltering badly and, during Eastwood's absence in Italy, the head of CBS, James Aubrey, had decided to cancel it. Aubrey was then fired himself and the series reinstated with Rowdy Yates promoted to trail boss.

Yates proved to be a more flexible and liberal-minded boss – he even took on the series' first black cowboy. But audiences were clearly as tired of the format as Eastwood, and the series ended – as it had begun – in mid-season. Only twenty-nine of the scheduled thirty-nine episodes were filmed – none of which ever reached British television – and on 8 February 1966 Eastwood received a pay-off from CBS of $119,000. As a result of the cancellation

61

Leone was able to bring the shooting date for his next Western forward and in May 1966, after a rest, Eastwood set out once more for Spain.

Provisionally entitled *The Magnificent Rogues*, the new film boasted a budget of $1,200,000 – six times that of *Fistful*; appropriately its final running time of 180 minutes (trimmed to 148 for the international print) would be almost double the length of the first 'Dollar' film, making it the longest of Leone's Westerns. Like *For a Few Dollars More*, it was an elaboration on its predecessor. Eastwood remained the Man With No Name, Lee Van Cleef was retained as the villain and another American actor, Eli Wallach, drafted into the story.

Wallach, a leading 'Method' actor of the American theatre in the fifties, had moved on to cinema performances, generally playing the heavy, like Van Cleef; it was his role as a cheerfully villainous Mexican bandit in *The Magnificent Seven* that brought him to Leone's attention.

The story, co-written by Leone, Vincenzoni and, Age-Scarpelli was not dissimilar to *For a Few Dollars More* – three characters of varying degrees of villainy contest with each other for a cache of stolen money. Unlike its predecessors, however, it was placed within a specific historical context – the American Civil War. This allowed Leone to indulge his pursuit of authenticity – many of the scenes are based on contemporary photographs and in the battle sequences the camera view is cluttered with period field pieces borrowed from the Madrid Army Museum.

Though Leone boasted that his Westerns were more authentic than Hollywood's, the device, as in *Fistful*, is used more as an expression of style than for historical truth; there are a number of blatant anachronisms, including a scene where No Name uses a rifle with a telescopic sight.

More importantly the Civil War gives Leone the opportunity to widen his critical stance. His characters, typically, have no personal interest in the conflict but even they are appalled by the mass slaughter of modern warfare: 'I've never seen so many men wasted so badly,' comments No Name after witnessing a full-scale assault. In comparison the violent events of Leone's West and the attitudes of the people living in it seem almost tame. It's no surprise that the eventual title of the film *The Good, the Bad and the Ugly* could decribe, interchangeably, many of the events of the story.

Specifically, however, it refers to the three main characters. 'Il Buono' is No Name, still in his role of bounty hunter; 'Il Brutto' is Setenza (Van Cleef), also known as 'Angel Eyes', a sadistic hired killer; while 'Il Cattivo' (Wallach) is Tuco, a garrulous, exuberant and wholly untrustworthy Mexican bandit.

As the film opens No Name and Tuco form a bizarre symbiosis. No Name regularly turns the bandit in to local lawmen, collects his bounty and rescues his partner at the point of death by shooting through the rope that hangs him. When Tuco eventually decides he is taking the greater risk and demands a bigger share of the proceeds, No Name abandons him in the desert, horseless and with his hands still roped together from his latest 'hanging'.

Meanwhile Angel Eyes is sharing a meal with his next victim, from whom he learns of the existence of 200,000 dollars worth of missing Confederate gold, stolen by a man who now calls himself Bill Carson. Knowing his fate, the victim hires Angel Eyes to kill his employer instead. The gunman accepts the job, shoots his victim – and an elder son who unwisely intervenes – returns to his employer and kills him too. He begins to track down Carson, initially by beating up his girlfriend.

Tuco has since survived a trek across the desert and, with three bandit companions, catches up with No Name in a hotel room close to the frontline. No Name disposes of the three gunmen as they burst through the door, only to be trapped by Tuco who uses the window. Gleefully revenging himself, Tuco gets his former partner to balance on a chair with his head in a noose hanging from a roof beam. It looks as if No Name's last hour has come when a shell from the front suddenly strikes the hotel. When the dust clears, No Name has escaped.

Later No Name is carrying out his hanging trick with another partner when Tuco puts a gun to his head. 'Sorry Shorty,' murmurs No Name as Tuco's replacement drops to an unexpected death. Now Tuco subjects No Name to the torture he suffered in the desert, dragging the bounty hunter behind him on a lengthy journey across endless dunes.

No Name is on the point of death when a runaway Confederate ambulance wagon appears, full of dead or dying soldiers. Tuco stops the wagon and learns about the missing gold from one of the wounded – Bill Carson – who tells him it is buried in Sad Hill cemetery. He is too thirsty to say in which grave. While a desperate Tuco runs for his water bottle, No Name crawls up to the dying Carson and learns the name of the grave as the man dies.

Now that each shares a half of the gold's secret, their partnership is resumed. Tuco takes No Name to a monastery run by Tuco's brother and the bounty hunter is nursed back to health. He and Tuco leave in Confederate uniform and are promptly captured by Union soldiers. They are sent to Betterville prison camp where Angel Eyes, having since enlisted on the Union side, is in charge. As soon as Tuco gives his name as 'Bill Carson' he and No Name attract his attention. He tortures the name of Sad Hill out of Tuco who is then taken away to be turned in for his bounty. He offers a partnership to No Name who accepts. With four of Angel Eyes' companions they leave for Sad Hill.

Tuco, meanwhile, escapes his gaoler and hurries toward Sad Hill. All seven arrive at a war-devastated town at roughly the same time, though No Name is the first to meet up with Tuco. The two quickly kill off Angel Eyes' companions but Setenza himself escapes. They hurry on to Sad Hill, pausing only to settle a military conflict over a disputed bridge which they dynamite.

They reach the cemetery where Angel Eyes is waiting and a three-way gunfight takes place; both No Name and Tuco aim for Angel Eyes who dies, at which point Tuco realises his gun is empty – No Name has surreptitiously emptied it. No Name forces Tuco to dig up the gold and then balance on an unsteady wooden grave cross with a noose round his neck attached to a tree branch. After dividing up the gold, the bounty hunter loads his share onto his horse and rides off into the distance, pursued by Tuco's screams of abuse. He disappears, then after a brief pause re-appears, raise his rifle, fires and severs the rope around Tuco's neck for the last time.

The Good, the Bad and the Ugly is the most accomplished of Eastwood's Italian Westerns, technically, thematically and in terms of pure entertainment. It's a dazzling kaleidoscope of stunning effects, abrupt reversals, wildly sardonic humour and some of Leone's most grandiose set-pieces, backed by Morricone's most elaborate and inspired score to date. Conventions of the Western and of cinema technique in general are taken gleefully for a ride, stretching the limits of both close to breaking point.

In the opening shot a distant panorama of a familiarly bleak landscape snaps into close focus as a face – as rugged and pock-marked as the surroundings – swings abruptly into mid-frame, like a kiddie's weighted punchbag on the rebound. Hardly has the audience adjusted to this bizarrely original shot when what appears to be a classic Western confrontation begins. The owner of the pock marks stands impassively at one end of a deserted, one-horse town, watching as two equally grim-faced individuals dismount at the opposite end. With gazes fixed and trigger hands poised, they walk towards each other. Only the whistling of the wind, the rattling canvas of an abandoned wagon, a dog's howl and the crunch of their boots disturb an eery silence. Closer and closer they move until they are barely feet away, on the boardwalk outside a run-down saloon. At the very last moment all three turn aside and fling themselves through the saloon's swing doors. There is a burst of gunfire and a snarling Tuco, gun in one hand and half-consumed chicken leg in the other, crashes through the saloon's window glass. A freeze frame captures him in mid-lunge; 'Il Cattivo' slashes across the screen in jagged red lettering.

As in *For a Few Dollars More* prefatory cameos introduce each of the main charac-ters – a device formalised even further in this case by the use of the freeze frame and an appropriate title. No Name earns his as he abandons Tuco in the desert. As the bandit yells abuse at his retreating back, No Name pauses and turns with an ironic smile. 'Such ingratitude,' he murmurs, 'after all the times I've saved your life.' If No Name is 'Il Buono' in this world then the 'Bad' must be pretty terrible and, of course, Setenza swiftly proves it is.

But it's the set-pieces that remain memorable: No Name's desert agony as his face peels and bubbles in the fierce heat while Tuco looks on from beneath a brightly coloured parasol; the moment in Betterville when a brutal guard forces an orchestra of prisoners to play in order to cover the screams of a fellow prisoner under torture (the tune is Morricone's haunting and elegaic theme that accompanies all the Civil War sequences); Tuco and No Name's capture by a detachment of ghostly 'Confederate' cavalry – in fact Union soldiers whose faces and uniforms have turned grey under a layer of trail dust, though the 'Good' and the 'Ugly' don't realise this until too late; Tuco's frantic search for the right grave in Sad Hill cemetery as the camera sweeps after him over an ever-widening vista of crosses; and the final three-way confrontation in a pebble-strewn, sun-bleached arena at the centre of the cemetery – surely the ultimate Western showdown – while Morricone's soaring theme and Leone's repeated close-ups build an extraordinary tension.

The humour, too – though as sardonic as ever – reaches new and more subtle

As Joe 'The Good' in The Good, the Bad and the Ugly, *1966*

64

heights. In *For a Few Dollars More* it tended to be too broad – No Name learns Mortimer's identity from the Prophet, an old man who lives in a shack he has refused to leave simply because the railroad has lain a track directly outside his door; as a result their conversation is punctuated by the thunderous roar of passing locomotives. Or it was too subtle: when Indio tries to escape with his stolen safe where does he end up but in Agua Caliente, literally 'hot water' in Spanish.

In *The Good, the Bad and the Ugly* in a scene cut from the international print, though the video version retains it, Tuco emerges from the desert and finds himself outside a gunsmith's shop. Inside he examines the shopkeeper's wares, then with loving care assembles his own customised revolver. After loading and testing it in a makeshift firing range at the rear of the shop, he asks the gunsmith, 'How much?' 'Twenty dollars,' the man replies, and pauses. 'Forty dollars' then with a sigh of despair: 'Two hundred dollars – it's all I've got!' Only then does the audience – and the unfortunate gunsmith – realise that the penniless Tuco is not asking the gun's price but committing a robbery.

There is a similar neat reversal of audience expectations when Tuco, having reached the shattered town en route to Sad Hill, discovers a bath tub in an abandoned saloon. Somewhat uncharacteristically he decides to take a bubble bath. As he splashes away a gunman approaches stealthily; it's the owner of the pock-marked visage who opened the film. Bursting in upon Tuco with a raised gun, he declares triumphantly: 'I've been looking for you for eight months . . . now I find you in exactly the position that suits me . . .' At which point flames erupt from beneath the bubbles and Tuco rises from the tub with a smoking handgun, hanging from a cord around his neck. 'When you have to shoot, shoot,' he advises belatedly, 'don't talk!'

Alternatively Tuco is the brunt of the joke when after killing off Angel Eyes' henchmen in the devastated town the bandit and No Name find the arch villain has flown, leaving a scrawled note. 'See you soon Idi . . . Idio . . .' struggles the near-illiterate Tuco. 'Idiots,' No Name fills in. 'It's for you.'

Not only are the jokes better but they are better integrated into the story, defining and refining the characters involved. No Name's sparring relationship with Tuco is a delicate balance between harsh necessity and an almost involuntary mutual affection – with necessity always winning out, as it has to in this savage environment. Both are conscienceless killers when the need arises – or when they believe it does – but only for the sake of survival: as Tuco reminds his priestly brother in the monastery, the only way to avoid starvation where they came from was to become either a priest or a bandit. Tuco even crosses himself, rather perfunctorily, after each killing.

No Name, too, displays a more human side. Apart from his disgust over the waste of the war, he finds time to give a young, dying soldier a last draw on his half-smoked cigar. When the man dies No Name immediately steals his poncho; nothing else would be expected from the Supreme Realist but the sympathetic gesture has been made. Similarly when Tuco

Top and bottom: *Two scenes from* The Good, the Bad and the Ugly *– with Eli Wallach*

66

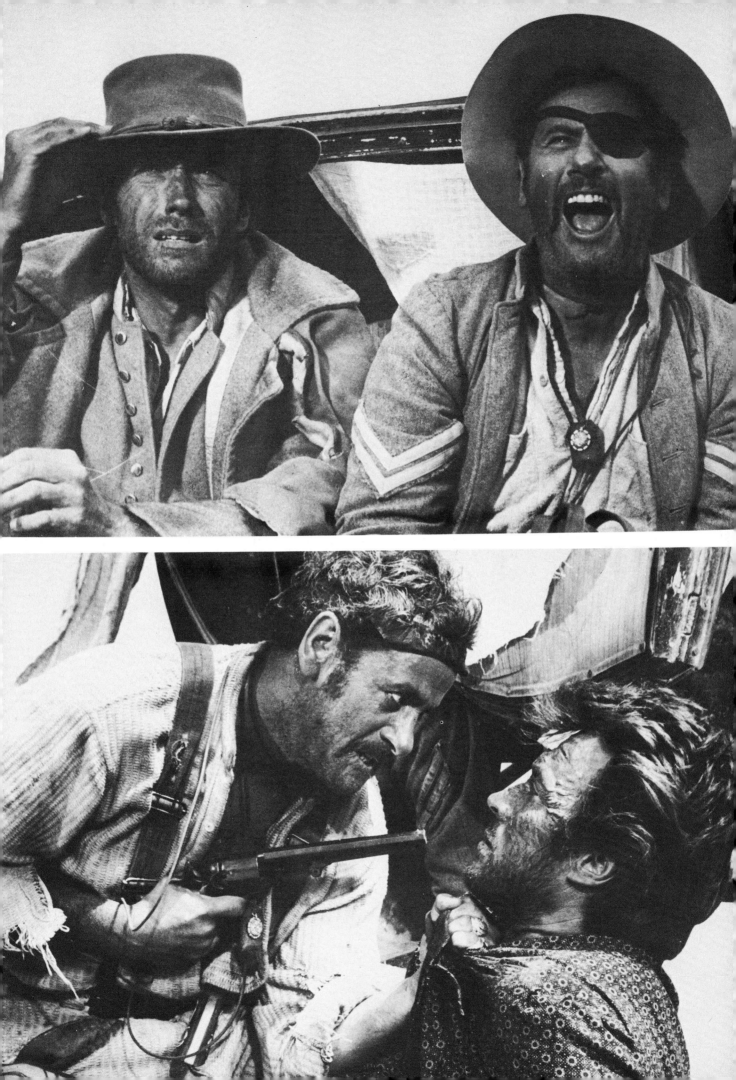

and No Name dynamite a bridge which Union and Confederate forces have been fighting over with enormous loss of life, they do it as much to please a drunken and disillusioned Union captain, who is equally appalled at the losses but helpless to prevent them, as to clear another obstacle on the way to Sad Hill.

The elaborate and treacherous fandango that No Name and Tuco dance around each other is the comic centre of the film and one of its chief joys. Unlike the Mortimer – No Name pairing in *For a Few Dollars More* it allows No Name to be his enigmatic, totally authoritative self; it's he who dreams up the mock hanging trick, he who manipulates the final confrontation at Sad Hill to his own advantage. When Tuco first tries to take his revenge for his abandonment in the desert, No Name leaps from his predicament, like the hero of a Victorian melodrama, in a single bound – and in a puff of convenient smoke. When Tuco is finally allowed his revenge by dragging No Name through the desert it is, we suspect, as much to redress the balance of audience sympathy for such a likeable character as the bandit as anything else.

Eli Wallach's frantic mugging in the role – a performance so wildly over the top it becomes compulsive – is a perfect foil for Eastwood's dry understatement. The third and last of his No Name roles was his most assured and fluent with a finely judged edge of self-parody that underlines Leone's intentions exactly. The partnership that had made Eastwood a star was to end at its highest point.

Eli Wallach played Tuco 'The Ugly' to Eastwood's Joe 'The Good' in The Good, the Bad and the Ugly

The Return of the Prodigal Cowboy

The arrival of *A Fistful of Dollars* in America was marked by that quality of unexpectedness and incongruity that was becoming a hallmark of Eastwood's career. It opened in eighty cinemas in New York on Thursday, 2 February 1967 – in the middle of a blinding snowstorm.

The critics, with few exceptions, hated it. Judith Crist of the *New York World Journal Tribune* dismissed it as a 'cheapjack production (which) misses both awfulness and mediocrity. It is pure manufacture . . . an ersatz Western dedicated to proving that men and women can be gouged, burned, beaten, stamped and shredded to death.' Other comments included: 'high blown cowboy camp', a violation of 'the happy romantic myth' of the West and a 'cold-blooded attempt at sterile emulation'.

Predictably the poor production values came in for a pasting: '. . . the movie suffers from the dreadfully mechanical inflections of the dubbing and the wearisome "universality" of the "Mexican" set,' complained the influential Andrew Sarris of *The Village Voice*. But inherent in almost all these criticisms was a sense of pique, if not outrage, that the Italians were presuming to usurp the most American of all cinema genres. If *Fistful* had been innovative in a more conventionally intellectual way – like *Yojimbo* or the Italians' own neo-realistic dramas of the forties – it would almost certainly have earned critical applause and success in the limited field of the art-house cinema.

But Leone's Westerns weren't like that all. They were works of popular, commercial cinema, tackling Hollywood on its own ground with its own weapons and – most galling of all – winning. For a moment, though, it did look as if popular taste might mirror the disapproval of the critical and film-making establishments. As in Italy, the film's popularity built by word of mouth, but build it did and the distributors, United Artists, soon found they had one of their most commercially successful films in years. *For a Few Dollars More* was released in May 1967 and *The Good, the Bad and the Ugly* early the follow-

71

ing year. Each outgrossed its predecessor by a large amount.

Critical opinion remained mostly dismissive – usually on the grounds of the trilogy's excessive violence and amorality. But views were changing. Reviewers became more aware of Leone's sardonic humour – with its implication that not all the ferocious events on screen were to be taken entirely seriously. Having slammed *Fistful* initially, and then praised 'the superiority of mass taste in America over that anywhere else in the world' for appearing to agree with him, Andrew Sarris now went to the other extreme, praising the religious imagery that litters all three films. When Tuco revenges himself on No Name in the desert in *The Good, the Bad and the Ugly*, 'the suffering becomes so intensely vivid and the framing so conscientiously poetic,' Sarris noted, 'that the audience is subjected to a kind of Cactus Calvary . . . the sheer duration of the suffering makes Eastwood a plausible lower-class hero whose physical redemption is the contemporary correlative of Christ's spiritual redemption.'

Pauline Kael of the *New Yorker* – America's most respected film critic – underwent a reverse process. She began by enjoying the films' larger-than-life quality, but as Eastwood's screen persona developed in movies like *Dirty Harry* and *Magnum Force* she re-appraised the 'spaghettis' – as the American critics now called them – and found some traits that disturbed her. Leone's Westerns

first eliminated the morality-play dimension and turned the Western into pure violent reverie. Apart from their aesthetic qualities (and they did have some), what made these Italian-produced Westerns popular was that they stripped the Western form of its cultural burden of morality. They discarded its civility along with its hypocrisy. In a sense they liberated the form: what the Western hero stood for was left out, and what he embodied (strength and gun power) was retained . . . This is no longer the romantic world in which the hero is, fortunately, the best shot; instead, the best shot is the hero. And that could be what the American audience for action films, grown derisive of the triumph of good, was waiting for. Eastwood's gun power makes him the hero of a totally nihilistic dream world.

Eastwood himself was inclined to agree. 'People don't believe in heroes,' he said. 'Everybody knows that nobody ever stood in the street and let the heavy draw first. It's me or him. To me that's practical and that's where I disagree with the Wayne concept. I do all the stuff Wayne would never do. I play bigger than life characters but I'd shoot the guy in the back.'

His own notices from the three films had ranged between the initial opinion of *Fistful's* producers ('Mr Eastwood shows a talent for squinting and mouthing a cigarillo': Judith Crist) to a guarded approval ('He should be good for many a year of hero': Archer Winsten, *New York Post*). But success with the public and an unprecedentedly healthy bank balance gave him a new assurance as an actor, and as a human being. It was time to fulfil a promise he had made to himself in his army days.

With Maggie he picked out a 200-acre site along the coast of the Monterey peninsula just outside Carmel. Moving into a house that already existed on the land, they began working on plans for a large ranch-style home overlooking the Pacific. Its size wasn't simply for appearance's sake. After thirteen years of marriage they had decided to start a family, surely the most extreme example yet of Eastwood's natural caution.

For the time being he had leisure time to fill. There were promotion tours for the 'Dollar' films, but Hollywood was far from beating a path to his door. Despite the burgeoning career of Steve McQueen, the film industry was still chary of television stars and Eastwood's Italian success might only be a flash in the pan. Finally it was the continued demand for more of the new star from Hollywood's European companies that prompted fresh action.

United Artists hired Eastwood for *Hang 'Em High*, a new Western which was clearly designed to be America's answer to the spaghettis. The budget was $1,600,000 – low by Leone's current standards – but Eastwood negotiated a fee of $400,000 plus a 25 per cent share of the net profits. What ever private opinions Hollywood might have, this alone indicated Eastwood's new status.

His influence did not end with the financial aspect. He lobbied, successfully, for the director to be Ted Post, a veteran of *Rawhide* who had never directed a feature film before. Post's technique and working methods had impressed Eastwood greatly; his choice of a familiar and tested face and his decision to give a newcomer his first opportunity were to become characteristics of the star's career.

The film's producers gave both Eastwood and Post solid backing with some of Hollywood's best known and most reliable supporting players, including Inger Stevens, Ed Begley, Ben Johnson, Pat Hingle, James MacArthur, Bruce Dern and Dennis Hopper (soon to startle Hollywood with one of the most successful 'sleepers' of all time, *Easy Rider*).

The gamble, if there was one, proved to be slight. Within ten weeks of its opening in August 1968 the film had recovered all of its production costs – a studio record in itself – and went on into a healthy profit. The critics were generally kinder to it than they had been to Leone's Westerns, but their views of Eastwood were largely unchanged – 'Mr Eastwood, with his glum sincerity, isn't much of an actor,' wrote Howard Thompson of *The New York Times*. What his performance proved, however – apart from his growing popularity in America – was that he could hold a major Hollywood production together virtually single-handed – since there is little else to unify this rambling and confused piece of cinema. The movie borrows a favourite Leone theme of revenge, adding spaghetti-style violence and historical accuracy, but the dry humour, the visual invention, the subversiveness of the Italian model has gone – replaced by a heavy-handed obsession with justice.

Eastwood gained an on-screen name – Jedediah Cooper, ex-St Louis lawman – for the first time in a major cinema role. When we meet him at the opening of the film he's almost reverted to a Rowdy Yates figure, nursing a herd of newly purchased cattle across the Rio Grande. Nine horsemen approach, led by Captain Wilson (Ed Begley), a rancher who accuses Cooper of rustling a neighbour's cattle and murdering him. Despite showing his bill of sale and describing the vendor of the cattle, Cooper is lynched and left for dead.

Moments later a roving US Marshall, Bliss (Ben Johnson) chances upon him, cuts him down, restores him to life and throws him into the tumbleweed wagon (the Western equivalent of a Black Maria) which he is delivering to Fort Grant.

This is the base of 'hanging-judge' Fenton (Pat Hingle) whose trademark is a public multiple gallows which can deal with up to six occupants at a time. Fenton is the sole government-appointed dispenser of justice for 70,000 square miles of Oklahoma and Indian Territory and eager to earn statehood for his area of jurisdiction.

After a night in Fort Grant's overcrowded and malodorous gaol, Cooper is taken to Fenton, in time to see the execution of the man who committed the crimes for which Cooper was lynched. Cooper is released but when he expresses a keen desire to revenge himself on the vigilantes who hanged him Fenton at first warns him against flouting the law and then offers him a job as a marshall. Cooper accepts.

His first task is to collect a prisoner from a nearby town. While there he recognises his own saddle, stolen at the time of the lynching, and approaches one of the vigilantes in the saloon. The man refuses to surrender, there is a gunfight and the vigilante is killed.

Back in Fort Grant another member of the lynching party gives himself in, identifying the rest as coming from the town of Red Creek. Cooper immediately rides there and arrests the first vigilante he sees – the town's blacksmith. En route to Captain Wilson's ranch, he's approached by a distraught young rancher who tells him rustlers have stolen his cattle and murdered his father and brothers. Reluctant at first to abandon his personal vendetta, Cooper joins a posse in pursuit of the rustlers, one of whom turns out to be another vigilante. The posse are eager to lynch them, but Cooper insists on taking them back to Fort Grant, a job he completes single-handed.

A delighted Fenton rewards him with a night in the local whorehouse where Cooper avails himself of inmate Jennifer (Arlene Golonka). Though he is keen to return to Red Creek, Fenton insists he stays for the trial of the rustlers and the mass executions that follow.

Meanwhile Captain Wilson's gang have split up, some to flee the territory, the rest – led by Wilson – to deal with Cooper personally. During the executions, they ambush Cooper and severely wound him. He is nursed back to health by Rachel (Inger Stevens), a local widow who mysteriously haunts the gaolhouse. In the course of a convalescent picnic, she tells Cooper that she is seeking the men who raped her and killed her husband. The couple become lovers.

As soon as he is fully recovered Cooper returns to Red Creek where Wilson and the remaining members of his gang have barricaded themselves in the captain's ranch house. He disposes of the gang one by one, but when he finally enters the house he discovers that a terror-stricken Wilson has committed suicide – by hanging himself from a rafter.

By now sickened by his vendetta, Cooper tries to resign but is persuaded by Fenton that justice, however imperfect, is a worthy goal. Cooper leaves in pursuit of the gang members who fled.

If the spaghetti Westerns had stripped the genre of its morality, *Hang 'Em High* tried to restore it – but in a highly confused manner. Cooper's desire for revenge is tempered, almost from the beginning, by the constraints of the law. Yet the law is shown to be as unsubtle in its processes as the actions of the lynch mob – Cooper pleads, unsuccessfully, for the lives of two young and impressionable members of the rustler gang he brings back to Fort Grant, then in protest refuses to watch their execution.

Dramatically, too, public and private justice are seen to be on a par. Cooper's abrupt and brutal lynching is matched by the bizarre, carnival-like atmosphere of Fenton's mass execution, with its communal hymn-singing, sales of iced beer and pathetic gallows addresses to the assembled multitude.

Almost everyone in the film is uncertain about their actions, from Bliss – the marshall who rescues Cooper and who then shoots and kills an escaping madman (Dennis Hopper) partly out of necessity and partly, one suspects, because the occupants of the tumbleweed wagon are urging him to 'Kill 'im! Kill 'im!' – to Rachel who until meeting Cooper doesn't seem to have thought through her own desire for revenge. Even Judge Fenton wrestles with his conscience and the Wilson gang, largely respected members of their community who are seen to have acted impulsively but in good faith when they lynched Cooper, only go after him when they realise the implacable nature of the law and Cooper's own desire for revenge.

None of this would have mattered too much if Cooper had been a figure apart from all this moral uncertainty – as No Name was. But Cooper is as much at sea as everyone else. He might look like No Name and even shoot like him, but the air of casual authority and the wry humour have gone. This is a man who goes on lyrically photographed picnics with attractive widows and pleads for a second kiss. The closest echo to his Leone heritage is his greeting to the first of the vigilantes he tracks down: 'You made two mistakes. You hung the wrong man, and you didn't finish the job.'

But in spite of a leaden pace the film did have its felicities. The grotesque set-piece of the mass executions – based on those carried out at Fort Smith by the real-life 'hanging' Judge Parker – rings true in an original way. Cooper's lynching, too, has a powerful impact, contributed in no small part by Eastwood's insistence on doing his own stunts, including a sequence where he is dragged across the Rio Grande by lariat. And in terms of performances Inger Stevens's quiet conviction lends the story an emotional depth which the script alone had not provided.

However jumbled the result artistically, the mixture was calculated to make Eastwood's No Name persona more acceptable to an American audience and in this it succeeded brilliantly. *Hang 'Em High* not only proved the rising star's 'bankability' in America, it provided an entrance ticket to the Hollywood Western. But Eastwood's ambitions extended far beyond a successful synthesis of Rowdy Yates and the Man With No Name. He wanted to exploit as wide a range of Hollywood's potential as possible, and that meant returning not only to the Old West but to the modern world as well. Ironically his chance to do so would come through Universal – the studio which had rejected him twelve years earlier.

The Siegelini Breakthrough

Coogan's Bluff was one of a number of film projects put to Eastwood in 1967 and, even

75

though a final script had not been written, its central idea appealed to him strongly. Set in the present, the story concerned a deputy sheriff from Arizona sent to New York to extradite a prisoner. To Eastwood it had two major attractions: firstly, it featured a 'Western' hero who moves into a modern, urban environment – effectively allowing him to make the same transition in his career; and secondly, the contrast between the hero's 'frontier' attitudes and abilities and the sophistication of city-dwellers seemed a fruitful one.

The choice of this particular film was illuminating. Having made a successful leap into the Hollywood Western – at least in commercial terms – Eastwood could easily have consolidated his career with a series of No Name impersonations, milking a current trend for all it was worth. His fees would have climbed with his popularity until public interest waned and an early and well-cushioned retirement beckoned.

Eastwood would certainly not be beyond accepting roles that presented a familiar image for a high financial return. But his first instinct on gaining the artistic freedom of Hollywood stardom was to take a completely fresh direction – to experiment.

That didn't mean, however, discarding his No Name persona – he would not feel confident, or foolhardy enough to do that for another two films. What he did was to take a leaf out of Sergio Leone's book, by extending what had now become an accepted screen image.

The result was to re-introduce the humour so conspicuously lacking in *Hang 'Em High* – not the wild, sardonic humour of Leone, but a quieter, dryer though equally laconic kind that was much closer to Eastwood's own personality.

Even more important, *Coogan's Bluff* allowed him to tackle in a more relevant way the moral aspects of his persona. No Name's ruthless self-sufficiency might be the only realistic way to respond to the anarchic world of the Leone Western, but how would a similar character stand up in an equally anarchic modern world, with its ever-increasing bureaucracy, its rising crime rates, and – in 1967 – the escalating unrest over Civil Rights and America's deepening involvement in Vietnam? Would audiences still cheer him on?

The moral tension created by an updated No Name was to play a crucial part in Eastwood's future career. For the moment, however, those themes were at the prototype stage – and creating havoc with the script in hand.

Eastwood's championing of Ted Post for *Hang 'Em High* had clearly taught him that he needed a more experienced hand on the tiller. The first choice as director was Alex Segal, again a man with limited feature film experience but an award-winning stage and television director. He and Eastwood were unable to agree over the final form of the script and Segal left. Other directors were suggested, including Don Taylor and Mark Rydell who in turn put up the name of Don Siegal. Siegel appealed to Jennings Lang, the Universal executive who was dealing with the film. Eastwood remembers the studio's logic for their pairing: 'They said I was "warm" in Italy, and (Don) was "warm" in France, so maybe the two of us would get along. I

Coogan's Bluff, *1968*

76

went looking at some of the films he'd done, a couple of television shows and the movie *The Killers*, and I was very impressed.'

So began a collaboration between star and director matched in importance only by Eastwood's experiences with Sergio Leone.

Despite an eighteen-year age gap there were remarkable correspondences between Siegel's career and artistic concerns and Eastwood's. Like the star, Siegel had been accepted by the Hollywood establishment only grudgingly and after a long period of time. After an English education at Cambridge and the Royal Academy of Dramatic Art, despite being born in Chicago, he'd joined Warner Brothers as an assistant film librarian in 1934. From there he had moved into film editing, eventually running Warner's montage department. In 1945 he revealed his film-making talent with two documentary shorts, *Star in the Night* and *Hitler Lives?*, both of which won Oscars. The following year he had his feature film debut.

Since then Siegel had specialised in fast-moving, economical, low-budget films, usually with a violent content; some of them, like the science-fictional *Invasion of the Body Snatchers* and the prison drama *Riot in Cell Block 11* became B-movie classics. His Hollywood reputation was as a proficient, low-budget director – with a status appropriate to his budgets.

Like Eastwood, however, his true worth had first been acknowledged in Europe – by writers in the French critical magazine *Cahiers du Cinema*. Rather to his surprise (he has a dry humour not unlike Eastwood's), he was identified as an *auteur*, literally an 'author' of the films he made, each of which was seen to bear indelible traces of his philosophy and style, regardless of their being made within the constraints of the studio system.

Siegel's universe was described as angry and pessimistic. His heroes – always highly masculine – boasted private moralities which were at odds with those of the world they lived in. Invariably, too, they were flawed in some way which usually led to their downfall, making many of them anti-heroes long before such figures were fashionable. Now, however, they were fashionable due in large part to the success of the Man With No Name.

Siegel's latest film – and his most commercially successful – was *Madigan*. Starring Richard Widmark – one of the few occasions Siegel had used a star name – the film told the story of a New York detective who bends the rules to track down a ruthless killer. Not only did its theme mirror *Coogan's Bluff*, especially in its hero's conflict with urban bureaucracy, but its depiction of New York was sharp, taut and highly atmospheric.

When Siegel was first approached he arranged to see Eastwood's Leone Westerns which he enjoyed and admired. But things did not run smoothly at once. Siegel worked on his own version of the *Coogan* story, by now the ninth draft, which Eastwood promptly rejected. Siegel was not pleased. Despite feeling 'like a prophet without honour in my own land', as he had once complained, he had chosen to work in low-budget films because they allowed him more artistic freedom than financially high-powered productions. He wasn't keen to abandon that freedom, and it was Jennings Lang who insisted that both men sit down and try again.

Together with Dean Riesner, a writer who had worked on *Rawhide*, Siegel and

Eastwood put together a tenth and final version, combining the best aspects of all the previous drafts. By the time they had finished they had developed a strong mutual respect; they had also become friends.

'He's straightforward and knows what he wants,' Eastwood commented later. 'He never gets bogged down, even in a disaster, and he likes to hear ideas. He has an ego like everyone else, but if a janitor comes up with something Don won't turn it down. He breeds an atmosphere of participation.'

Siegel was equally complimentary of his star.

> I found Clint very knowledgeable about making pictures, very good at knowing what to do with the camera. I also found that he is inclined to underestimate his range as an actor . . . .He doesn't require and I don't give him much direction . . . Clint knows what he's doing when he acts and when he picks material. He has very good ideas about setups and things, and I call them Clintus shots. Now I'll try to figure out a shot to top it and if I do it's called a Siegelini shot . . . Many times his ideas will lead me into another channel of thought, and I'll come up with a new approach . . . It's a peculiar relationship. He doesn't treat me as the producer or director and I don't treat him as the star – what we're trying to do is tell a story as well as we can.

What also delighted Siegel was Eastwood's adherence to his anti-heroic image. 'Clint has an absolute fixation as an anti-hero,' he told an interviewer. 'I've never worked with an actor who was less conscious of his good image.'

The fruits of their co-operation can be seen in the opening moments of *Coogan's Bluff*. A panoramic view of a bleak and featureless desert, backed by rugged mountains, could be the first shot of a Leone Western. A scruffy-looking Indian in a loincloth climbs higher up a rocky hillside, rifle in hand – the weapon even has a telescopic sight. He then notices someone approaching across the desert, a distant cloud of dust too far off to be identified. The camera moves closer – and we see Clint Eastwood, entering the film like No Name from the wilderness, but dressed now as a modern sheriff, riding a high-powered jeep; dark glasses have replaced the familiar cigar.

Braking, he spots the Indian's discarded western clothes – boots with the reservation stamp, a shirt and trousers. Clearly a manhunt is in progress. Unaware of, or simply unheeding, the fact that the Indian's rifle is trained on him, Eastwood drives at speed toward the hillside where the man is hiding, swerving to a halt in a shower of dust as the Indian opens fire. When the dust clears, the jeep is empty. Thoroughly disconcerted, the Indian turns from side to side, emptying his magazine clip in the direction of a sudden noise. When he turns back, Eastwood is standing there, his gun trained. He tosses the Indian's trousers onto the ground and utters the film's first and typically laconic line of dialogue: 'Put your pants on, chief.'

As the Indian bends to pick them up, Eastwood takes the opportunity to sink a blow into the man's gut, doubling him

Overleaf: *With Susan Clark in a scene from* Coogan's Bluff

79

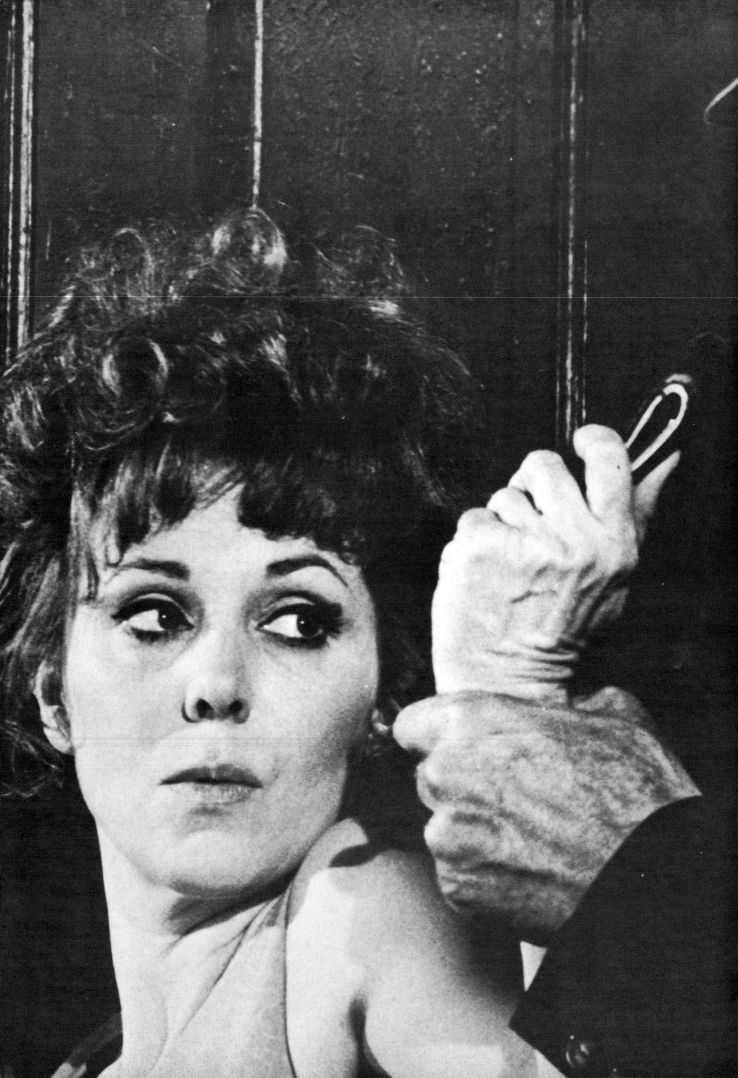

over. The pace and economy of the scene-setting and the action is Siegel's, the characterisation is Eastwood's. No Name's ruthless certainty and understated authority is back with a vengeance. Deputy Sheriff Coogan is as much a part of this scorched western landscape as No Name was of his; he rides through it with self-sufficient ease and his mastery of it is symbolised by the courageous, swift yet apparently effortless way in which he subdues the Indian – a figure who by historical and cultural right should be most at home here.

But this version of No Name doesn't live in a world where gun power and cunning need be a man's only justification for his actions. This is modern Arizona, a real world with all its moral and legal constrictions, and ambiguities. Not that that bothers Coogan overmuch as he drives his prisoner back toward town and parks outside an isolated farmstead.

Handcuffing the Indian to a porch rail – and denying him a cigarette – Coogan goes inside to make love to a married girlfriend whose husband is away on business. It's here, as he languishes in a pre-coital bath tub, that his middle-aged boss, Sheriff McCrea (Tom Tully) finds him, berates him for leaving the road block to which he was assigned and bawls him out for his treatment of the Indian: 'That's a prisoner out there, not an animal you can tether to a rail!'

His punishment for acting in such an independent fashion is to go to New York to fetch another prisoner, James Ringerman (Don Stroud), a task generally regarded as a boring chore. This is the price of independent action – however successful – in this world.

It's a conflict that grows on his arrival in New York. In his stetson, bootlace tie and cowboy boots, he drops from the skies by helicopter onto the roof of the PanAm building – a beautifully compressed image of American West meeting East. In Arizona, Coogan's frontier-style individuality paid dividends; here his dress alone makes him stick out like a sore thumb – and his attitudes are about to prove just as incongruous.

A running joke develops as he is repeatedly addressed as 'Tex' and with increasing exasperation he explains that he comes from Arizona, a taxi driver cheats him and he quickly runs into a legal impasse. Detective Lieutenant McElroy (Lee J. Cobb) informs him that Ringerman has taken an overdose of LSD and is now in Bellevue prison hospital. He can only be handed over to Coogan after a complex judicial procedure. Coogan will have to stay over for a few days.

In the same police station, Coogan spots Julie Roth (Susan Clark), an attractive social worker. A male client she is talking to deliberately takes liberties, eventually fondling her. To the liberal-minded Julie, tolerance, reason and understanding will solve this problem: 'Nothing you can say or do is going to shock or offend me.' To Coogan, this is simply a punk pushing his luck. After due warning, he punches the man, who flees. Julie is outraged, but Coogan, with insistent charm, persuades her to have lunch with him, and eventually returns with her to her flat. His attempt at seduction almost succeeds when a client calls.

The following day Coogan decides to ignore the red tape and bluffs his way into Bellevue where he sees Ringerman – a man, we learn, he had originally arrested after an eight-day hunt – and Ringerman's rather fey girlfriend, Linny Raven (Tisha Sterling). Ringerman whispers something to her as he leaves with Coogan and in the lobby of the PanAm building Linny and some of Ringerman's associates knock Coogan unconscious. Ringerman escapes.

McElroy visits Coogan in hospital and angrily warns him off the case. Undeterred, Coogan discharges himself and visits Ringerman's mother but only succeeds in blowing the cover of a police officer already keeping her under surveillance. An exasperated McElroy brings him in and orders him to take the next flight home. As Coogan leaves he meets Julie again and they go for a walk in nearby Tryon Park where Coogan discloses some of the reasons for his ruthless attitudes. 'The colour of pity', he tells her, 'is red.' The red of his own blood, spilled when he once – for humanitarian reasons – allowed a prisoner to see his wife after his arrest; the woman had a six-inch blade up her sleeve and it ended up in Coogan's stomach. 'So much for pity,' he says.

A more sympathetic Julie invites Coogan home to dinner. But as she prepares a meal, Coogan discovers that Linny Raven is one of her clients. He leaves abruptly, tracking the girl down to a discotheque. She takes him back to her flat and seduces him, with little difficulty, then leads him to a poolroom, where Ringerman's associates are waiting.

In a brilliantly choreographed and photographed scene of extraordinary violence, Coogan takes on all six, apparently killing one, before escaping just as the police arrive. Battered and bloody, he returns to Linny's apartment and bullies the truth out of her: Ringerman's hiding place is a building known as the Cloisters

in Tryon Park, on a high point called Coogan's Bluff.

Linny leads Coogan there and a chase ensues, at first on foot and then on stolen motorbikes along the steep paths of the public park – another example of Eastwood performing his own stunts. Ringerman is captured after a rugby-style flying tackle from the back of a bike, just as McElroy and the police arrive. Coogan growls that he is making a citizen's arrest but he agrees, finally, to go through with the judicial procedure that will give him his prisoner.

McElroy sees him off at the PanAm heliport, thanking him with a grudging but genuine respect. Julie, too, waves goodbye – she is dressed entirely in red. Sitting next to a handcuffed Ringerman in the departing helicopter, Coogan takes out a cigarette – and then offers one to his prisoner.

The film is a tightly woven network of contrasts and correspondences, all throwing fresh light on Coogan and the attitudes he embodies. His hard-hat ruthlessness is matched by Julie Roth's tolerant liberalism, his naive straightforwardness by McElroy's world-weary acquaintance with the complexities of urban justice: 'I know,' the lieutenant mocks, when he visits Coogan in hospital. 'A man's gotta do what a man's gotta do.'

Clear-cut frontier ethics are seen to be laughable in this context, but Coogan's philosophy is far from condemned. The New York detectives might dismiss his instinctive method as 'woodcraft' ('Animals, people,' Coogan tries to explain, 'they don't act much different when you're hunting them' – which in turn puts his treatment of the Indian into a different, more understandable perspective); but the

83

film takes on a mood of genuine wistfulness when Coogan looks over the Manhattan skyline from Tryon Park and tries 'to picture how it was before people fouled it up'.

Both sides are affected by Coogan's visit. McElroy comes to respect the man he derided as 'Tex' or 'Wyatt'; Julie sees him off in a red outfit, the colour which symbolises a key aspect of Coogan's personality and which is an indication of how close she has come to him. Coogan himself, eventually, accepts the city's methods and something of Julie's more tolerant attitudes – he offers his second quarry the cigarette he would not have dreamed of giving to his first.

And yet the film did go back to the moralistic, if hypocritical, attitudes of the Western from which, according to Pauline Kael, Leone's 'spaghettis' had liberated it. Coogan's actions might result in censure and confusion but they manifestly work; he does get his man, and in a very entertaining fashion.

There is one scene in the film which, more than any other, suggests Coogan's moral rightness, regardless of almost anything he does. His visit to the discotheque where Linny Raven hangs out is shot as a quick-fire montage, taking full advantage of Don Siegel's experience in that field. It becomes a vision of what was then a trendy, psychedelic hippy culture, full of garish, pop-art designs and pounding rock music, painted faces and writhing bodies. Here Julie Roth's liberalism turns into mere licence, on a par with ancient Rome. Projected nudes flit across the walls, a topless dancer descends on a trapeze, homosexual couples embrace. And Coogan, the tallest man on the floor in his stetson, strides through with obvious dis-

belief and distaste – as alien to this culture and as grotesque an intrusion as the fleeting image of a gigantic spider (taken from the early Eastwood film *Tarantula*) which briefly appears on the walls. Suddenly Coogan's image of the clear-cut, clean, inviolate Western hero seems infinitely superior to the frenzied and corrupt world about him.

It was clearly a view intended by both Siegel and Eastwood. Siegel was to describe Eastwood as having 'that indefinable something that is the best in America. He's cleancut, he's strong he's resolute, he's honest.' Eastwood, too, expressed a liking for the Coogan-style characters. 'That's why, maybe, I carry them to other extremes than my predecessors. In other words, in the complications of society as we know it today, sometimes a person who can cut through the bureaucracy and red tape . . . who thinks on that level is a hero. A man who thinks on a very simple level and has very simple moral values appeals to a great many people.'

He was certainly right about the appeal. *Coogan's Bluff* was a commercial as well as a critical success and it drew some of Eastwood's finest reviews to date, particularly from *Time* magazine: 'Clint Eastwood performs with a measure of real feeling in the first role that fits him as comfortably as his tooled leather boots.'

With Don Siegel's direction, Eastwood had brought his screen persona home to America. The pattern for future success – and controversy – was set, but for the

Coogan is forced to defend himself when attacked by thugs at a poolhall, Coogan's Bluff

84

moment he felt the need to consolidate his career both in terms of finance and box office. In 1968 the most straightforward way to do that was to appear in an international blockbuster, which is exactly what Eastwood did.

Coogan and Julie falling in love in Coogan's Bluff

By the sixties the traumatic events of World War Two were sufficiently distant to have taken on the aura of myth – and that ambiguity which is characteristic of the most potent fairy stories or folk tales. To the new youth culture the war was an awful warning that such things should never have been allowed to occur again – and yet that was exactly what appeared to be happening in Vietnam. To many of the older generation, who had actually experienced the conflict, there was the attraction of nostalgia; for all its deprivations and tragedy, it was the most exciting and memorable time of many lives.

The cinema was well aware of this and of the filmic possibilities of the war story; it offered high adventure – on an epic as well as a personal scale – visual excitement, and a reasonably clear-cut morality. Unlike World War One, whose true ghastliness did not really reach the screen until BBC TV's harrowing *Great War* documentary series in 1964, World War Two presented a straightforward conflict between evil-minded, ruthless, black or grey-uniformed Nazi 'baddies' (or even more inscrutably treacherous Orientals) and tough but fair-minded Allied 'goodies'. War might be hell but the violence was plainly justified because it was intended to preserve civilisation, so we might as well sit back and enjoy it.

It was a wide-screen, updated version of the Old West, where the violence of the white-hatted hero – who fortunately turned out to be the toughest, fastest-drawing man around – was OK because it paved the way for stability and progress, justice and truth.

The decade began with a blockbusting, no-expense-spared epic, *The Guns of Navarone*, which pictured the war as high adventure. The highest grossing film of 1961, it nodded towards tragedy by killing off most of its major characters in the course of their heroic deeds, but its audience appeal

Left: *Eastwood played Lt Morris Schaffer in* Where Eagles Dare, *1969.* Overleaf: *Ingrid Pitt, Clint Eastwood, Mary Ure and Richard Burton in a scene from* Where Eagles Dare

was based firmly on tension-filled excitement and the spectacular special effects of the climax when the gigantic guns of the title are finally blasted into the night sky.

The Great Escape, which made a star of Steve McQueen in 1963, followed a similar path. But by the mid-sixties the mood was changing. In *The Dirty Dozen*, the most commercially successful film of 1967, there were as many heroics and explosive special effects, but the main characters were now vicious criminals, acting as much out of self-interest as patriotism. By the end of the decade the most popular films – *M*A*S*H*, *Patton*, *Catch-22* (all among the top ten money-earners of 1970) – would adopt a clear anti-war stance, picturing those who took up arms willingly as fools, madmen or crooks.

Eastwood's essentially Western screen persona could plainly fit in well with this new war-as-rip-roaring-adventure genre. He was to make two war epics at the end of the sixties, *Where Eagles Dare*, released in 1969 and *Kelly's Heroes*, released in 1970. Both were highly successful commercially and both accurately attuned to public taste, the first as an all-action, suspenseful display of superheroics, the second with a more humorous, satirical edge and a much more equivocal attitude to war and heroism.

Where Eagles Dare had a promising provenance in a script written by Alistair MacLean, author of *The Guns of Navarone* – even though he completed it in just six weeks. The film was set in motion by London-based producer Elliott Kastner who sold it first to Richard Burton and then MGM.

Burton, it was rumoured, accepted because he wanted to appear in a film his young sons could see and enjoy. Since the shooting would take place in Austria and in England with a largely British cast, MGM insisted on including a big American name. They approached Eastwood, who was compensated for second billing below Burton by a fee of $800,000.

With that peculiar absence of logic all too common to such large scale productions, Brian G. Hutton – a thirty-three-year-old ex-television director who had never tackled a project of this size before – was signed to direct. It proved, however, to be an inspired gamble. He papered over the gaping credibility abysses in Mac-Lean's convoluted script with a crisp pace, a sense of fun and a flair for presenting explosive action.

The story, which alternated a series of double and then triple crosses with bouts of equally improbable, though highly dramatic action, was in need of such qualities. Burton played Major John Smith, the British commander of a commando unit ordered by Turner (Patrick Wymark), the head of MI5, to rescue a captured American general from an apparently impregnable fortress high in the Bavarian Alps. The general knows the Allied plans for the invasion of Europe which the Nazis may discover at any moment.

Eastwood played his second in command, Lieutenant Schaffer, ostensibly a member of the American Rangers. With five companions they parachute into the area of the fortress. One man is killed in the drop and Smith suspects he may have been murdered by a double agent in the unit. Smith approaches a British intelligence agent Mary Ellison (Mary Ure) in a nearby town and enlists her help in a plan to enter the fortress, where she is working as a maid.

92

Before the plan can be carried out, however, another member of the unit is mysteriously killed and Smith and Schaffer are captured by the Germans in a local tavern. With the help of a diversionary fire, they manage to escape and mount their sneak attack on the fortress – a remote, mountain-top retreat which can only be approached by cable car.

They succeed in rescuing the general but are forced to surrender when their three companions are captured. It is now revealed that the American general is in fact an actor and the purpose of the whole mission has been to unmask Nazi agents in the Allied high command, including a member of Smith's unit. The three captured commandos are shown to be double agents – as is Smith himself, who then discloses that he is in reality a triple agent. Schaffer, in turn, is not a Ranger but a professional assassin whose task it is to clear up all the confusion, permanently.

Smith, Schaffer, Mary Ellison and the fake general stage a dramatic escape from the fortress, whose climax is a fight between Smith and a Nazi on the roof of a descending cable car. With the aid of a stolen bus, they flee to a nearby airport, pursued by the Germans. A plane is waiting and its crew includes the MI5 supremo, Turner. As they head for home, Smith proves that Turner is the leading Nazi agent they have been looking for and offers him the chance of an honorable death by committing suicide. Turner promptly throws himself out of the plane.

Despite a performance that was in many ways a regression from the subtleties of *Coogan's Bluff*, Eastwood earned the most glowing reviews of his career so far. His own opinion may be judged by the title he generally gives the film – *Where Doubles Dare*. But there was a highly effective contrast between the laconic, very physical style of the American star (who typically cut down his own dialogue to the minimum) and the wordier, classical acting style of Burton and other British cast members, including Michael Hordern, Donald Houston and Peter Barkworth. As a result it was left to Burton's swelling tones to explain the complexities of the plot while Eastwood was left to do the killing – most impressively in a submachine gun battle which marks their escape from the fortress. Ironically the body count was far higher than in any of his previous films, including the 'spaghetti' Westerns, but no one seemed to mind in this comic-book context.

The two leading actors got on as well together off-screen as on. Isolated in the remote Schloss Hohenwerfen in Austria, as well as a London he had never visited before (British pubs earned his swift approval), Eastwood formed a strong friendship with the Burtons who at that time consisted of Richard and Elizabeth Taylor. The relationship was to give rise to a future film project. Elizabeth Taylor liked the idea of working with Eastwood and showed him a script called *Two Mules for Sister Sara*, essentially a two-handed Western for a male and female lead. It was earmarked for a convenient gap in both their schedules, though it would be another twelve months before it got off the ground.

The reason was largely due to an unprecedented pace of work on Eastwood's behalf: two years of concentrated effort that were to give him an unassailable position at the box office and the bank.

Within a month of returning from Europe, he was off again – to spend five

PW-252-20

94

months on location at the small town of Baker in north-east Oregon. There he co-starred in *Paint Your Wagon*, another epic production and his first, and last, musical.

The choice was more than a little eccentric. No one had gone out of their way to suggest that Eastwood had a neglected singing talent – though he had made one record in his *Rawhide* days, a cowboy ballad called 'Unknown Girl', which sank without trace. His fee, too, was considerably less – at $250,000 – than he had received for *Hang 'Em High*.

Personal reasons may have been more important. Because of his work on *Where Eagles Dare* he had missed the birth of his first child – Kyle Clinton Eastwood – by four days, an event made even more tense than usual by the fact that a previous pregnancy had ended in miscarriage. Baker was a car drive away from Carmel. In addition the opportunity to work once more among the mountains and forests he had known as a teenager must have had its appeal.

The role, too, represented something of a challenge for Eastwood. As the introspective, dependable prospector 'Pardner', he was a No Name without the ruthlessness or the sardonic humour – a difficult act to pull off.

In casting Eastwood and Lee Marvin – a major star since his Oscar-winning performance in *Cat Ballou* in 1963 – as leads, Paramount, the studio in charge, hoped to guarantee box-office appeal, but their chief motive for setting up a musical was to

With Lee Marvin in Paint Your Wagon, *1969*

emulate the success of *The Sound of Music*. That 1965 hit had recently overtaken *Gone With the Wind* as the biggest money-earner in the history of cinema, and musicals like *My Fair Lady* and *Thoroughly Modern Millie* had continued to do very well.

The musical Paramount chose to film was a fifties Broadway success by Lerner and Loewe, set in a goldrush town of the Old West – the setting in which both Eastwood and Marvin had first made their marks. The director was to be Joshua Logan who had made the musicals *Camelot* and *South Pacific*.

Paramount had hoped to sign Julie Andrews, then the world's top box-office attraction, but she preferred to star in her husband Blake Edward's current production *Darling Lili* which was also being made by Paramount. As an alternative, though by no means an obvious one, the studio hired Jean Seberg as the female lead. Plucked from obscurity at the age of seventeen, amid much publicity, to star in Otto Preminger's 1957 version of *Saint Joan* – which proved to be a resounding flop – she had pursued her career in Europe. There she had struck lucky in Jean-Luc Godard's revolutionary *A Bout de Souffle* in 1960. Though she was no more known for musicals than her fellow principles, she was well-liked by European audiences and added to the film's international appeal.

The appeal of the plot, having grown somewhat outdated since the show's first appearance on stage, was increased by creating a ménage-à-trois situation for the three main characters. Eastwood and Marvin played the soft-spoken Pardner and the rumbustious and frequently drunken Ben Rumson who team up during the California gold rush. Despite moderate success, Rumson feels the need of a wife

and purchases Elizabeth (Jean Seberg) from a Mormon who has two. However Elizabeth's beauty – and the fact that women are in extremely short supply causes trouble in the small mining town where they all live. To alleviate the situation Rumson is deputised to hijack a wagon-load of six French whores who are en route elsewhere. In his absence Pardner and Elizabeth inconveniently fall in love.

When Rumson returns and finds out, the two men fight but Elizabeth resolves the problem by agreeing to be a wife to both. The triangle works well until a party of straight-laced settlers, the Fentys, are rescued from a blizzard and move in with the threesome.

The newcomers are deeply shocked by the unusual marital arrangement and even more disturbed when their son Horton (Tom Ligon) starts to take after Rumson.

Meanwhile the gold is running out and the prospectors are moving on. Rumson and Pardner devise a secret plan to continue living there with Elizabeth by digging a series of tunnels beneath the town to recover the gold dust which has filtered through the floor boards over the years. Elizabeth, however, is stricken with guilt at her double marriage – mainly due to the influence of the Fentys – and turns both Rumson and Pardner out.

At this point the town – now riddled by tunnels – collapses. Rumson decides to leave in search of fresh adventures. Pardner remains with Elizabeth to settle and take up farming.

Off camera with Jean Seberg, Paint Your Wagon

In spite of some spectacular photography and well-staged musical numbers, the film was not an artistic success. The plot appeared largely static, the Eastwood–Marvin pairing failed to strike sparks and Jean Seberg lacked the weight for such an overblown production. Eastwood handled his two solo songs 'I Still See Eliza' and 'I Talk to the Trees' largely by talking his way through them in a soft voice. Marvin achieved much the same result with a deep growl, which unpredictably pushed his recording of 'I Was Born under a Wandering Star' to the top of the British pop charts.

But in the face of indifferent reviews it was Eastwood who won the accolades: 'He has a casual, soft elegance that instantly makes him a friend to the audience,' enthused Rex Reed. 'I found myself looking forward to his one-dimensional underplaying out of sheer gratitude.'

In the light of the remainder of his career, *Paint your Wagon* remains a curious aberration. At the time it was a valuable object lesson to the ambitious star.

Paint Your Wagon earned $15 million on its release in late 1969, a sum that should have guaranteed commercial success. It didn't because its production costs – originally budgeted at a generous $14 million – rocketed close to $20 million by the time the film was finished.

The freewheeling expense appalled Eastwood. 'It was a disaster,' he complained in an interview with Rex Reed. 'It didn't have to be such an *expensive* disaster. We had Lear jets flying everyone in and out of Oregon, helicopters to take the wives to location for lunch, crews of seven trucks, thousands of extras getting paid for doing nothing, everyone living in ranch houses – twenty million dollars down the drain and most of it doesn't even show on the screen!'

Even worse he loathed the squabbling that arose over the final cut. 'I saw that film in four versions: the director's version, the producer's version and then the coalition of all the studio executives and their versions. The director's version, the first one, was actually the best one. But that wasn't the one that was released.'

To Eastwood's mind taking personal control of his films was not only a better guarantee of artistic success but of commercial success too, which made his next project doubly pleasurable. It was *Two Mules for Sister Sara* and it re-united him with Don Siegel. It was also a co-production between Universal and Eastwood's own production company, Malpaso. He would do only one more film solely for another studio – MGM's *Kelly's Heroes* – his second war film and his final blockbuster.

Eastwood's opinion of his 'epic' performances may not be the highest, but they served their function. By the end of 1968 he had amassed sufficient funds to make Malpaso possible; he was also the fifth most popular box office star in America. By the end of 1970, when *Kelly's Heroes* was released, he had risen to second position, behind Paul Newman. For that reason it's convenient to look at *Kelly's Heroes* out of sequence.

Scripted by British writer Troy Kennedy Martin – who had been responsible for BBC TV's *Z Cars* series – and with Brian Hutton again in the director's chair, it was potentially the most promising of all Eastwood epic films – a fact of which he was all too aware by the time the movie was completed.

Set in post D-Day France – though

filmed on a five-month location stint in Yugoslavia – it combined the derring-do elements of *Where Eagles Dare* with more strongly delineated characters, broad comedy and even more explosive special effects. But its implications were far deeper than the MacLean-scripted film.

Here war has become a commercial enterprise, with unpleasant side effects. Eastwood's Private Kelly – actually an ex-lieutenant, demoted after he became the scapegoat for somebody else's blunder – learns from a captured German officer that a secret horde of gold bullion, worth $1.6 million, is concealed in a French bank. Unfortunately the bank lies behind enemy lines.

During a three-day respite from combat, he persuades his squad sergeant, Big Joe (Telly Savalas), Crapgame (Don Rickles) – a supply sergeant and king of the black market – and Oddball (Donald Sutherland) – an unconventional tank commander – to join him in a private war to liberate the gold. After several battles, they succeed – though they end up by drawing in most of the American army in the immediate area with promises of a share in the proceeds. Meanwhile the local American commander – unaware of the men's true reasons for such enthusiasm – cheers them on and enters the French town as a conquering hero as Kelly's 'heroes' leave by the back door with the gold.

Self-interest governs everyone in a world as anarchic as anything Sergio Leone invented. When the German officer who

Donald Sutherland as Oddball, and Clint Eastwood as Kelly in Kelly's Heroes, *1970*

will lead them to the gold is captured from the neighbouring, occupied town of Nancy, Big Joe has no interest in military secrets. 'I just want to know the best hotel,' he tells the prisoner. 'Think of us as tourists.' He adds: 'We're not worried about the German army. We've enough troubles of our own.' A view borne out immediately as they are inadvertently shelled by an American mortar battery.

The squad's three-day rest is only possible because their young captain wants to arrange the transport home of a looted yacht. Crapgame instantly checks the price of gold on the Paris exchange when the deal is offered to him, and Oddball – a man who disguises his tanks as wrecks in order to avoid combat – decides: 'For one point six million dollars we could become heroes for three days.' He adds, in much the same way as a gangster might commend a superior form of tommy gun: 'A Sherman can give you a very nice edge.'

Finally, when only a single Tiger tank keeps the Americans from their goal, the Panzer commander inside is persuaded to surrender when he is told what he is defending and offered a share. 'Business is business, right?' declares Big Joe.

The Leone-like quality of this world is underlined in an overt parody of a 'spaghetti' set-piece as Kelly, Big Joe and Oddball – guns in hand – advance across the town square to present their deal to the Tiger's occupants. Electric guitars twang, Morricone-style, on the soundtrack.

Even the American general (Carroll O'Connor) has his price, which is military glory. When he enters the liberated French town the jubilant citizens mistake him for Eisenhower and he is so overwhelmed he does nothing to dissuade them.

Death, however, is treated in a conven-tionally comic book fashion. As Oddball's Sherman tanks demolish a German rail-way depot, cheerful music, including 'I've Been Working on the Railroad', booms from a loudspeaker attached to the lead tank. After the ruthless massacre of a German troop column, the squad – and an elegaic theme on the soundtrack – mourn the deaths of just two of the Americans. Kelly is noticeably the first of the squad to turn away and get moving again.

Eastwood's quiet underplaying made him an excellent straight man, against which the exuberant performances of his colleagues could be judged. Only Donald Sutherland's portrayal of Oddball as an anachronistic hippy – forever begging his more pessimistic comrades to 'come on with the positive waves' – threatened to upset the balance.

The film emerged as an entertaining, spectacular and rather hypocritical romp and a sound commercial success. But Eastwood was far from happy with it. 'That film,' he said in an interview for *Playboy* in 1974, 'could have been one of the best war movies ever. And it should have been; it had the best script, a good cast, a subtle anti-war message. But somehow everything got lost. The picture got bogged down in Yugoslavia and it just ended up as the story of a bunch of American screw-offs in World War Two. Some of the key scenes got cut out. I even called up Jim Aubrey, who was then the head of MGM, and said: "For God's sake don't run that picture for critics until Brian, the director, has had a chance to do some more work on it. You're going to cut off maybe millions of·dollars in box office receipts." Aubrey said he'd think it over, but I'm sure when he hung up the phone he said to himself: "What does this frigging actor know about millions of dollars? Forget it.'' It was released without further work and critically it did badly.'

Eastwood might have further justified his opinion by pointing out the success of another war epic made at the same time, and dealing with much the same theme. *Catch-22* was a black comedy and unequivocal in its condemnation of war and the attitudes it gave rise to; there was even a sequence when one wheeler-dealer character makes a business arrangement with the Germans to bomb his own airfield. Unlike *Kelly's Heroes*, *Catch-22* was among the top ten money-earners of 1970.

Eastwood played a private hell-bent on promotion in Kelly's Heroes

Romantic Problems 6

Two Mules For Sister Sara
The Beguiled
Play 'Misty' For Me

Can There Be A Mrs No Name?

A horseman rides out of a gorgeous sunrise, trailing a pack horse. As the day lightens, he moves through a landscape of wild and spectacular beauty, his passage registered by equally solitary inhabitants of the same wilderness: a tufted owl, a jack rabbit, a snake slithering for cover, a mountain lion poised on a high rock.

As the hoof of his horse crushes a tardy tarantula, the camera cranes upward to reveal a lean, unkempt figure in dusty leather hat, a soiled bandana and a poncho-like waistcoat. His ragged beard and a squinting gaze complete a familiar picture. No Name is back in a frontier setting – though he now has a surname, Hogan, and the country is Mexico. A dramatic incident quickly re-establishes his credentials.

As Hogan approaches a ridge a woman's cries draw him to the crest. Below, three drunken men are preparing to rape a half naked woman. Shots from Hogan's handgun give him their attention. They try to persuade him to join in but as one moves toward cover, Hogan shoots two of them dead.

The third grabs the woman, using her as a shield. Hogan's reaction is to disappear behind a large boulder. There he reaches inside his waistcoat, retrieves a stick of dynamite, lights the fuse and tosses it casually over his shoulder.

It falls at the feet of the last would-be rapist. Stunned, the man hesitates, then panics and runs – to be shot in the back by Hogan, who ambles down the side of the ridge, picks up the still smoking dynamite and snaps off the fuse – which has only an inch or two left to burn – with a smile of supreme confidence.

It's his last moment of total certainty for the remainder of the film. While he takes the opportunity to relieve the corpses of their money and supplies, the woman dresses and fetches the mule she was riding. When Hogan turns back to her he finds he has rescued a nun, Sister Sara.

Two Mules For Sister Sara is a westernised, or semi-latinised variation on *The African Queen*, in which a strong-willed and devious female outwits and eventually subdues an apparently invulnerable male,

cajoling him into a form of heroic and romantic action he would otherwise never have considered. Eastwood's Hogan is No Name with a background, a disillusioned veteran of the American Civil War persuaded to run arms to the rebel army of Mexico currently engaged in a war of independence against occupying French forces. His reward is to be half the French treasury held by the garrison at Chihuahua. Like No Name, his motive is purely financial. As he tells his employers, he's a 'Hogan patriot'. His idealism died in the Civil War. 'Everybody,' as he says to Sara, 'has got a right to be a sucker once.'

Sister Sara, meanwhile, shows every sign of being a confirmed *Juarista*, a supporter of the Mexican leader Juarez. It's this that throws her once more on Hogan's mercy when he attempts to leave her behind after rescuing her. A troop of French cavalry approach and Sara explains that they are searching for her. Out of respect for her calling, Hogan helps her to get away.

From this point an uneasy partnership is formed. Hogan makes no bones about his attraction to Sara as a woman but since she is also a nun he feels himself unable to make a sexual approach. Sara, in turn, encourages him to keep his distance. At the same time her behaviour is seen to be far from nun-like: she takes surreptitious puffs at Hogan's cigars, swigs whisky with enthusiasm and reveals a very worldly vocabulary.

But the partnership proves fruitful. Sara provides Hogan with a plan to overcome the Chihuahua garrison and together they

Previous page: *Shirley MacLaine portrays a prostitute masquerading as a nun in* Two Mules For Sister Sara, *1970.* Left: *Eastwood as Hogan in* Two Mules For Sister Sara

105

blow up a French supply train. Sara also removes an arrow from Hogan's chest after an attack by hostile Indians. It's when they reach Chihuahua, however, that Hogan is revealed to be just as much of a 'sucker' as he was in his Civil War days. Sara suggests a sneak attack can be made on the garrison through a tunnel that runs into its dungeon; previously, she explains, the garrison building was a monastery and there was a subterranean link with the local bishop's house. When they arrive at the 'bishop's house', however, it turns out to be a brothel and Sara is its most accomplished inhabitant.

Outraged, Hogan is nevertheless unable to disguise his growing affection for Sara, and reluctantly he allows her to accompany him in a ruse to infiltrate the garrison as part of the *Juarista* attack. Hogan pretends to surrender her to the French authorities. Soon after they gain admittance the battle begins. After a desperate struggle the Mexicans win. Hogan carries the French strongbox back to the brothel in a wheelbarrow and uses it to break open the door of Sara's room where she is titivating herself in a bath. He swiftly joins her.

In the last shot of the film Hogan leads Sara back into the desert, and presumably to America – only now his pack horse is piled with hat boxes instead of weapons and Sara, still astride her mule, is dressed in a gaudy scarlet gown. Her expression is one of haughty triumph. Hogan has plainly become the second of Sister Sara's two mules.

After the relative failure of *Paint Your Wagon*, *Sister Sara* gave Eastwood the opportunity to attempt romantic comedy in what must have seemed a more reliable format. It was also intended to give him the chance to work with Elizabeth Taylor, who had brought him the script. In practice, however, neither of these intentions were fulfilled.

Shooting was scheduled to begin in Mexico in spring 1969 when Elizabeth Taylor withdrew from the project. According to producer Martin Rackin, she had wanted to bring along her customary and very large entourage, and also insisted on working in close proximity to Richard Burton – conditions which could not be met in the remote desert location. Hurried negotiations brought in Shirley MacLaine who had just starred in *Sweet Charity*, another musical like *Paint Your Wagon* which had not achieved the success hoped for by its makers.

At face value she was a good choice. Most of her major roles had been as the whore with a heart of gold and she was an accomplished comedienne. But her acting partnership with Eastwood proved to be competent rather than inspired and a two-handed story like this one needed that extra lift.

Part of the problem was illness. Most of the non-Mexican cast and crew suffered from stomach complaints – the legendary Montezuma's Revenge. Only Eastwood emerged unscathed, by confining himself to a diet of pineapples and papayas.

There was also tension between Shirley and Don Siegel and between Siegel and producer Rackin. Though the director had been happy to work with Eastwood again, it had meant taking over a story that had already been developed by someone else – the veteran director Budd Boetticher.

The result was an awkward pace and a lack of tension which fail to disguise a threadbare quality in the plot; the dramatic incidents are widely spaced and seem largely arbitrary – Hogan and Sara do a great deal of travelling and talking to remarkably little effect.

Siegel, himself, only expressed satisfaction with two sequences: the opening, where the animals Hogan passes in the wilderness can be regarded as emblems of aspects of his character – as well as demonstrating how much a part he is of his environment – and the climactic garrison battle. 'I shot it as a montage, right out of my Warner Brothers days. I had every shot tilted in the opposite direction from the one before. I worked very hard on making that battle sequence work because there was really nothing in the story that justified it. My goal was to make it justify itself by being very exciting.'

Eastwood was happiest with the scene where he drinks himself into near oblivion to enable Sara to extract the Indian arrow from his chest – a process that involves igniting a trail of gunpowder lain in a groove in the arrow shaft while the nun simultaneously knocks the arrow out through his back with a sharp tap from a gun butt. The incident deftly combines comedy, high drama and a certain amount of horror, though, like the rest of the film, it generally failed to impress the critics.

Two Mules For Sister Sara was a financial success, but a minor one according to Eastwood's own, increasingly impressive commercial standards. Clearly the public preferred not to see his screen persona suffer a defeat. But the problem *Sister Sara's* relative failure raised was a much larger one than a simple miscalculation, and Eastwood's next two films – one of which he directed himself – can be seen as attempts to produce a solution.

Stated simply, the problem was romance. Eastwood's No Name persona was the embodiment of self-sufficient self-reliance. In its purest Leone form, he outwitted or shot the men who threatened his survival; women, who would clearly be an encumbrance in the 'spaghetti' West, were disregarded – or used as laconically as the men were for purely sexual reasons (in a brief scene cut from the original version of *The Good, the Bad and the Ugly*, No Name is discovered in bed with a Mexican whore).

Eastwood's updated No Name, Deputy Sheriff Coogan, similarly regarded attractive females as another form of prey, to be trapped and discarded, regardless of the charm and Old West good manners displayed en route. Any display of genuine affection – which must at some point result in an emotional commitment – could only dent the apparent invulnerability of the No Name persona.

Eastwood could simply have lived with that fact. The strong, silent type would always have its appeal to a large section of his female audience: as his co-star in *Coogan's Bluff*, Susan Clark remarked: 'Part of his sex appeal is the constant mystery: how deeply does he feel; how deeply is he involved with life?' But, like playing hard to get, its charm could not be inexhaustible and Eastwood has always been aware of the need to move on.

His attempts to introduce a romantic element had till now only resulted in a lacklustre film like *Paint Your Wagon* or the confused characterisation of *Hang 'Em High*. *Sister Sara* had simply pitted a virtually undiluted No Name (the film even had a score by Ennio Morricone) directly against a female counterpart. Shirley MacLaine's 'nun' is as skilful in ensuring her own survival as Hogan; only their weapons differ and his expertise with the gun is ludicrously inadequate to deal with her capacity for emotional and sexual manipulation. The mere fact that Hogan has entered the arena with her is a mark of her victory. If Leone had been directing, the story would have been over in the first five minutes.

It would not be for another seven years and Eastwood's highly personal film *The Gauntlet* that his screen persona would have evolved sufficiently to resolve this dilemma – and then largely through the vulnerability of his co-star Sondra Locke. For the present the most obvious solution was to reverse the Hogan–Sara relationship, to make Eastwood the expert at emotional and sexual manipulation. The result was one of the most extraordinary and uncharacteristic of his films, *The Beguiled*.

Universal owned the rights to the original novel by Thomas Cullinan, which Eastwood had read during the filming of *Two Mules*, passing it on to Don Siegel. It was a strange, haunting tale of repressed sexuality and near-Gothic horror, set in the American Civil War, and quite unlike anything Eastwood had ever tackled before. For that reason he was chary of accepting it, but Siegel's enthusiasm eventually persuaded him. While the star went to Yugoslavia to fulfil a contractual obligation with *Kelly's Heroes*, Siegel – now doubling as his own producer – worked to set up the film.

Filmed in a genuine Civil War mansion near Baton Rouge, Louisiana, the movie details the effects of the sudden intrusion of a wounded Union soldier, Corporal John McBurney (Eastwood) into the cir-

With Sister Sara in Two Mules For Sister Sara

108

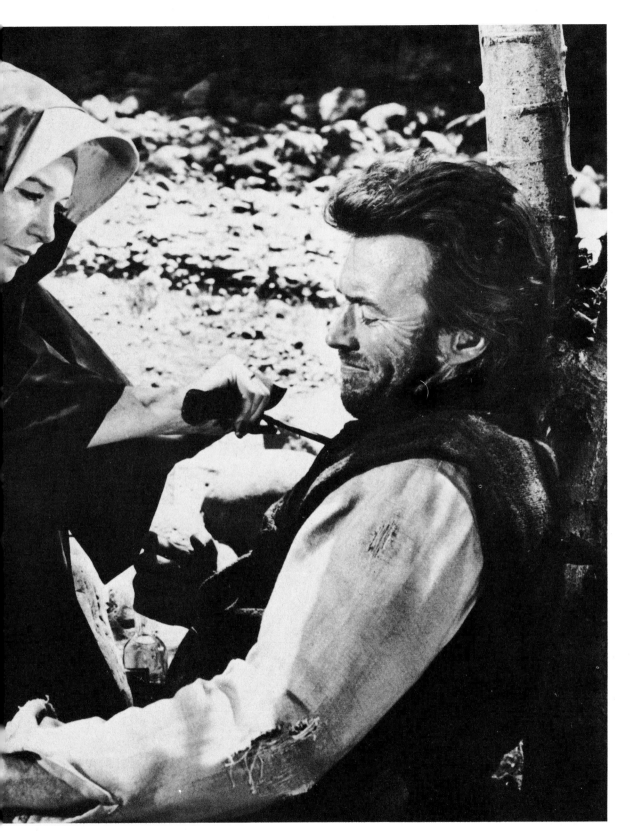

cumscribed lives of a household of Southern women.

'McB' – as he comes to be known – is discovered with a broken leg in woods near the Farnsworth Seminary for Young Ladies by a ten-year-old pupil, Amy (Pamelyn Ferdin), who is out gathering mushrooms. He has been left behind by the changing tide of the war and the area is now in Confederate hands.

His arrival causes great alarm at the seminary where in spite of their isolation the occupants are deeply insecure. Martha Farnsworth (Geraldine Page), the authoritarian headmistress, is at first anxious to hand the soldier over to the Confederate forces: there is an agreed signal – a blue rag attached to the seminary's iron gate – which will alert passing patrols. But her timid young assistant Edwina Dabney (Elizabeth Hartman) convinces her that imprisonment would inevitably entail the death of such a badly wounded man.

The two women decide to keep McBurney hidden away, nursing him until he is well enough to be given up. When a Confederate patrol pays a visit, Martha reveals nothing, though she is unable to keep the secret of McBurney's presence from her own pupils. One of them, Carol (Jo Ann Harris), a precocious and attractive seventeen-year-old, instantly desires him.

As McBurney begins to recover he realises he is too weak to escape and his only means of avoiding capture is to retain the sympathies of the women, to 'beguile' them using his good looks and charm to persuade each in turn that she alone will enjoy his favours. He has already won over

Clint Eastwood and Shirley MacLaine relax between scenes on the Mexican film-set of Two Mules For Sister Sara

110

Amy by kissing her and showing her kindness. Carol is already aroused and only needs to be kept at bay. The subservient Edwina also feels an attraction for him and McBurney encourages her by shrewdly playing on her fantasies: 'Do you ever think of yourself as a sleeping beauty, waiting for a prince to free you?' he asks. Clearly she does and McB conveniently fits the princely role.

Martha proves his most formidable challenge, but flashbacks reveal an apparently incestuous relationship with her brother who fled from home. McBurney contrives to suggest that he might be a substitute and is even offered a partnership in the running of the seminary.

His 'beguiling' of these frustrated and neurotic women reaches a peak, however, on a night when he must finally choose whose bed he enters. The sensible choice is between Martha and Edwina but, hesitating between their bedrooms, McBurney is waylaid by the seminary's 'hussy', Carol. She is plainly the most seductive, the most sexually desirable of all and, out of straightforward desire and a false sense of his own power in this all-female society, he follows her to her attic room. The result is disaster.

Carol's laughter brings Edwina up from the floor below and she discovers McB in the seventeen-year-old's bed. As he tries to escape, the humiliated assistant pushes him down the stairs, her timid demeanour cracking as she shrieks after him: 'You lying son of a bitch, you bastard, you filthy lecher! I hope you die!'

Equally humiliated, Martha examines the man's leg, newly shattered in the fall, and declares it gangrenous. With Edwina's help she takes the unconscious McB into the dining room and with a hacksaw amputates his leg. When he awakes he is horrified and all trace of his 'beguiling' charm vanishes. As soon as he is sufficiently recovered he goes on a drunken rampage, commandeering the seminary's only gun in order to dominate the women by force instead of sexual guile. He calls Edwina a 'virgin bitch', exposes Martha's incestuous past and alienates his only constant friend, Amy, when he wantonly destroys her pet tortoise, Rudolph.

That evening at dinner a sobered McBurney is contrite, but his earlier actions have panicked the women. At Martha's suggestion they have prepared him a favourite meal, containing mushrooms that Amy has picked. It is clear that the embittered ten-year-old has included poisonous toadstools.

To everyone's surprise McBurney announces that he has made his final choice. He intends to leave with Edwina and marry her. But by then he has sampled the 'mushrooms'. As he realises from the women's horrified looks what has happened, he falls dead.

Stunningly photographed in soft browns and blues by newcomer cinematographer Bruce Surtees, the film is plainly much more a Siegel than an Eastwood creation. McBurney's charm and manipulative subtlety is a long way from the Man With No Name; he might be temporarily triumphant here but he is as potentially, and actually, self-destructive as any of Siegel's former anti-heroes. The bleakness of this world isn't of a kind that a self-sufficient hero can survive and exploit, as No Name could in Leone's desolate West. It

As John McBurney in The Beguiled, *1971*

112

2029-64

expresses itself in a pervasive and corrosive pessimism, from the genteel decay of the seminary itself to McBurney's almost insanely foolish acceptance of Carol's favours – the only real flaw in a tightly woven plot. Like Hogan, he's trapped from the very beginning – in Siegel's own words 'a huge, powerful, beautiful man . . . made helpless – by a bunch of sparrows'.

In this world the most intimate relationship, the most apparently dependable – between a man and a woman – is in reality the most treacherous of all. Siegel intended the film to demonstrate that 'women are capable of deceit, larceny, murder, anything. Behind that mask of innocence lurks just as much evil as you'll find in members of the Mafia. Any young girl, who looks perfectly harmless, is capable of murder.'

It's not surprising that he's been accused of being a woman-hater, but his pessimism is by no means limited to one sex. McBurney is not only dishonest in the emotions he appears to show, he lies about his past too, claiming to be a peace-loving Quaker when flashbacks reveal that he relished the opportunity to murder and destroy that war gave him. A visiting Confederate officer is as keen to seduce the seminary women as to protect them; Martha's brother is incestuous and probably a deserter, Edwina's father is described as a philanderer. The only decent members of the male sex are either missing or dead.

Yet, for all his flaws, McBurney does bring the possibility of life and hope to the seminary women – a fact symbolised in the opening of the film when the sepia tones of contemporary Civil War photographs give way to full colour as the camera first shows the soldier's wounded and bloody leg. At the end of the film, as the women bury his body in the garden, the colour seeps out of the film, and their lives, once more. Their misplaced passions have proved just as destructive as McBurney's, but while his might have ended in rude but energetic life, theirs can only end in sterility and decay.

Siegel justifiably describes it as his best film. It was very consciously an art-house picture and the director showed that he could be as successful with a largely static atmospheric and highly emotional tale as he could with action and suspense. *The Times* called it 'a remarkably beguiling film' and Eastwood earned some of the finest critical reviews of his career. Writer De Witt Bodeen dubbed it 'his best film, in which he gives a real performance, one that has nothing to do with the Man with No Name characterisation or any of the strong but silent Gary Cooper derivates'.

He was right – unfortunately for the box office. When *The Beguiled* opened in summer 1970 it swiftly became one of Eastwood's few commercial failures. Eastwood himself blamed Universal, with some justification. Publicised as a typical Eastwood vehicle – 'Clint Eastwood has never been in a more frightening situation,' promised the ads – it was given a blanket release, and only succeeded in puzzling and then alienating his traditional fans.

By the time the distributors had realised their mistake and placed the film in the art-house where Siegel had originally intended it to be shown the impetus of the

Geraldine Page and Elizabeth Hartman help Union Soldier Eastwood in a scene from The Beguiled

114

publicity had been lost. Later Eastwood was to admit

> it would have been a more successful picture if I hadn't been in it. It was advertised to appeal to the kind of people who were my fans from the action pictures, and they didn't like seeing me play a character who gets his leg cut off, gets emasculated. They wanted a character who could control everything around him. The other people, those who might have liked the film, never came to see it.

Eventually those 'other people' did come, especially in Europe where Siegel's reputation was high, and the film developed a cult stature which has since brought it into profit. But Eastwood had learned the lesson that box-office success can bring as much artistic restriction as artistic freedom. 'To me,' he concluded, 'an actor's success comes not from the magnetism of his personality but more from his ability to select material that would be commercial with him in it.'

Never again would he attempt such a radical departure from the No Name persona which had first earned him fame. But that did not mean he would deliberately curtail his desire to experiment creatively. On the contrary, he now made the most important leap in the dark of his career – by deciding to direct his first film, starring himself.

A Self-Propelled Superstar

The name Malpaso appears on the credits of Eastwood's earliest post-'spaghetti' films but at that time it was no more than a device to reduce the star's tax burden.

Eastwood's ambition, however, had always been to increase his own control over his career. As he joked to an interviewer: 'My theory was that I could foul up my career just as well as anyone else could foul it up for me, so why not try it?'

In fact by creating his own production company he hoped to put into practice a philosophy of film-making built up over years of watching the mistakes and the profligacy of others.

'I had this great urge to show the industry that it needs to be streamlined,' he explained, 'so it can make more films with smaller crews. The crews will be employed more, so there'll be just as much work. What's the point of spending so much money producing a movie if you can't break even on it?'

His views were shared by Robert Daley, an accountant Eastwood had become friendly with in 1954 when they both worked for Universal and for a time lived in the same apartment block. Daley was equally impressed with Eastwood's phlegmatic attitude to success and when the star asked him to run Malpaso at the end of the sixties he was happy to accept.

He was quickly joined by Fritz Manes as an associate producer. Then working in television, Manes was one of Eastwood's oldest friends; they had even been at school together.

The third recruit was another familiar face, Sonia Chernus, who had helped Eastwood to make his *Rawhide* breakthrough; she left CBS to become Malpaso's script editor. Eastwood's business manager, Irving Leonard, became president. Judie

With Elizabeth Hartman as Edwina in The Beguiled

116

Hoyt, a receptionist-cum-personal assistant completed the tight-knit team.

The result was one of Hollywood's most cost-efficient and successful production companies. Operating out of offices at Universal and later in a bungalow-cum-dressing room at Warner Brothers, with excursions into trailers while shooting was in progress, it mirrored Eastwood's personal attitudes in its economy of style, its cautious reliance on the familiar and the tested, its deliberately co-operative 'family' atmosphere, and a total lack of pretension.

'We don't have a staff of twenty-six and a fancy office,' the star has said. 'I've got a six-pack under my arm and a few pieces of paper and a couple of pencils, and I'm in business. What the hell, I can work in a closet.' Even the company name expressed Eastwood's laconic wit. 'Malpaso' is the name of a creek bordering the Eastwood property at Carmel, but it can equally well be taken as an ironic reference to the star's decision to work for Sergio Leone – in Spanish the name means 'bad step' or 'bad move'.

By 1970 Eastwood felt confident enough to set up his first Malpaso-produced film. The links with Universal would remain – *Sister Sara* had been the first of a three-picture deal with the studio – and it would distribute the new film and have some say in the casting. The starring role would obviously be Eastwood's but the studio betrayed its unease at his decision to direct by insisting he take a percentage of the profits in place of a straight fee. Ironically this arrangement would eventually net him a much larger amount.

The story he chose came characteristically from both a friend and a source which no one else had taken seriously. It was an untitled sixty-page treatment written by Jo Heims, a former secretary of Eastwood's

Play 'Misty' For Me, as it came to be known, was in many ways an odd choice after the poor reception of *The Beguiled*. It was a psychological suspense thriller, more typical of Alfred Hitchcock than of a star who had made his reputation with action films.

Its attraction in production terms was more obvious. It was a relatively low budget film with a small cast the fledgling director could control easily. There were no studio sets, which not only cut costs but simplified the design decisions, and Eastwood used locations he knew intimately – the Carmel area, including his own property.

As a further safeguard he surrounded himself with professionals he knew well; Bruce Surtees and Carl Pingitore, respectively cinematographer and editor from *The Beguiled*; Dean Riesner, ex-*Rawhide* and *Coogan's Bluff*, as script doctor; and even his directorial mentor, Don Siegel who nervously agreed to take a small supporting role.

'A lot of people thought I was using him in the picture as a buffer,' Eastwood later recalled. 'Subconsciously maybe that was the idea; "I know I've got a really good director on the set if anything goes wrong." ' He gave substance to that theory by making Siegel's biggest scene the first he shot; Siegel left as soon as it was finished, claiming, 'He doesn't need me.'

Eastwood picked a modern role for his directing debut. He played Dave Garland, a disc jockey with a local radio station whose late-night programme is a schmalzy mixture of verse-reading and mood music with a strong romantic bias. It's a bias he shares, in the sense of being a dedicated sexual predator. His romantic excursions have aliented the one woman he cares for, Tobie Williams (Donna Mills), who has left her clifftop house on an extended trip to forget him.

One night at a local bar run by Murphy (Don Siegel), one of Garland's favourite haunts, the disc jockey finds it remarkably easy to pick up an attractive young woman called Evelyn Draper (Jessica Walter). Invited back to her apartment, he recognises her as an anonymous caller who regularly requests Errol Garner's 'Misty' on his programme. When it becomes clear that the girl is sexually interested, Garland tries to explain that his love life is already over-complicated, but Evelyn insists that she only wants a one-night stand. In the morning Garland leaves believing the affair is over.

Evelyn, however, begins to turn up uninvited at Garland's home, pursues him in the street and finally stages a suicide attempt in his bathroom in order to force him to let her stay. She refuses to believe that Garland is not in love with her and by her increasingly bizarre behaviour shows herself to be unbalanced.

Tobie, meanwhile, has returned and Garland tries to resume his relationship with her. Evelyn witnesses their reconciliation and immediately returns to Garland's home, vandalising it in a frenzy of jealousy and stabbing the cleaning woman who interrupts her. The woman survives but Evelyn is arrested and later institutionalised.

Free of her influence, Garland and Tobie's relationship steadily improves but Tobie is still unwilling to make the commitment of a joint household until she is convinced that Garland's predatory days

are over. Eager to reassure her, Garland accepts this and the inconvenience caused by a succession of different flatmates at Tobie's house; it's too expensive for her to afford alone and she won't sell because it's an inheritance.

One night Garland receives another request for 'Misty' on his programme. It's from Evelyn but she assures him that she is cured now and en route to a new life in Hawaii. She includes a cryptic reference to an Edgar Allan Poe poem Garland has read over the air.

Later that night, as he sleeps alone, he wakes to the sound of 'Misty' playing on his record player. Evelyn is poised over his bed with a large knife which plunges into his pillow as he throws himself aside. When he picks himself up, she has gone.

Garland learns from detective sergeant McCallum (John Larch), the policeman in charge of Evelyn's case, that she had been released on bail two days previously. McCallum decides to sit in on Garland's next show in case Evelyn rings again. She does, re-quoting the Poe poem and threatening to kill Tobie.

Unable to leave the studio, Garland sends McCallum to check up on Tobie at her home. A few minutes later Garland finally understands the meaning of the Poe references. The poem is 'Annabel Lee', Tobie's new flatmate, who has only just moved in, is called Annabelle.

Meanwhile, at Tobie's house, Evelyn has revealed her true identity. She ties up Tobie and greets McCallum with a pair of scissors with which she stabs him to death. Putting on an old tape of his show, Garland hurries from the studio. At the house Evelyn attacks him with a butcher's knife. With only his bare hands to defend himself, he eventually lands a blow on her jaw.

It sends her crashing through a French window and over a balcony onto the rocks at the foot of the cliff outside. As Garland and Tobie cling together, his recorded radio show reaches another of Evelyn's requests for 'Misty'.

Interestingly, the film takes some key aspects of the theme of *The Beguiled* – sexual and romantic obsession, the reality of male dominance in sexual relationships, the reality of female independence – and reworks them in terms of Eastwood's successful screen image. Dave Garland may not enjoy the absolute, totally anarchic freedom and invulnerability of the Man With No Name, but he's a local celebrity whose programme gives him a sexy image which he exploits ruthlessly in his private life. Like No Name, he's a figure who provokes both censure and admiration, a confident and self-reliant 'stud' who cuts as damaging a swathe through the emotional lives of his women friends as Deputy Sheriff Coogan did with the laws of New York. Like Coogan he also operates by a personal code (as he explains to Evelyn when she calls unexpectedly: 'I'm trying to tell you there's a telephone. I pick it up and I dial. You answer and I say, "What are you doing?"') but it's a selfish code that arouses a psychotic obsession in one woman and alienates another who offers a deeper and more rewarding relationship.

Garland's dilemma was clearly close to Eastwood's heart. In his *Playboy* interview he confessed that he had gone through a similar kind of relationship at the age of twenty-one and he told another interviewer: 'In addition to the psychotic, horror element, (*Misty*) made a nice comment on the relationships of individuals to each other and the misinterpretation of commitment.'

The dilemma, however, is only finally resolved in the closing shot of the film and then under conditions of extreme duress. Tobie Williams may be the sexual and romantic partner Garland eventually realises he needs, but in dramatic terms Evelyn is the female we remember. Her energy is based on obsession and psychotic dependence but it's the equal of Garland's – something Evelyn hints at when she sees a portrait of Garland painted by Tobie and criticises it for not showing enough passion in the eyes.

Evelyn's is the superior intelligence, too: as she tells Tobie when she belatedly realises the identity of her new flatmate – 'God, you're dumb!'

By contrast Tobie is a bit wet. Her one attempt to put Garland out of her life only results in her moving into her boss's home a few miles up the coast. Garland's romantic interludes with her are the weakest and least assured scenes of the film, marked by some arbitrary cutting and a tendency to pan away to spectacular but distracting views of the Monterey coastline.

Part of the problem is the writing – Tobie isn't much more than an attractive cipher – and the superlative playing of Evelyn by Jessica Walter – a performance that gave the film its power and which Eastwood has praised lavishly and rightly. But the question of a credible and satisfactory sexual-romantic dimension for Eastwood's screen persona remained unanswered.

That said, the film was an accomplished and stylish debut with a good sense of atmosphere and impressive handling of the scenes of violence. Rather to Eastwood's surprise, the critics generally expressed approval: 'a surprisingly auspicious directorial debut,' wrote Andrew

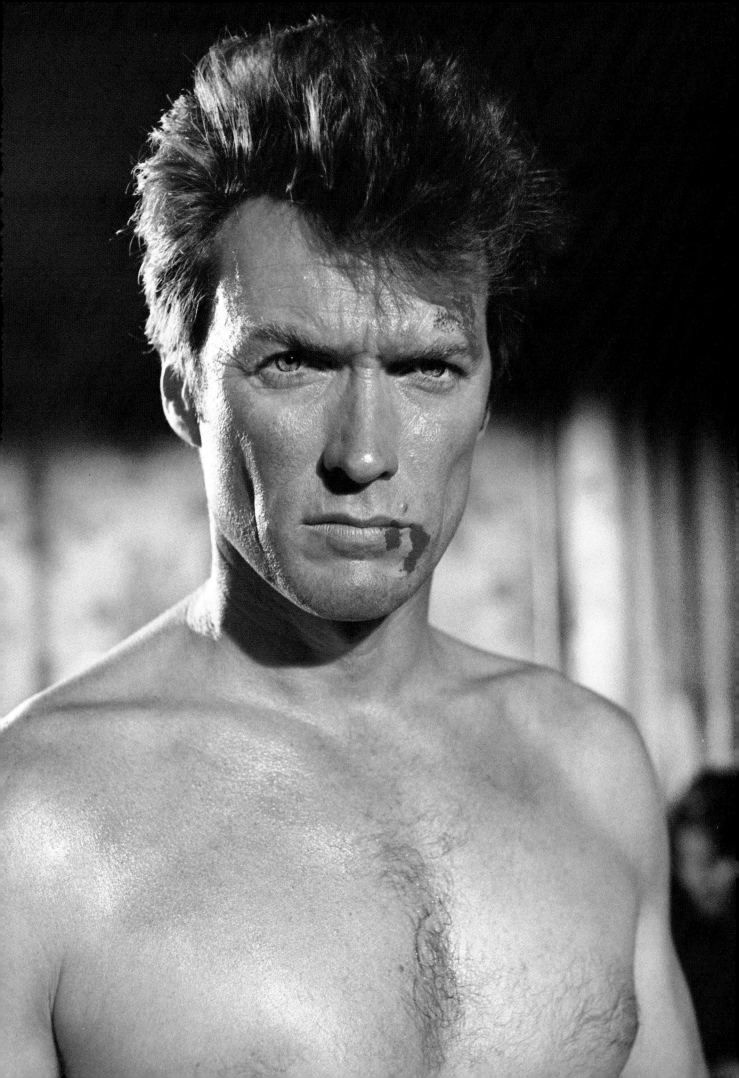

Sarris of *The Village Voice*. 'He has obviously seen *Psycho* and *Repulsion* more than once,' noted *Time*, 'but those are excellent texts and he has learned his lesson well.'

Eastwood had certainly succeeded in his own terms. The film was finished four days early and for $50,000 less than its projected budget of $950,000. He managed it by taking leaves out of Don Siegel's directorial manual – doing as much forward planning as possible, rehearsing his actors thoroughly before the cameras started rolling and shooting only enough to cover himself adequately, thus reducing time and effort in the cutting room later.

His philosophy of involving every member of his deliberately small crew also paid dividends.

If you explain what effect you are striving for instead of merely saying 'Put that case over there' or 'Set that lamp down there', your crew will become totally involved, [he explained later]. I had the distinct impression at first that they were all waiting for me to prove myself as a director. But that lasted exactly one day. By the second morning we were all working together as a totally involved, compatible unit.

His cast agreed. 'He's not insecure like some directors who impose things on you because they are nervous,' said Jessica Walter. 'He made me feel I could do it, whatever it was, and he left the role up to me. He has faith in people.'

He had faith in his audience too, and it was justified. *Play 'Misty' For Me* was a resounding commercial success, grossing over $5 million.

With co-star Jessica Walter in a scene from Play 'Misty' For Me, *1971*

Magnum Opus 7

Dirty Harry
Magnum Force
The Enforcer

No Name Puts Down Roots

With the first cut of *Misty* completed, Clint and Maggie flew to Italy where *The Beguiled* was about to open. Eastwood has always regarded Italy as his 'good luck' country and this visit proved it with a vengeance. He had recently been voted the leading international attraction at the Italian box office and his arrival provoked outbursts of almost hysterical adulation. Italy, after all, had discovered him and the star in turn had given Italian commercial cinema an unprecedented international standing.

At the premiere of *The Beguiled* in Milan's Cinema Misure – where the film earned the praise it had conspicuously lacked in the States – fans surrounded Eastwood's car, calling *niente funghi* – 'no mushrooms', in joking reference to McBurney's demise. A gala in his honour was held at Milan University where Eastwood chatted to students and was presented with a bronze medallion for his artistic contribution to the Italian film industry. He responded modestly and with pride, fully acknowledging the debt he owed to Sergio Leone and his compatriots. He enjoyed himself too, but such a high profile was alien to Eastwood's nature and, when he left, it was with a sense of relief.

Back in the States he had more privacy – but less recognition too, a point exemplified by his appearance on the cover of *Life* magazine on 23 July 1971: 'The world's favourite movie star is – no kidding – Clint Eastwood,' read the strap line. The 'no kidding' said it all. Eastwood was still an outsider to the media establishment – a genuinely 'popular' star whose appeal was direct to his audience; word of mouth had sold, and continues to sell, more Eastwood films than any carefully concerted advertising campaign. Like John Wayne, who beat Eastwood into second position as the top US box office star of 1971, Eastwood boasted such a powerful and resonant screen presence that fans regarded the man and the performance as indistinguishable. Once asked to define a Clint Eastwood picture, Eastwood replied that it was any film with him

123

in it. It was intended as a deadpan rebuff to critics, but his fans would have taken him at his word.

Eastwood is in a position that confounds criticism. Analysing a mythic figure is much more difficult than taking apart an individual performance that may never be repeated: John Wayne was a major star for forty years but he had to don an eyepatch and a self-consciously 'acting' style to win his Oscar for *True Grit*. To Eastwood's credit, he has taken far greater artistic gambles than the 'Duke' ever considered but his screen performances show the same ease, the same apparent lack of effort. Eastwood has shown himself to be a highly competent actor in a variety of roles, but not a great one; his vocal range is too limited, his physical presence too emphatic to take on the chameleon quality of an Alec Guinness or a Lawrence Olivier. What he can do – in the guise of the cool, supremely self-sufficient, highly individual character of No Name – is create a figure which stirs echoes in the minds and wishes of cinema-goers all over the world. Despite the realism of the violence that surrounds him, the actuality of the settings through which he moves, he's essentially a fantasy figure – an embodiment of impossible dreams, something Eastwood himself understands well: 'A guy sits in the audience. He's twenty-five years old and he's scared stiff about what he's going to do with his life. He wants to have that self-sufficient thing he sees up there on the screen. But it will never happen that way.

Previous page: With Don Siegel, who directed Eastwood in Dirty Harry, *1971*

126

Man is always dreaming of being an individual but man is really a flock animal.'

Eastwood had starred in nine films since his 'spaghetti' days and in spite of his success none of those productions had presented his screen persona with the dramatic impact of the Leone trilogy. As a result he was still very much an immigrant star – his peculiar qualities had been forged on an Italian and an international stage and as such were regarded with mild suspicion by his native critics. The Man With No Name had yet to prove that he was a genuine American, with a distinctive, national appeal. 1971 was to be the year when No Name finally became naturalised – and in a way that forced the critics to take notice.

Dirty Harry first came to Eastwood from Warner Brothers in the form of a script entitled *Dead Right* by a husband and wife writing team, Harry Julian Fink and R. M. Fink. It was a rogue cop story and at one point Frank Sinatra had been eager to star in it but it was a physically demanding role and a hand injury prevented him. Interested, Eastwood called in Don Siegel who immediately shared his enthusiasm.

It was Siegel who had first brought No Name into a modern, urban American environment, picturing him as a kind of frontier 'throwback' who could still function, if uneasily, in the uncomplicated wastes of Arizona. With *Dirty Harry* the decision was taken to place No Name squarely in the present day. He is still out West – in fact as far west as you can go in America, on the Pacific coastline – but now the frontier is occupied by one of the world's most modern cities, San Francisco.

There, Eastwood's Inspector Harry Callahan is a man who shares No Name's kill-or-be-killed philosophy, symbolised by the outsized handgun he carries, a forty-four magnum. Violent and unpleasant as the modern world can be, however, it doesn't justify the trigger-happy habits of No Name, so Callahan retains Deputy Sheriff Coogan's adherence to a different morality from those who surround him. He believes in justice of a simple, direct and usually instant kind. As he tells San Francisco's liberal-minded mayor: 'When an adult male is chasing a female with intent to commit rape I shoot the bastard. That's my policy.'

His justification for such an attitude is the feebleness of the existing legal institutions – the film makes specific reference to two real-life court rulings, *Miranda* and *Escobedo*, which allowed criminal suspects to go free because arresting officers had not informed them of their legal rights – and the monstrous nature of the criminals he faces.

The most monstrous of all is called Scorpio, named after a real-life killer called Zodiac who terrorised San Francisco. The film opens as Scorpio (Andy Robinson), hidden on the roof of a tower block, trains his silenced rifle on a young woman swimming in a rooftop pool in an adjoining building. He fires and the girl dies. When Callahan, a detective with the homicide squad, discovers the sniper's firing position he also finds a note addressed to the city, demanding $100,000. 'If I do not hear from you it will be my next pleasure to kill a Catholic priest or a nigger,' it concludes.

The mayor (John Vernon) and Callahan's superior, Lieutenant Bressler (Harry Guardino) decide to play for time – a move that Callahan opposes outspokenly. He wants to arrange a personal meeting with the blackmailer and he gives an indication of the likely outcome in an incident which

occurs later that day. Over lunch in a hamburger bar Callahan becomes suspicious of a car parked outside a neighbouring bank. He asks the bar owner to ring the police and tell them a raid is in progress, but before they can arrive violence erupts. As the bank raiders run for their car, Callahan attempts to arrest them. They open fire, peppering his leg with shotgun pellets. With the aid of his magnum, Callahan efficiently disposes of the getaway car and all but one of the raiders. The following day he is given a new partner, Chico Gonzales (Reni Santoni), a sociology graduate, a choice which he accepts grudgingly. Meanwhile a helicopter patrolling the rooftops of the city spots Scorpio about to shoot a black homosexual. He is challenged but escapes.

That night Callahan and Gonzales patrol the streets. Spying on one suspect, Callahan is accused of being a peeping tom and only rescued from angry bystanders by Gonzales. Later Callahan rescues a would-be suicide from a rooftop when he goads the man into assaulting him. Callahan responds with a punch and lowers the unconscious man to safety. The night ends with the news that Scorpio has struck again, shooting a ten-year-old negro boy.

The following night Callahan and Gonzales stake out a Catholic church where a late-night service is being held. Scorpio appears on an adjoining rooftop and a gun battle takes place. Again the killer escapes, shooting an officer dead en route. The next day the city receives another note from him, demanding $200.000. Scorpio has kidnapped a fourteen-year-old girl and buried her alive with oxygen to last until three the next morning. He encloses one of her teeth, removed with a pair of pliers.

The mayor agrees to pay and Callahan

volunteers to deliver the money. Privately he and Gonzales decide to remain in touch by radio. Scorpio leads Callahan all over the city from phone booth to phone booth until they eventually meet in Mount Davidson Park. There, a masked Scorpio beats up Callahan and takes sadistic relish in telling the detective that the girl is already dead. He is about to kill Callahan when Gonzales arrives. Gonzales is wounded but Callahan plunges a knife into Scorpio's leg as he escapes.

Callahan learns from a doctor in hospital where Scorpio has gone for treatment that the killer lives at the nearby Keazar Stadium. Callahan breaks in, corners Scorpio and shoots him in the leg, treading on the wound until the killer reveals the whereabouts of his victim. The girl is found dead but because of Callahan's illegal methods Scorpio is released. Callahan takes to following Scorpio in his own time, convinced he will strike again. In retaliation the killer pays a negro to beat him up and then accuses Callahan of doing it.

Shortly afterwards Scorpio hijacks a school bus and again demands $200,000 and a waiting plane. A frightened mayor assures him that this time the money will be paid at once. An outraged Callahan refuses to act as messenger. The hijacked bus is approaching the airport when Callahan leaps from a bridge onto its roof, causing Scorpio to crash. Callahan pursues him through an adjoining gravel works, swapping bullets. Scorpio makes a last stand on a jetty overlooking a flooded excavation, using a young boy who has been fishing as a shield. Callahan promptly shoots the killer in the shoulder, freeing the boy.

Scorpio drops his gun and Callahan offers him the chance to pick it up again – a gamble on whether or not the detective has used up all six bullets in his magnum. Giggling, the killer grabs for his weapon and Callahan's last shot blasts him into the water below. Staring down at the body, Callahan removes his police star and in disgust tosses it after the killer.

Dirty Harry was premiered in December 1971 and was an immediate and staggering success. By the end of 1972 it had grossed $16 million, making it the fifth highest earning film of that year and the most successful film Eastwood – and Siegel – had made to that date. It was also the most controversial of both their careers.

If Eastwood had accommodated his image to fit Siegel's conception in their first rogue cop collaboration, *Coogan's Bluff, Dirty Harry* reversed the process. The underlying concerns of director and star are still similar, but the film is unmistakably Eastwood's. Unlike Coogan, Harry Callahan isn't in the least altered by his clash with criminals and legal bureaucracy; on the contrary, the events of the film only confirm him in his attitudes, to the extent that he finally rejects both the police force and, by implication, the establishment which it represents.

Callahan strides through the movie like a mythic colossus; he casually blows away two armed bank robbers, wounds a third and demolishes their getaway car in a short break during his lunch hour and while he's still chewing a mouthful of hot dog; he foils a suicide attempt in minutes after being hoisted up the side of a six

Two scenes from Dirty Harry

129

storey building and while the massed services of the city mill about impotently at street level; he materialises on the bridge above Scorpio's hijacked bus, dressed in black and wearing dark glasses, like an avenging angel – and wearing his Sunday best, as if he were going to a funeral, or an execution; and when he tortures Scorpio on the vast, floodlit expanse in the middle of the Keazar Stadium, the camera retreats skyward into darkness and mist as the killer's screams rise to a peak – suggesting the operation of elemental and inhuman forces, something too terrible for mortal eyes to witness.

Callahan's moral righteousness is backed up by a righteous sword – his magnum, a weapon given an almost fetishistic gloss which fully exploits its phallic qualities: as Scorpio, in disarming him, coos: 'My, that's a big one.' Callahan's weapon takes on the dimensions of a force of nature that demands propitiation. When he approaches the last of the foiled bank robbers who lies wounded on the pavement, his hand within inches of the loaded shotgun he has dropped, Callahan taunts him with the power he can unleash: 'I know what you're thinking. Did he fire six shots or only five? Well, to tell the truth, in all this excitement I've forgotten myself. But, seeing as this is a forty-four magnum, the most powerful handgun in the world, that will blow your head clean off, you've got to ask yourself a question. Do I feel lucky? Well, do you, *punk*!'

The speech takes on the vestments of a personal and very violent credo – especially when it's repeated to Scorpio in the closing moments of the film: Scorpio, unlike the bank robber, believes he *is* lucky and suffers the consequences.

The law as it stands seems wholly inadequate confronted with such an overwhelming moral force. When the district attorney berates Callahan, he expresses the frustrating complexity of a more modern morality: 'You're lucky I'm not indicting you for assault with intent to commit murder. Where the hell does it say you have the right to kick down doors, torture subjects, deny medical treatment and legal counsel? Where have you been? Does *Escobedo* ring a bell? *Miranda*? I mean, have you heard of the Fourth Amendment? What I'm saying is that man had rights!' 'Well,' replies Callahan, 'I'm all broken up about that man's rights.' Because they have been violated, all of Callahan's evidence is inadmissable, the law cannot touch Scorpio. 'Well,' declares the detective, 'then the law's crazy.'

A judge, conveniently in the same office, tries to make the legal position clearer. Callahan's response is to champion the rights of the victim. 'She's raped and left in a hole to die. Who speaks for her?' The DA claims that his office does – a task at which it is patently not very good – and Callahan's own argument receives a boost when the DA admits: 'I've got a wife and three kids. I don't want him on the streets any more than you do.'

The attitudes encapsulated here released a storm of protest. To many critics the film was a plea for vigilante justice, a sop to the law-and-order advocates who helped to re-elect Richard Nixon in 1972 after the violence and disorder of the anti-Vietnam war campaign. To Pauline

The tough, relentless detective, Harry Callahan

130

Kael – the most vociferous of these critics – it was a

right-wing fantasy ... *Dirty Harry* is obviously just a genre movie but this particular genre has always had a fascist potential and it has finally surfaced. If crime were caused by super-evil dragons, there would be no *Miranda*, no *Escobedo*; we could all be licensed to kill like *Dirty Harry*. But since crime is caused by deprivation, misery, psychopathology and social injustice, *Dirty Harry* is a deeply immoral movie.

Eastwood denied the accusation:

It's just the story of one frustrated police officer in a frustrating situation on one particular case ... Most of the films coming out then were extremely anti-cop. They were about the cop on the take, you know. And this was a film that showed the frustrations of the job, but at the same time it wasn't a glorification of police work ... There's a reason for the rights of the accused, and I think it's very important and one of the things that makes our system great. But there are also the rights of the victim. Most people who talk about the rights of the accused have never been victimised; most of them have probably never got accosted in an alley. The symbol of justice is the scale, and yet the scale is never balanced; it falls to the left and then it swings too far back to the right.

This apparent defence of the film only fuelled the controversy, despite Eastwood's assurances that he was a political moderate. Pauline Kael detected a strong anti-liberal bias in the film. Scorpio has long hair and seems to be some kind of hippy; he wears an anti-war badge prominently. The judge who explains matters to Callahan in the DA's office also happens to be a lecturer at Berkeley, then a centre of student radicalism. When Scorpio screamed for his legal rights, under Callahan's torture – 'Puerto Ricans in the audience jeered – as they were meant to.'

But, under Don Siegel's direction, things simply aren't that straightforward. Callahan might represent a hard-hat, redneck morality – as a colleague tells his new, Mexican, partner: 'Harry hates everybody. Limeys, micks, hebes, fat dagoes, niggers, honkies, chinks, you name it' – but Scorpio chooses his targets from the same catalogue of prejudice, blacks, homosexuals and women, all of whom he treats with similar contempt. His haircut and lifestyle – what little we see of it – suggest a student background, but his boots are laced in military fashion and his expertise with a variety of firearms is considerable.

Like Coogan and Ringerman, Callahan and Scorpio are identified with each other. Both are loners who have no apparent life beyond the events of the plot – Callahan, we learn, had a wife but she was killed in a drunken driving accident; both pursue their roles with the same ruthlessness and the same apparent lack of motive – Callahan's barely suppressed hatred and disgust of the criminal community may be more likely than Scorpio's homicidal mania but neither is given a specific cause.

When Callahan follows Scorpio after his release, the killer spends his sparetime ogling nudes in topless bars in the red light area of San Francisco that Callahan claims to loath – 'I'd like to throw a net over the whole lot of them,' he tells his new partner on their first patrol through it. But in following up a suspect, a nude woman in a

132

window detains Callahan long enough to be accused of peeping-tommery. And when Scorpio shoots up the Catholic church, he misses the gunman's arrival on the building opposite because he is too busy watching a lesbian encounter in a flat below.

Callahan and Scorpio can be regarded very much as mirror images of each other: they need each other to justify the extremes they represent. Neither are in fact tolerable and Callahan's final rejection of his police badge – an act Eastwood initially objected to – is Siegel's acknowledgement of that.

Siegel's justification for apparently deliberate taunts at the liberal and anti-liberal establishment is to undermine both, to point out that what a person professes and what he or she actually does aren't necessarily the same. He commented on the peace badge Scorpio wears: 'it seems to me that it may remind us that no matter how vicious a person is, when he looks into the mirror, he's not capable of seeing the truth about himself.'

Scorpio wears a peace badge yet kills mercilessly. San Francisco's legal establishment claims to represent justice to all but following its principles would have meant throwing away the life of the fourteen-year-old kidnap victim. Harry Callahan heroically saves the city from a gang of desperate bank robbers but the power he uses to do so is wielded with a relish that verges on Scorpio's sadism – when the wounded robber who has declined Callahan's offer to reach for his shotgun begs to know whether the detective did or did not have a sixth bullet in his magnum, Callahan smilingly points the weapon at the man's head and presses the trigger on an empty chamber.

And yet, at the end of all this, in purely dramatic terms Scorpio is manifestly a villain just as Callahan, for all his faults, is the hero who swiftly and efficiently defeats him. As Siegel commented : 'It's a simple story basically.' Simple it may be in basis but its collective effect was to find the nation's most sensitive nerve and play on it remorselessly. Law-and-order advocates saw in Callahan's methods an argument for a no-holds-barred approach to crime prevention. Liberals saw the film confirming their worst right-wing fears of the police establishment. Eastwood's existing fans saw their hero at last acting out his No Name fantasies, almost undiluted, on streets they could recognise. A whole new audience who had barely heard of Eastwood, or not taken him seriously, joined the box-office queues to find out what all the fuss was about.

But for the bank robbery sequence, the film was shot on location and Eastwood enjoyed himself working on the streets of his home town. When Siegel fell ill with influenza he shot the would-be suicide sequence himself, completing it with justifiable pride in a single night when six had been allowed for in the schedule. As in the leap from the bridge onto Scorpio's hijacked bus, he insisted on doing – and being seen to do – his own stunts, something which added greatly to the already considerable power of the film.

Despite Don Siegel's insistence that Harry Callahan and the San Francisco Police Department part company, com-

Overleaf: *Eastwood feels equally at home behind or in front of the camera*

mercial good sense alone demanded a reprise for the character. Malpaso were to revive him twice, each time with greater commercial success, but Siegel was to direct neither. It would be eight years before he worked with Eastwood again and on a very different kind of project from *Dirty Harry*.

There is no question of personal disagreement in this; the two men remained as friendly and mutually respectful as ever. Siegel had simply taken the star as far as he could for the moment, redefining his screen persona in as important and radical a way as Sergio Leone had done seven years previously. Eastwood, in turn, had absorbed all that Siegel could teach him as a director – as he was soon to show in his second self-directed movie *High Plains Drifter*, released in 1972. For the purposes of clarity, however, it's convenient to leap the intervening years and follow the progress of Eastwood's newly naturalised screen persona, Inspector Harry Callahan.

'A Man's Got to Know his Limitations'

A disgruntled Harry Callahan, freshly demoted to the SFPD surveillance department for his controversial methods, is taking a break at San Francisco airport where an ex-policeman runs a snack stand. As he munches into a taco, the detective becomes aware of signs of alarm among airport officials. Following them, Callahan learns that two gunmen have hijacked an airliner on the tarmac and are demanding a quarter of a million dollars ransom and an overseas pilot. The money is ready and the officials are waiting for the arrival of the FBI. 'May I make a suggestion?' offers Harry.

Moments later he strides out onto the tarmac – in pilot's uniform and carrying a briefcase packed with notes. On board the hijacked plane, the gunmen search him and urge him forward to the cockpit where he slips into the pilot's seat. As the terrified crew look on, a gunman settles behind Callahan, presses a handgun to his head and orders him to take off.

At Callahan's request the co-pilot sets the aircraft in motion. As it begins to roll down the tarmac, he hands control over to the detective. The taxiing goes on and on to the increasing bemusement of the crew. At last the most senior member can no longer contain his alarm. 'Excuse me, captain,' he enquires shakily, 'this may sound silly, but can you fly?' Callahan's response is a broad smile. 'Nope,' he says. 'Never had a lesson.'

In the stunned silence that follows he wrenches over the wheel, throwing the hijacker off balance. Snatching his gun, Callahan knocks him insensible and dives into the passenger compartment where the second gunman is just picking himself up. He sees Callahan's gun and retreats into a toilet. Yelling at the passengers to keep down, the detective fires through the toilet partition. The gunman tumbles out, dead, and the hijack is over.

Magnum Force, released in 1973, showed Harry Callahan in the same heroic form as before, now dealing with hijackers – who then dominated the world's headlines – as efficiently as he dealt with bank robbers in *Dirty Harry*. But, under the direction of

With director Ted Post on the set of Magnum Force, *1973*

136

Ted Post, the film doesn't postulate the world view of Don Siegel's original. It's a much more intimate film, shown in the tighter camerawork, the frequent use of close-up and the relative humanising of Harry Callahan. The hijacking vignette allows him to display the sardonic, don't-give-a-damn humour of No Name – in the Siegel version he was only allowed one joke, and that a defensive jibe aimed at the over-liberal mayor ('When a naked man is chasing a woman through an alley with a butcher's knife and a hard-on I figure he isn't out collecting for the Red Cross,' he declares).

He has a home – characteristically a bleak and unprepossessing apartment where he can usually not be bothered even to turn on the light. He has friends – policemen or ex-policemen, including their wives and children. He has a social standing independent of his day-to-day work – even if it only consists of being the most frequent winner of a target shooting competition for a police benevolent association.

He even has a girlfriend, though in order not to damage his invulnerable image the girl, who lives in the same apartment block, has to make the advances: 'What's a girl have to do to go to bed with you?' she asks. 'Try knocking on the door,' Callahan suggests.

When the separated wife of a colleague, a mature woman with a family who is already a friend, makes a pass the relationship offered involves a much greater intimacy and degree of commitment than mere sex, and a wooden-faced Callahan is only saved by a fortuitous phone call recalling him to work.

But the most important adaptation to Callahan's image is that the flouter of legal rules that did not accord with his own higher sense of justice now becomes the defender of those same rules. In an obvious rebuff to the criticisms of *Dirty Harry*, the villains of this film are not conventional criminals but the police themselves, an elite vigilante squad who decide to execute members of the underworld that the law, for technical reasons, cannot touch.

The film opens with a virtual reprise of the Scorpio incident when Carmine Ricca, a corrupt union leader and racketeer, is released from custody after a murder charge has been dismissed. At his home an anonymous police officer watches on television as outraged demonstrators surround Ricca's car. The officer puts on his uniform and leaves. Shortly afterwards Ricca's car is pulled off the road by a motorcycle policeman who alleges the driver has committed a traffic offence. As Ricca and his associates taunt the officer, he draws his gun and shoots them all dead.

More killings follow, a pool-side massacre of gangsters and their girlfriends, a pimp who has murdered one of his girls by forcing drain-cleaner down her throat. Callahan is reinstated and ordered to work under Lieutenant Briggs (Hal Holbrook) who professes to loath Callahan's violent methods. At first Callahan suspects a fellow officer and good friend, Charlie McCoy (Mitchell Ryan) of being the killer; he is clearly on the verge of a nervous breakdown and bitter about the restraints of the law – 'These days a cop kills a hoodlum on the street,' he complains, 'and he might as well just dump the body someplace.' But McCoy is himself killed by the vigilantes when he meets one escaping from the scene of another slaying.

Meanwhile Callahan has become

acquainted with four young traffic police-men, all Vietnam war veterans who are expert shots and go around as a group. He begins to suspect them, despite Briggs' insistence that gangland assassins are responsible. When the group's leader, Davis (David Soul), beats him in a target shooting competition, Callahan takes the opportunity to examine a bullet from Davis's revolver and discovers that it was fired from the same gun which killed McCoy.

Later the group approach him and admit their responsibility. 'We're only rid-ding society of killers that would be caught and executed anyway if the courts worked the way they were supposed to,' says Davis. 'It's not just a question of whether or not to use violence. There simply is no other way, Inspector. You of all people, should know that.' They ask him to join them but Callahan does not rise to the bait. 'I'm afraid you've misjudged me,' he tells them. Minutes later he spots a bomb in his mail box and carefully defuses it. His black partner, Early Smith (Felton Perry), is less vigilant and dies in a blast at his home.

Callahan telephones Briggs who comes round immediately. With the bomb as evi-dence they set off for police headquarters but Briggs pulls a gun and announces that he is the true leader of the vigilantes. His argument for his actions sounds suspici-ously like Callahan's: 'The legal process has broken down and somebody has to protect society. It's as simple as that.' Cal-lahan now is forced to present the liberal counter-argument: 'When the police start becoming their own executioners, where's it going to end, eh, Briggs? Pretty soon you start executing people for jaywalking, and executing people for traffic violations.

Then you end up executing your neigh-bour because his dog pisses on your lawn.' Briggs taunts him for sticking with a use-less system. 'Briggs,' he replies, 'I hate the goddam system. But until someone comes along with some changes that make sense I'll stick with it.'

A similar trick to that Callahan used on the aircraft hijackers enables him to knock Briggs unconscious, but they are pursued by three members of the vigilante squad on motorcycles. Callahan forces one off the road and takes refuge in a naval yard. A chase through the bowels of a disused air-craft carrier results in Callahan stabbing a second; the third dies when he attempts a spectacular motorcycle leap from carrier to dockside – a leap Callahan only just completes – and plunges into the harbour.

Briggs, meanwhile, has recovered and has regained his gun. The deaths of his associates don't worry him: 'There's a lot more where they came from, believe me,' he says and declares his intention to prose-cute Callahan for their murder. 'It's going to be my word against yours. Who's going to believe you? You're a killer, Harry. A maniac.' But during their conversation Callahan has secretly reactivated the mail-box bomb and as Briggs drives away the car is blown apart.

As in *Dirty Harry* Callahan and his vil-lainous opponents are identified with each other, and not simply because they both happen to be policemen. The four vigi-lante cops are as handsome and clean-cut as Callahan (Harry's nickname arises from the unsavoury nature of the tasks he is given rather than any slur on his per-sonal habits or hygiene); they shoot as well, they're as dedicated and their black leather uniforms, gleaming white helmets and dark glasses give them the same fetishistic glamour that Callahan gets from his magnum. Like the similarly clad motorcycling angels of Jean Cocteau's 1950 fantasy *Orpheus*, they are representatives of death – as much avenging angels as ever Callahan was. They have the ambiguous appeal of black-uniformed Nazis – particularly in the blond-haired, blue-eyed, Aryan good looks of David Soul's Davis, their leading light. The ambiguity isn't just moral, either.

Again like Callahan they are loners, constantly preferring their own company, which gives rise to suspicions of homosexuality. In a neat reversal it's Callahan who excuses them this charge. 'If the rest of you could shoot like them, I wouldn't worry if the entire department was queer,' he says.

Naturally enough he starts out by admiring them. 'You sure show a sense of style,' he tells them, though significantly it's the same phrase he uses to describe the manner in which the pimp kills his prostitute with drain cleaner. Callahan himself comes under only half-joking suspicion: 'No one hates hoodlums as much as he does,' remarks his partner. And Callahan's own statement that 'there's nothing wrong with shooting as long as the right people get shot' is a sentiment the vigilantes would instantly endorse.

The difference is that, like the bad guys in a Western, they sneak up on their victims and shoot them down when they are unaware of danger; Callahan shoots his wrongdoers when they are in the process of doing wrong, either by committing a crime or resisting arrest with bullets. He explodes onto the screen as a concrete embodiment of the audience's pent-up indignation and frustration and provides an instant emotional release. His victory over the vigilantes is an emotional and dramatic, not a moral one. As Pauline Kael says in her predictably unfavourable review of the film, when 'Harry keeps saying . . . "A man's got to know his limitations" . . .it's not a comment on himself but on his enemies' failure to recognise that he's the better man. Harry is tougher than the elite cadre, just as he was tougher than the mad hippie killer.' When Callahan watches the last vigilante plunge to a watery grave and kicks his white helmet after him, he concludes: 'Briggs was right. You guys don't have enough experience.' But the experience they lack is not so much in threading their way through the moral complexities of a policeman's lot as in fighting dirty with an old pro like Harry Callahan.

The film has its moral cake and eats it in a way Don Siegel ultimately refused to do in the original *Dirty Harry*. The result is a much less resonant film but one that plays more directly to the gallery with much greater violence and of a more spectacular kind. Scorpio's one-shot swimming pool killing here becomes a bloody massacre with automatic pistol and plastic explosive; elsewhere a man is blasted at point blank range through a two-way mirror; a steel girder crashes through a getaway car's windscreen, obliterating the driver; when one gangster is shot down in his penthouse apartment a naked young man and woman, apparently making love for his benefit on a nearby waterbed, are filled with holes too, the girl's body smashing through a picture window and hurtling to the street below.

As Harry Callahan again in Magnum Force

140

Though the critics, particularly Pauline Kael, found this objectionable, the gallery didn't, paying nearly $7 million to see the film in the first week of its release. Yet the biggest commercial success of the *Dirty Harry* series was still to come.

The Enforcer, filmed toward the end of 1975, reproduced the bare bones of the now well-established formula but without the subtlety or the moral depth – however confused – of its predecessors. Part of the reason was the direction of James Fargo, formerly an assistant director of some of Eastwood's previous films and now given the opportunity to direct his first feature; his work was competent rather than inspired with some awkwardness in the pacing.

Another problem was the script. *Magnum Force* had been written by Michael Cimino – the future Oscar-winning director of *The Deerhunter* as well as Eastwood's own *Thunderbolt and Lightfoot* – and by John Milius, already a director, who had contributed Callahan's 'do you feel lucky, punk' credo to *Dirty Harry*, though without a credit. Both were men of high talent whose personal philosophies chimed well with the themes of the picture. *The Enforcer* was scripted by Eastwood's old *Rawhide* companion Dean Riesner and Stirling Silliphant, a much respected screen and TV writer and though their work remained faithful to the Callahan image it did not extend it.

Advertised as 'the dirtiest Harry of them all', the film re-introduced Callahan teasingly as he is called to a restaurant where a customer has apparently just had a heart attack. The detective's reaction is to take one look at the unconscious man then heave him unceremoniously to his feet and drag him to the door past the appalled customers. The man, it transpires, is simply a con man who stages such 'attacks' to avoid paying his bill. The joke is on the audience for doubting the value of Callahan's violent methods.

They are further vindicated when his next call takes him to a liquor store siege where four desperate gunmen are holding staff and customers to ransom. Their spokesman demands a getaway car with a radio and freedom from pursuit. Callahan's reaction is to provide the car – by driving it through the store window and picking off all four gunmen with his magnum.

This brutal efficiency predictably provokes outrage in Callahan's superior, a Captain McKay (Bradford Dillman) whose liberal convictions are based less on principle than self-seeking ambition. He accuses Callahan of using excessive force: 'For your information, Callahan, the minority communities have just about had it with this kind of police work.' 'By the minority communities,' the detective replies, 'I suppose you're talking about the hoods.' 'It so happens,' insists McKay, 'they are American citizens too. They happen to have rights.'

Callahan is left to re-state the premises of *Dirty Harry*: 'And what about the lady with the shotgun stuck in her ear? Or doesn't she count any more? What the hell is going on around here? What kind of department are we running when we're more concerned with the rights of criminals than of the people we're supposed to be protecting?'

Again his methods and his insubordination earn him demotion. McKay is a petty bureaucrat whose only stated police experience is in personnel, where Callahan is despatched. There he crosses swords with a female representative of the mayor's office who is keen to see minorities – specifically women – given promotion. Her brief is to 'winnow the Neanderthals out of the department' and bring it 'into the mainstream of twentieth-century thought'. She is as prissily self-important as McKay, an easy target for an enraged Callahan who stresses the impracticality of putting under-experienced officers on the street. He savages a young woman officer Kate Moore (Tyne Daly) who is up for inspector when he finds out that her background is entirely administrative. Her inexperience, he argues, would gravely endanger any future partner she has. 'That,' he says, 'is a hell of a price for being stylish.'

His argument wins because, in dramatic terms, we have seen it justified.

The villains of this film are appropriately updated. They are the People's Revolutionary Strike Force – a clear echo of the real-life Symbionese Liberation Front whose violent activities were snatching headlines in the mid-seventies. Unlike their counterparts, however, the PRSF merely mouth revolutionary sentiments; they are vicious, cardboard-cutout 'bad guys' who are only in it for the money and their leader, Bobby Maxwell (De Veren Bookwalter) is a brutal and sadistic killer whose blond-haired, blue-eyed prettiness suggests not the misguided Nazi morality of *Magnum Force's* Davis but unrepentent homosexuality. Callahan becomes involved when Maxwell stabs his ex-partner, De Georgio (John Mitchum), to death when he surprises the gang raiding an arms warehouse. Callahan is reinstated with homicide and given a new partner – the inexperienced Inspector Moore. 'Oh shit,' is his succinct comment.

The PRSF have meanwhile demanded a million dollars from the city, threatening terrorist outrages if they don't get it. Callahan and Moore are visiting a local hospital when they witness the first – a bomb explosion in a washroom – and spot the black PRSF member who placed it. After a lengthy chase over the rooftops, Callahan corners him in a church – to the indignation of the priest. This arrest confirms McKay's unfounded suspicion that black militants are responsible and Callahan and Moore visit a local black militant leader, Black Ed Mustapha.

Mustapha is contemptuous of the white race but non-violent. He agrees to help Callahan if Callahan will put in a good word for one of his followers arrested on a minor charge.

Their meeting is the most significant in the film. Like Callahan, Mustapha is frustrated and embittered by the status quo and subscribes to what he believes is a higher ideal. As he tells Callahan, 'You're on the wrong side . . . You go out and put your life on the line for a bunch of dudes who wouldn't let you in the front door any more than they would me.'

'I'm not doing it for them,' replies Callahan, but when asked who he *is* doing it for avoids the question: 'You wouldn't believe me if I told you.'

The truthful answer is that he's doing it for himself, for Harry Callahan, because he's the hero of this story and he's also Clint Eastwood with the in-built moral authority of his screen persona. He's first and last an individual, the ultimate and inviolable loner who never compromises his individuality by committing himself to one side – at least in a political sense.

The two men part, having reached an uneasy mutual respect. Minutes later McKay arrives with dozens of policemen and marches Mustapha and his followers away, convinced he's solved the PRSF problem. To further his own career by making the mayor (John Crawford) look good, he suggests that Callahan and his new partner be given public credit for the arrests – as a vindication of the new mayoral policy of putting women officers on the streets. Disgusted, Callahan turns in his badge. Inspector Moore runs after him, though without resigning, and when she offers to help a deeper and even flirtatious relationship begins to develop between them.

It's the most human aspect of Callahan we're shown over the entire trilogy, a genuinely supportive man-woman relationship based not on sexual attraction but on a shared attitude to their work. Moore jokes about her 'women's intuition' but she also teases Callahan gently about his male chauvinistic image – 'cold, bold Callahan with a great big forty-four' – thus defusing any lingering sexual tension. Disarmed, he suggests 'a few beers', as he might to a male colleague and concludes: 'You know, whoever draws you as a partner could do a hell of a lot worse.'

Meanwhile the mayor pays the price of his 'stylishness' when the pseudo-revolutionaries kidnap him and hold him to ransom for $5 million. Callahan posts bail for Mustapha who gives him the name of a female member of Maxwell's gang, Wanda. He traces her to the church where he arrested the black bomber. When he tries to force information out of the priest, who is sympathetic to the PRSF's avowed cause, Wanda appears disguised as a nun and armed with a rifle. Moore turns up at the appropriate moment and saves Callahan's life.

In an abrupt, and rather glib change of heart, the priest recants – 'I closed my eyes to all this' – and leads Callahan and Moore to Maxwell's hide-out at Alcatraz. The two detectives invade the island and in a prolonged gun battle through the corridors of the ex-prison Moore is killed by Maxwell and Callahan blasts Maxwell with a LAWS rocket, a form of miniature bazooka, which destroys the guard tower where the killer – rather foolishly – has taken refuge. As the grateful mayor promises endless letters of commendation, McKay arrives overhead in a helicopter, promising to accede to all of Maxwell's demands.

Callahan's cry as he despatches Maxwell – 'You fucking fruit!' – expresses his hatred for a man who has killed two of his partners but his accusation of homosexuality – on no apparent evidence – betrays the woolliness of writing that has characterised the film. Till now Harry has been content to 'hate everybody' and 'punk' was the epithet he applied universally and democratically. Calling Maxwell a 'fruit' smacks of playing directly to a prejudiced gallery and Pauline Kael seized on it instantly. 'Is this the last outpost of the Western hero,' she wrote, 'killing homosexuals to purify the cities?'

The Enforcer lived up to its advertising by being the 'dirtiest Harry' in that it was the crudest made of the trilogy. Its broad outlines, however, struck a powerful chord with the public; five years after its release it had notched up a staggering $24 million at the American and Canadian box offices alone, making it the third most successful film Eastwood has ever made.

But in terms of artistic development it was something of a throwback for the star. His performance – with able support from Tyne Daly – was well up to his monolithic

144

best but there were hints of tiredness as he worked to bring life to over familiar material. He was already looking for a deeper, more satisfying expression of his screen persona and in his next film, *The Outlaw Josey Wales*, he was to find it.

On the run as Dirty Harry Callahan in The Enforcer, *1976*

Back in the Saddle 8

Joe Kidd
High Plains Drifter

One of the enduring and creditable aspects of Eastwood's personality is that he plainly learns lessons. After the commercial failure of *The Beguiled* he has never again given a screen performance in which he does not demonstrate, at some stage, the precise qualities that have made him a star. There is always a moment – usually violent – that makes the audience gasp or burst into surprised laughter or both. It's a moment that is succinct, brilliantly worked in dramatic terms and quintessentially Clint Eastwood. By such moments he has kept faith with his audience in a way few other major stars have managed to do. They sparkle, even among the dullest and most intractable material. *Joe Kidd*, the film he made immediately after *Dirty Harry*, is an excellent demonstration.

It is another Western, set in Leone territory on the American side of the Mexican-American border. The local Mexican population, led by Luis Chama (John Saxon), are being systematically cheated of their land rights by American land barons. Frustrated by the indifference of the law, they riot at the court house in the New Mexico town of Sinola, burn the land records and threaten the judge. He is rescued by Joe Kidd (Eastwood) who has been gaoled overnight on a drunk and disorderly charge.

Frank Harlan (Robert Duvall), one of the biggest American landowners, arrives in town and offers Kidd $500 to help track down Chama. At first Kidd refuses, but then discovers that Chama's men have stolen horses from his property and agrees to Harlan's offer – for $1000. As the hunt progresses, however, it becomes clear that Harlan, who has since hired a small army to accompany them, is a ruthless killer. When he takes the population of a small Mexican village hostage and threatens to shoot them one by one until Chama gives himself up, Kidd switches sides. With the aid of Chama's girlfriend Rita Sanchez (Stella Garcia) he tries to persuade Chama to give himself up to the law, but Chama proves to be as ruthless as Harlan. Kidd promptly captures him and attempts to bring him back into Sinola.

147

Harlan's men, meanwhile, are waiting in town. A gun battle ensues between the Mexicans and the Americans which Kidd brings to a spectacular conclusion by driving a locomotive through several buildings. Chama finally agrees to surrender to the sheriff and Kidd despatches Harlan in the courthouse where he has taken refuge.

Arthur Knight in *Saturday Review* accurately pointed out the film's basic flaw: 'Joe Kidd, in his single-minded purpose of turning the corrupt Mexican over to a corrupt justice, is demonstrably mad.'

He's certainly not very bright. He has No Name's expertise with firearms but little of his devious intelligence. At the end of the film he takes on Dirty Harry's aura of self-righteous judge, jury and executioner rolled into one when Harlan sneaks into the apparently deserted courthouse and the judge's chair suddenly swivels, revealing Kidd with a levelled gun. He's photographed from a low angle to lend menace and authority and in a style quite alien to the rest of the film. When the sheriff tries to intrude, Kidd bawls at him to get out – Kidd's court is in progress, but it's no more legitimate than Harlan's or Chama's and plainly deeply hypocritical.

These contradictions might have been less important if Kidd had been a more ruthless figure himself, but for the remainder of the film he is fair-minded and comparatively amiable. Eastwood's performance is one of his more relaxed and assured with fine touches of humour – something the critics were swift to praise: to Roger Greenspun in the *New York Times* he demonstrates 'a kind of authoritative normalcy, an actor's gift to an ordinary film that at least gives him reasonable room to breath.'

Malpaso hired John Sturges to direct; he had made several notable Westerns, including *The Magnificent Seven* and the excellent *Bad Day at Black Rock*, but here he appeared to be attempting to recreate with Eastwood the kind of role that had made Steve McQueen a star in the director's 1963 success *The Great Escape*: 'the same brand of humorously low-keyed, bottled-up violence,' as one critic put it. It simply wasn't compatible with Eastwood's distinctive moral authority.

But there were enough 'Eastwood' moments to make the film a healthy box-office success: in gaol, as the picture opens, Kidd is taunted by a fellow prisoner who refuses to let him share the saucepan of beans he is heating for breakfast; as Kidd leaves to go to court the man jeers at him again and Kidd instantly snatches the saucepan and throws its contents into the other's face. Too stunned for a second to react, the man finally flings himself at his attacker, and with impeccable practicality Kidd smashes him in the face, with the empty saucepan.

Meeting Harlan's girlfriend Elma (Lynn Marta) for the first time, Kidd attempts and almost carries off an instant seduction. 'How long were you in gaol?' she enquires breathlessly. 'Two days,' he replies. 'What would you be like after two months?' she wonders. He grins. 'We wouldn't be talking now.'

Eastwood's next film – the second Western he made in 1972 – had as many fan-pleasing moments, but unlike *Joe Kidd* it found a director who succeeded in satisfac-

John Saxon and Clint Eastwood in a scene from Joe Kidd, *1972*

148

torily fusing the ruthless intelligence of No Name with moral righteousness of Dirty Harry – Eastwood himself. In the process he finally laid the ghost of the Man With No Name – quite literally.

High Plains Drifter is not only a superlative Western but a ghost story too. The opening shot sets the scene for both with an economy reminiscent of Don Siegel and a pictorial ingenuity, and beauty, that Serge Leone might have envied.

A telephoto lens picks out a lone rider as he emerges from a desert waste. Seen at the very limit of vision where the ochres, tans and yellows of the landscape separate and stratify in the heat haze, the distant figure seems to materialise out of the mingled elements of earth and sky. Eery, high-pitched music, reminiscent of Ennio Morricone's more tension-filled moments, accompanies this unsettling manifestation.

But as the rider enters the small, lakeside mining town of Lago he takes on more solid and familiar form. Dusty, scruffily bearded with a cold, squinting gaze, this stranger could have stepped straight from the frames of a 'spaghetti' Western. His measured progress down the town's single street, followed by a tracking camera which picks out the expressions of the townsfolk – a mixture of unease and uncertain recognition – recalls No Name's entry into San Miguel. Only one thing disturbs his icy equanimity – the sudden cracking of a whip, whose significance becomes clearer later.

In the town's saloon three heavies loom

With Rita Sanchez (Stella Garcia) in Joe Kidd

150

menacingly as he takes a drink. 'Flea-bitten range-bums don't usually stop in Lago,' says one. 'Life here's a little too quick for them. But maybe you think you're fast enough to keep up with us.' 'I'm faster,' the stranger replies, 'than you'll ever live to be.'

The sparse dialogue has a teasing ambiguity – as the stranger quickly proves. Seated in the barber shop, where the nervous and avaricious barber vainly attempts to boost the stranger's expenditure, he's again approached by the heavies. This time their threats are overt; they want him out of town. The stranger's response is swift and bloody. A concealed gun barks from beneath the white sheet tucked into his collar and all three heavies fall dead.

Unmoved by his actions, or the astonished looks of the townsfolk, the stranger rises and leaves. Outside the town whore Callie Travers (Mariana Hill) flounces past him, deliberately knocking into his shoulder and using that as an excuse to berate him with such a sudden ferocity that it smacks of an equally powerful sexual interest. Astonished at first by this outburst, the stranger takes her at her unspoken word, drags her, loudly protesting, into the nearby barn and promptly rapes her, an act to which she rapidly acquiesces.

Back on the street the town dwarf, Mordecai (Billy Curtis), provides the stranger with the last props of his No Name persona. He offers a thin black cigar and asks, 'What did you say your name was?' 'I didn't,' replies the stranger.

Meanwhile the townsfolk are deeply worried by the imminent release from gaol of three gunmen – predecessors of the heavies killed by the stranger – who have

vowed revenge on the town. Their solution
is to approach the stranger for help, offering in return unlimited credit in the town.
He agrees and goes on a spending spree,
taking over an entire floor of the local hotel
and promoting Mordecai to sheriff.

He makes plans to defend the town,
instructs the citizens in tactics and
arranges target practice for them, but their
initial delight turns to unease as his
demands become more arbitrary and
extreme. He commandeers food and drink
for a picnic in the main street and has a
barn torn down to provide wood for the
picnic tables. He orders that the entire
town be painted red. 'When we get done,'
complains one citizen, 'this place is going
to look like hell.' It's clearly the stranger's
intention. He crosses out 'Lago' on the
town sign and substitutes 'Hell' in red
letters.

In the meantime flashbacks in the form
of recurring nightmares suffered by both
the stranger and Mordecai establish that
the town's former Marshal – Jim Duncan
– was whipped to death in the main street
by the three gunmen who are about to
leave gaol. Though the killers were impris-
oned for the murder, the townspeople witnessed the crime and made no attempt to
stop it. Duncan, it transpires, discovered
that the mine which is the source of Lago's
prosperity is on government not private
land and was about to inform the authorities. The sheriff now lies in an unmarked
grave. 'They say the dead don't rest without a marker of some kind,' Mordecai

As The Stranger in High Plains Drifter, *1973*

153

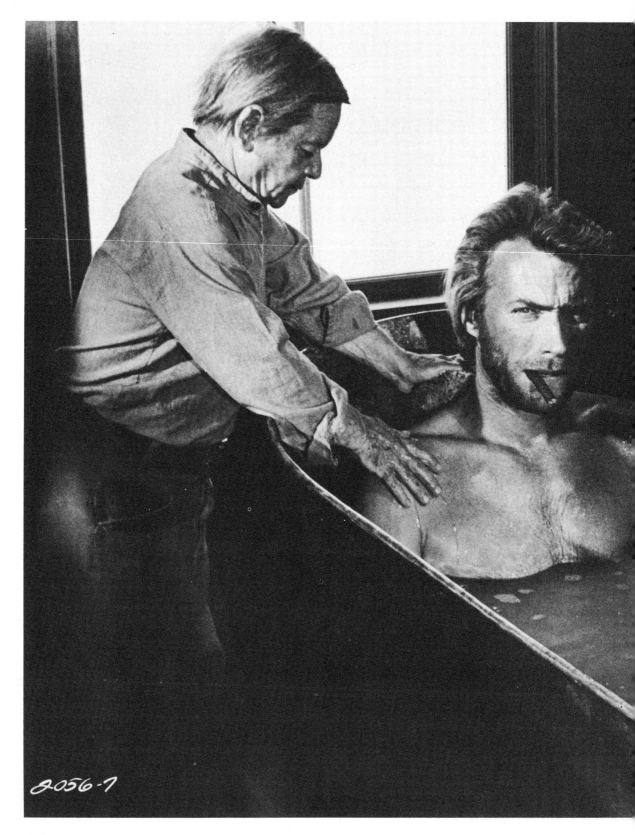

154

informs the stranger. 'He's the reason this town's afraid of strangers.' The stranger agrees; no man, he says, can rest easy in an unmarked grave.

The townspeople start to crack under the pressure of his demands. One night, after he's enjoyed an intimate dinner with Callie Travers, a group of them burst into his bedroom and mercilessly beat the figure lying in his bed. It turns out to be a dummy. The stranger has been waiting for them on a low roof outside the bedroom window and casually tosses a burning stick of dynamite inside.

Now he talks of leaving the town to its fate, but the terrified citizens offer him $500 a head. 'Five hundred dollars an ear,' he replies. They hurriedly agree. His next demand is that he has the town's hotel to himself. The residents are immediately turfed out, including the manager whose room the stranger takes for himself – along with the manager's wife, Sarah Belding (Verna Bloom). She and Mordecai are the only citizens who tried to stop Duncan's murder. In the morning, after she has made love with the stranger, she tells her husband that their marriage is over and she is leaving Lago.

The three gunmen are released from gaol and immediately take up their old ways, murdering a group of cowboys for their horses. As the time of their arrival draws near the stranger, contrary to his agreement, rides out of town. The killers make their entrance, greeted by a sheet

Mordecai (Billy Curtis) scrubs The Stranger's back in a scene from High Plains Drifter

155

draped across the main street at the stranger's request and with the words 'Welcome home boys' painted on it.

The townspeople's plan of defence crumbles at the first shot and the gunmen run amok, killing and looting at will and eventually setting half the town aflame. As night falls they collect the terrified citizens together in the saloon and taunt them. Their vengeful gloating comes to an abrupt end as a whip cracks suddenly in the darkness outside. One of the gunmen goes toinvestigate and a whip fastens around his neck. In seconds he is whipped to death on the same spot where Duncan died.

A second gunman follows and is hung with the same whip. When the leading killer, Stacey Bridges (Geoffrey Lewis) goes outside the stranger is waiting. They draw and Bridges dies, crying in terror, 'Who are you?'

In the morning the stranger rides out of town – now a smouldering ruin – the way he came. His route takes him past the graveyard where Mordecai is at work. 'I never did know your name,' the dwarf asks. 'Yes, you do,' the stranger replies tersely and as the camera pans to follow him it picks up Jim Duncan's graveyard cross. It now bears lettering: 'Marshal Jim Duncan – Rest in Peace.' The film ends with a repeat of its opening shot, only now the stranger retreats until his distant image breaks apart and dematerialises in the swirling heat haze.

No Name has become literally the avenging angel Sergio Leone had hinted

Eastwood doubled as star and director in High Plains Drifter

he might be in the 'spaghetti' Westerns. As such his moral credentials are impeccable. Unlike Dirty Harry, who had to justify himself constantly in a realistic situation, the drifter has a supernatural licence to kill in the mythic context of the Old West. But it's not exercised indiscriminately.

He kills the three heavies when they are on the point of killing him. He rapes Callie Travers only after she has savaged him and at her unspoken request – a point underlined when she takes over a day to seek her revenge, emptying a revolver at the stranger as he sits in the barber's bath tub; he sinks under the water, untouched by the bullets that splash around him, and surfaces to ask Mordecai: 'I wonder what took her so long to get mad?' 'Maybe because you didn't come back for more,' the dwarf suggests.

He offers the town a genuine chance to avoid its fate and they muff it, as they muffed the chance to save Marshal Duncan. He offers friendship to the one man who still agonises over the Marshal's death – Mordecai – and elevates him into the position of moral authority he deserves. He becomes a substitute husband to the one woman who feels the same and gives her the strength to see her husband's moral cowardice clearly.

He satirises the townspeople's selfishness and greed; his first act on being granted unlimited credit is to give blankets to an Indian the storekeeper is about to throw out of his store and sweets to the Indian's children. When he unceremoniously deposits the hotel's residents on the street and the town preacher berates him for his lack of charity, the stranger suggests that the dispossessed can be accommodated in the homes of their fellow citizens. The preacher agrees – adding

that they will be charged at no more than normal hotel rates.

Eastwood himself described the film as a morality play and it does correspond to the mediaeval pattern with Mordecai as the comic chorus, who is also the wise fool, and citizens whose predominant characteristics bear more than a passing resemblance to the seven deadly sins: the overweight and slothful sheriff, the avaricious and envious barber, the wrathful and lusty Callie Travers, and so on. The story has the directness and simplicity of such plays too, and its clarity finds expression in the unusual setting in which Eastwood chose to film it.

Lago was constructed in eighteen days on the shores of the almost unnaturally blue waters of Lake Mono, in the high clear air of the Sierra Nevada, close to California's Yosemite national park. No attempt was made to age the look of the buildings. Their newly planed boards gave Lago the authentic, just-arrived appearance that must have been common to many frontier settlements, but they also suggested the all-too-temporary nature of the town. Perched between a wilderness and the dazzling blue abyss of the lake, it added to the bizarre, slightly unsettling atmosphere of the film.

Eastwood completed the filming in a little under six weeks, two days within schedule – a more impressive feat than it sounds because the painting of the town and its eventual destruction meant that the story had to be shot in sequence. As with *Play 'Misty' For Me* he used video-tape to check his own performance and he further accelerated the film-making process by editing as he went along, installing all the necessary equipment in a small log cabin close to the location.

But *High Plains Drifter* was more much more than a triumph of logistics. In a single film Eastwood leapt into the first rank of the cinema's directors. Gone were the awkwardnesses and uncertainties of *Misty*; the camerawork is inventive and assured, the storytelling economical and well-paced, the performances crisp and accurate. One could argue that Eastwood was making it easy for himself by covering ground he knew almost too well; there are obvious homages to both Leone and Siegel but they are subsumed into a new and distinctive style that is peculiarly Eastwood's.

He had moved beyond both his mentors, skilfully and intelligently using his improved directorial skills to exploit the mythic aspects of his own screen persona more effectively than any other director had managed. The result was the ultimate redefinition of No Name – the earthly superman has finally achieved supreme invulnerability by taking on supernatural powers. The only problem is that he has had to die to make that possible.

To develop his screen image further Eastwood would need to find a new and equally resonant reincarnation. Almost four years were to pass before he succeeded and, as a director, matched the new and exacting standard he had set himself in *High Plains Drifter*.

The period between 1972 and 1975 – from the completion of *High Plains Drifter* to the start of filming *The Outlaw Josey Wales* – was in many ways an odd one for Eastwood. Privately his life was enriched by the birth of a second child, Allison, on 23 May 1972. Commercially he achieved unprecedented success; both *Magnum Force* and *The Enforcer* were among the top ten highest earning films of the years in which they were released; 1973 saw Eastwood as Hollywood's top box office star.

Creatively, however, his choice of films reveals uncertainty. His most successful performances were re-explorations of his Dirty Harry persona, but the three other films he made at this time – *Breezy, Thunderbolt and Lightfoot* and *The Eiger Sanction* – show him searching for some new and more fruitful cinematic image. Each was a characteristically bold foray into a completely new genre – respectively, romance, 'buddy' movie of the sort that had brought Paul Newman and Robert Redford success in *Butch Cassidy and the Sundance Kid*, and James Bond-style spy saga. Although

Thunderbolt and Lightfoot and *The Eiger Sanction*, were solid commercial successes they demonstrate a confusing mixture of experimentation and creative staleness. *Breezy*, however, was both a commercial and a critical failure. In making it Eastwood contradicted his own definition of an Eastwood film as being one with him in it. It was the first film he directed which did not also star himself.

There is a recurring pattern in Eastwood's career of following success with experimentation, but there seemed little obvious reason for choosing to do *Breezy*. It was a sentimental tale of love between a middle-aged, divorced, real-estate executive, Frank Harmon (played by William Holden) and a footloose seventeen-year-old (Kay Lenz, then a young television actress), the Breezy of the title. He encounters her hitch-hiking outside his plush Los Angeles home and gives her a lift, chiefly to clear the neighbourhood of such a scruffily unconventional character.

In the car he finds her conversation irritating though he is forced, reluctantly, to

2059.40

162

co-operate with her when they go to the aid of an injured dog. That evening she re-appears at Harmon's door, claiming to look for a guitar she left in his car. She persuades him to invite her in and to allow her to take a bath but when she asks to stay the night he sends her away.

The following night she appears yet again – in the custody of two police officers. She has told them that she is Harmon's niece to avoid a vagrancy charge. Harmon confirms her story and this time she stays the night. The following night romance blossoms and they make love.

Though happy in themselves, their relationship provokes tension with both their friends. Harmon eventually decides it cannot go on and ends it. But shortly afterwards the husband of a woman friend dies in a road accident. In the woman's grief Harmon is confronted with real loneliness and realises he has been foolish to deny Breezy's love. He finds her again and their relationship resumes.

Scripted by Jo Heims, who had written *Play 'Misty' For Me*, the leading role seems to have been intended for Eastwood. If so, its attraction could well have been that of a possible solution to the romantic dilemma posed by films like *Misty* and *Two Mules for Sister Sara* and still largely unsolved. But when it came to the crunch he balked at the idea. 'I've never done a love story,' he said, 'so I'm staying behind the camera.' In the event it was a wise decision.

Eastwood's handling of the film was deft and highly competent, skilfully avoiding

Previous page: *Eastwood in* Thunderbolt and Lightfoot, *1974.* Left: *Eastwood, director of* Breezy, *1973, with his discovery, Kay Lenz, who played the title role*

163

the obvious sentimentality of the story. But he could not avoid its equally obvious triteness. The central relationship is well-observed but unexceptional and neither Jo Heims' script nor Eastwood's direction could give it any greater resonance.

Now approaching his mid-forties, Eastwood may well have felt a need to make a comment on his awareness of encroaching middle age and his changing attitudes to the younger generation. Nothing in his career, however, had prepared him for a sympathetic understanding of the young; on the contrary, in films like *Coogan's Bluff* and *Dirty Harry* the alternative youth culture had virtually been written off as a sign of rampant decadence, giving rise to long-haired homicidal maniacs like James Ringerman and Scorpio. It was no surprise that Eastwood's portrayal of Breezy and her friends should ring false.

Breezy opened to lukewarm reviews – no indication of commercial failure with many of Eastwood's films – but it suffered a further setback when a brief shot of a bare breast earned it an R-rating, effectively forbidding it to a large section of Breezy's own generation. Then, as now, cinema audiences were largely composed of men and women in their twenties and early thirties and the problems of a middle-aged estate agent aroused no great empathy or enthusiasm.

Significantly the two films that followed *Breezy* – *Magnum Force* and *Thunderbolt and Lightfoot* – both touch on similar themes of youth and age, experience and inexperience and with increasingly sympathetic portrayals of the younger generation – though the price of that acceptance in both cases is death. The four young vigilante cops of *Magnum Force* win Harry Callahan's admiration to the extent that he's willing to excuse their possible homosexuality. 'We're the first generation that knows how to fight,' their leader, Davis, tells him. Unfortunately, though their hearts are in the right places, their fighting methods aren't and their inexperience in combat proves fatal.

Lightfoot, the young co-hero of *Thunderbolt and Lightfoot*, earns the friendship of the older, more experienced Thunderbolt and achieves the one concrete ambition of his rootless life – paying cash for a brand new, white Cadillac, only to die in the car from a head wound.

Thunderbolt and Lightfoot was not a wholly successful film, except in financial terms, but it is one of the most boldly experimental Eastwood has ever made. In making it the star went further than he had ever done before in encouraging new and exciting talent. The script was by thirty-one-year-old Michael Cimino – co-scripter of *Magnum Force* – and so impressed Eastwood he offered the young screenwriter the opportunity to direct it. The role of Eastwood's co-star went to twenty-five-year-old Jeff Bridges, an actor who had first made his mark in Peter Bogdanovich's *The Last Picture Show* in 1971, and Eastwood's unusually self-effacing performance gave the young actor the lion's share of the film's dramatic opportunities.

Though it is chiefly a 'buddy' movie – and in its lyrical evocation of male friendship a prototype of Cimino's Oscar-winning *The Deerhunter* – it is many other things too: a 'caper' movie (what plot there is revolves around a cleverly organised robbery of an apparently impregnable vault), a 'road' movie after the pattern established by *Easy Rider*, and a tale of revenge.

It is also the only example in Eastwood's work of what has been called the New American Cinema, a cold, clear, detached approach to American society and to the American landscape, more characteristic of European cinema than of the conventions of Hollywood. Films like Bob Rafelson's *Five Easy Pieces* and *The King of Marvin Gardens*, Terence Mallick's *Badlands* and Hal Ashby's *The Last Detail* – all made around this time – focused attention on a neglected hinterland, unfashionable but no less fascinating aspects of their native land which had little to do with the glossy, conventionally dramatised products of the Amercian Dream peddled by Hollywood and network television.

The America portrayed here by Cimino is a pristine wilderness, an eye-beguiling landscape of Eden-like valleys, remote and spectacular gorges, endless wheatfields and vast skies. It's both real and unreal, a landscape of dream. When the two main characters are forced to abandon their car in an isolated canyon of awesome beauty, Lightfoot summons up a passing riverboat like an old-time cowboy saddling a fresh mount or a knightly hero seizing a new destrier and it bears them away in a matter of minutes. Appropriately it is called 'Idaho Dream' and from its deck Thunderbolt reveals his own frustrated dream of wealth, a robbery which misfired, and puts in motion what will eventually lead to the realisation of Lightfoot's similar fantasy.

The inhabitants of this landscape are equally strange and startling. The two men accept a lift from a maniac driver who keeps a caged racoon on his front seat and a boot full of white rabbits which he releases only to blast at point blank range with a shotgun. Lightfoot encounters a pretty female motorcyclist on the road and her immediate reaction to his greeting is to start beating against the side of his van with a hammer. His temporary job as a landscape gardener is enlivened by the lady of the house who poses stark naked at her living room window. A middle-aged couple shuffle an apparently unending stream of credit cards to pay for petrol at a garage while the disgruntled attendant imagines that the entire American economy is dependent upon a single little old lady with just seventy-five dollars and twenty-five cents and a majority holding in everything.

The bizarrely original mood is established in the opening scene. The sound of hymn-singing rises from a small, white-painted, clapboard church, pictured against a clear blue sky and the luminous yellow of an Idaho wheatfield. A battered car approaches and pulls up outside. A sweating, middle-aged man, dark-suited and overweight, steps out, checking the church notice board before he moves to the entrance.

The pastor, we have seen, is John Doherty and our first surprise comes as we see him at the pulpit, reminding the Mid-Western congregation that they are all imperfect. It's Eastwood – dressed as never before in a dog collar and spectacles with slicked back hair.

The film cuts to a nearby used car lot where Lightfoot, a young drifter, feigns a limp to impress the dealer as he tries out a $3000 Pontiac Firebird. The dealer is still uncertain if the young man is telling the truth about a wooden leg when Lightfoot stamps on the accelerator and steals the car.

Back in the church the pastor concludes his sermon by wishing peace and goodwill toward men. At which point the middle-

165

aged man whips out an automatic and begins shooting at him. Doherty bolts through a hail of bullets and is pursued across the adjoining wheatfield. As he reaches the road, Lightfoot appears in his stolen Firebird, ignores Doherty's frantic signal to stop and instead veers into the corn and flattens his still firing assailant. Doherty leaps at the departing car, which still shows no sign of stopping for him, and is borne away, clinging onto the passenger door. In a moment he has hauled himself inside – at the cost of a dislocated shoulder – and the odd partnership is underway.

Doherty, it transpires, is the 'Thunderbolt' who successfully raided the Montana Armoury vault with the aid of a 20mm cannon. He and another member of the gang, who has since died, hid the proceeds, fearing that the three other gang members would spend the money too quickly and announce their guilt. As a result 'Thunderbolt' has been constantly pursued by them. He gradually reveals this to Lightfoot as they travel and are shot at by the remaining gang members, the vicious Red Leary (George Kennedy) and the amiable buffoon, Eddie Goody (Geoffrey Lewis). Thunderbolt decides it's time to recover the money which has been hidden in an old school. When he and Lightfoot arrive there they discover that it has been demolished and a new building stands in its place.

Leary and Goody now catch up with them and Thunderbolt eventually convinces them he has not been a cheat. Lightfoot then suggests they re-enact the original robbery and the four men take jobs to finance the project.

The raid is carried out with split-second timing and initial success. Leary and Thunderbolt invade the vault manager's home to obtain the combination for its outer doors and use a cannon to blast their way into the vault itself. Lightfoot masquerades as a woman to distract a security guard.

But as they make their getaway they are spotted by police. Goody is badly wounded and thrown out of their car by Leary, who then knocks Thunderbolt and Lightfoot unconscious, kicking the young man repeatedly in the head because he has been the butt of the youngster's youthfully insolent manner. Leary takes off with the money, hotly pursued by the police, and crashes through the window of a store which is guarded at night by savage Dobermanns. The dogs kill him.

Left with nothing, Thunderbolt and Lightfoot leave the area on foot. In the morning they are confronted by the schoolhouse where Thunderbolt hid the proceeds of the original raid. It has been moved intact to a new location where it is now a museum. Inside they find the money still hidden. Thunderbolt uses it to buy a new white Cadillac but when he picks up Lightfoot the young man's speech is slurred and he is partially paralysed from the beating Leary gave him. 'I feel we accomplished something, a good job,' he says. 'I feel proud of myself, man. I feel like a hero.' They are his last words. Thunderbolt snaps the celebratory cigar he is smoking and drives into the distance.

Throughout the themes of friendship, age and youth, experience and inexperience are cleverly intertwined. Thunderbolt's text for his church sermon is 'the wolf shall dwell with the lamb, the leopard shall lie down with the kid', On the word 'kid' the film cuts to introduce Lightfoot. Thunderbolt is plainly the sleek and efficient leopard. He repeats the quotation

166

when Lightfoot first suggests restaging the vault robbery and the cantankerous Leary voices initial objections. 'What's that – a poem?' asks Goody. 'No,' says Thunderbolt, 'a prayer.' A prayer that isn't answered.

Leary rejects Lightfoot's friendship but holds to Thunderbolt's because it was forged years before in the fires of the Korean War in which they both served. Lightfoot's response to this is mockery that includes more than a grain of truth. 'I had a dream about you last night,' he tells Leary. 'I dreamt you said hello to me.'

When Lightfoot first offers friendship to Thunderbolt, the older man demurs. 'Kid, you're ten years too late,' he says. 'You're as young as you feel!' Lightfoot calls after him. Thunderbolt only returns because he has spotted Leary in a nearby bus station. The two men stop at a motel and Lightfoot swiftly picks up a local girl, Melody (Catherine Bach), and her friend Gloria, for Thunderbolt. Thunderbolt's response is less than enthusiastic; his one-night-stand days are over. When he beds Gloria, the young girl is plainly a little too much for him. 'Take it easy, Gloria,' he groans. 'You're killing me.' Next morning at breakfast a bright-eyed and bushy-tailed Lightfoot tells a baggy-eyed Thunderbolt: 'You stick with me, kid. You can live forever!' Thunderbolt's only comment is another quotation: 'The clock uncoils the working day/He wakes up feeling is youth is gone away.'

The homosexual implications of male friendship aren't avoided either. 'We've got to stop meeting like this,' jokes Lightfoot when Thunderbolt returns to his car after seeing Leary at the bus station. 'People will talk.' Lightfoot excites Leary with his description of the nude woman at the living-room window on his landscaping job and then climaxes his tale by giving the older man a mock kiss. Later, as part of the vault raid, he has to transform himself into a mock 'woman', convincing enough to fool a sexually frustrated security guard. 'Oh you sexy bitch,' he tells himself in the mirror. 'I could go with you myself.'

Lightfoot starts the film as another example of the decadent youth culture – 'You hippy son of a bitch!' the cheated used-car dealer shouts after him. By the end his loyalty to Thunderbolt and his dedication and determination to carry through the raid (ironically, and rather unfairly, his transvestite role turns out to have been unnecessary; the security guard's console does not register the break-in) have made him a 'hero'. Similarly Thunderbolt is revealed to be genuinely heroic earlier on; he has told Lightfoot that Leary is a Korean war hero who saved his (Thunderbolt's) life; when the raid goes wrong Lightfoot realises that the opposite is in fact true.

Lightfoot may be able to match Thunderbolt's qualities of friendship and determination but his youthful inexperience is his undoing. As they ride away in the white Cadillac their triumph seems total. 'We won, didn't we?' says Lightfoot. Thunderbolt has seen too much to reach such an unequivocal conclusion. 'I guess we did,' he replies. 'For the time being.' Most of the relevant quotations, as the above shows, come from Lightfoot. He has the best lines, he is the more dramatically interesting character and Jeff Bridges took full advantage of his opportunities. And that, through no fault of Bridges, is the film's major weakness.

In a subordinate position – as he had

been in *Paint Your Wagon* and *Two Mules for Sister Sara* – Eastwood's screen persona shrinks. His withdrawn self-sufficiency seems almost peevish when he is not in a situation where he can use it to dominate his environment. In *Thunderbolt and Lightfoot* he only becomes truly alive as he plans and carries out the robbery; suddenly he is a dynamic and admirable figure, clearly brighter and more efficient than anyone who surrounds him; he is manifestly in charge. For the bulk of the film, however, he is unable to suggest a deep enough response to Bridges' uninhibited performance. Their relationship is unbalanced, incapable of displaying the emotional resonance that would have made Cimino's script something more than simply clever.

That said, Eastwood's willingness to make the film, and in the way that he did, is a remarkable testament to his personal qualities. Few other actors in the superstar bracket would have had the courage, or the generosity, to give rising talents their heads in such an open-handed way.

But he also had the shrewdness to realise that experimentation could only go so far before the reputation he had built up so assiduously was put at risk. Which made him retreat to safer and more familiar ground for the next film – though only in a metaphorical sense.

For the first time in his directorial career Eastwood followed the conventional Hollywood path and chose a story which was already an established success in another form. *The Eiger Sanction* by Trevanian became a bestselling novel on its publication in 1973. It was an unremarkable James Bond-style fantasy, short on credibility and long on uninhibited sex, a mixture of wisecracks and violence given substance by an integral and apparently authentic account of mountaineering. The hero was a professor of art at an American university who pays for a private and ever-increasing collection of artistic masterpieces by carrying out 'sanctions' – revenge killings – for a secret US intelligence agency. His particular qualification for such work – apart from physical skills – is a pathological condition which makes him incapable of feeling guilt.

Superficially the character has a number of correspondences with Eastwood's screen persona. He kills as coldly and conscienscelessly as No Name and has the same sardonic sense of humour. He shares Harry Callahan's contempt for his employers and expresses it with a similar kind of inventive insolence.

But he doesn't face any of the obvious threats or frustrations that justified the violence of those characters. He lives comfortably in a comfortable modern world and his only motive is unalloyed greed – only partially mitigated by the fact that its object is great art, which indicates a certain sensitivity, but even that is indulged entirely selfishly in the secrecy of an underground vault.

The film's script attempts to alleviate this by having the hero rail – rather unconvincingly – against the rottenness of a system which has no qualms about employing people like him. It can't, however, conceal the gaps in a slack and unlikely plot. When an agent is assassinated in Zurich, the agency head – an invalid albino called Dragon (Thayer David), who for medical

Eastwood as Jonathan Hemlock in The Eiger Sanction, *1975*

168

reasons is forced to live in permanent semi-darkness – recalls his chief assassin, Jonathan Hemlock (Eastwood) from retirement with the promise of a double fee. Hemlock only agrees because he is anxious to buy a painting by Pissarro which has recently come on the black market.

He flies to Zurich, shoots one of the agent's two assassins and meets an attractive black stewardess, Jemima Brown (Vonetta McGee) on the flight home. They sleep together and in the morning Hemlock's fee, and Jemima, are missing. It transpires that Jemima is also a Dragon employee.

Dragon offers to raise Hemlock's fee to $100,000 – five times the original sum – if he will 'sanction' the second of the agent's assassins. All that is known about him is that he has a limp and he will be a member of an international team attempting to climb the treacherous north face of the Eiger that summer. Hemlock refuses until he is told that the murdered agent was a personal friend. He also learns than an old enemy, Miles Mellough (Jack Cassidy), was instrumental in the murder and can be sanctioned too.

Accepting the job, Hemlock – an experienced mountaineer – begins training at a climbing school in Arizona run by an old friend, Ben Bowman (George Kennedy). Bowman, it turns out, has been chosen as the ground man for the Eiger climb. During Hemlock's time at the school he is visited by Miles Mellough. Mellough knows that Hemlock is after the second assassin, but he is also aware of the assassin's identity. He offers to exchange it for an undertaking that Hemlock will spare his life. Hemlock refuses to give an answer and Mellough makes an attempt on his

life. In retaliation Hemlock lures him into a remote part of the surrounding desert, kills his ever-present bodyguard and leaves him to die of thirst.

Bowman and Hemlock join the three other members of the climbing team in Switzerland and they begin their climb with Hemlock no wiser as to the identity of the assassin. Bad weather turns the expedition into a disaster and only Hemlock survives. Bowman leads the rescue team and there comes a point when Hemlock must cut a vital supporting rope in order to swing within Bowman's grasp. It's then that Hemlock notices that Bowman has developed a limp, marking him as the second assassin. Earlier events have identified Hemlock as the sanctioner, though in a manner that only his victim would recognise. Hemlock has no choice but to trust his old friend, and is saved.

On their return from the mountain Bowman admits his guilt and also that he acted in complicity with Miles Mellough who was blackmailing him. The Zurich murder had not been intended – at least by Bowman. Back at Hemlock's hotel Dragon telephones to congratulate him, assuming that the sanctioner was unable to identify the second assassin and so sanctioned all three members of the climbing team. Hemlock does not enlighten him and he and Bowman call it quits.

Hemlock displays the randy charm of a Joe Kidd or a Deputy Sheriff Coogan, the ease in killing of No Name and the moral wrath and ambiguous bigotry of Harry Callahan. Like Dirty Harry who professes all manner of prejudice yet is partnered, successively, by a Mexican, a black and a woman, Hemlock is sexually attracted to a black girl, Jemima, and an Indian girl, Bowman's pneumatic daughter 'George'

Attempting to scale the north face of the Eiger with Meyer (Micheal Grimm) in a scene from The Eiger Sanction

(Brenda Venus), who plays an active part in his training in Arizona. Yet when he finds that Jemima has stolen back the payment for his first sanction after sleeping with him, he condemns her, hypocritically, as a whore, despite her insistence that making love to him was not part of her brief and that she wishes to continue the relationship.

He sneers at Miles Mellough, another former friend who betrayed him, but his contempt is as much for the fact that Mellough is outrageously homosexual as it is for the man's dishonesty. Miles even boasts a small lap dog named Faggot which appropriately deserts him, hopping into Hemlock's jeep as his master is abandoned in the waterless desert.

In the context of a story that is as much hokum as *Where Eagles Dare*, Hemlock's attitudes operate in a vacuum; he is simply a bullying and unprincipled snob. And for that reason, in directing the film, Eastwood concentrates the major part of the dramatic tension on the one true challenge that Hemlock does face – the mountains he climbs and, in particular, the Eiger.

Eastwood had always insisted on doing

171

his own stunts whenever possible but *The Eiger Sanction* is a stunting tour de force. He was determined to make the film in authentic locations, balking only at the actual north face of the Eiger itself, and before shooting began prepared himself with three weeks' intensive training at Yosemite National Park. It was a courageous decision for a man in his mid-forties who had never climbed before, and his brief experience convinced him that he would have to direct himself; trying to follow someone else's direction halfway up a sheer rock face would not have been practical.

Eastwood's initial choice for director had in fact been Don Siegel, who refused on practical grounds, though it's difficult to see how such a story could have appealed to the veteran director; when the film was completed he admitted as much. In the event the film proved the most difficult and dangerous to make that Eastwood had ever attempted. On only the second day of shooting one of a number of professional mountaineers taking part, a young British climber called David Knowles, was killed in a rockslide. Eastwood, who witnessed the accident, was appalled but became determined to complete the film, in part as a tribute to the dead man and despite his own freely admitted fears.

As a result the climbing sequences are the most distinctive and impressive aspect of the film. When, during the training in Arizona, Eastwood and George Kennedy heave themselves on to the flat top of an isolated butte, rising hundreds of feet into the desert air, the helicopter-borne camera retreats, showing the actors alone and unaided in a highly precarious position. When Hemlock dangles over a deep abyss on the face of the Eiger, it is clearly Eastwood and not a double on the end of the rope.

Though professional climbers might gibe at the actual techniques and climbing methods on display, there is no doubt of the dramatic and visual excitement of such moments. In general the critics gave Eastwood due credit for them, while pointing out that they did not redeem the slack and rambling nature of the remainder of the film, which ran for over two hours.

Commercially, however, it did well and with *Thunderbolt and Lightfoot*, released in the same year, maintained Eastwood's popularity as America's second biggest box-office attraction of 1974; only Robert Redford, still basking in the Oscar-winning success of *The Sting*, could nudge him from the first position.

Eastwood as director and star of The Eiger Sanction *makes-up co-star Jean-Pierre Bernard*

172

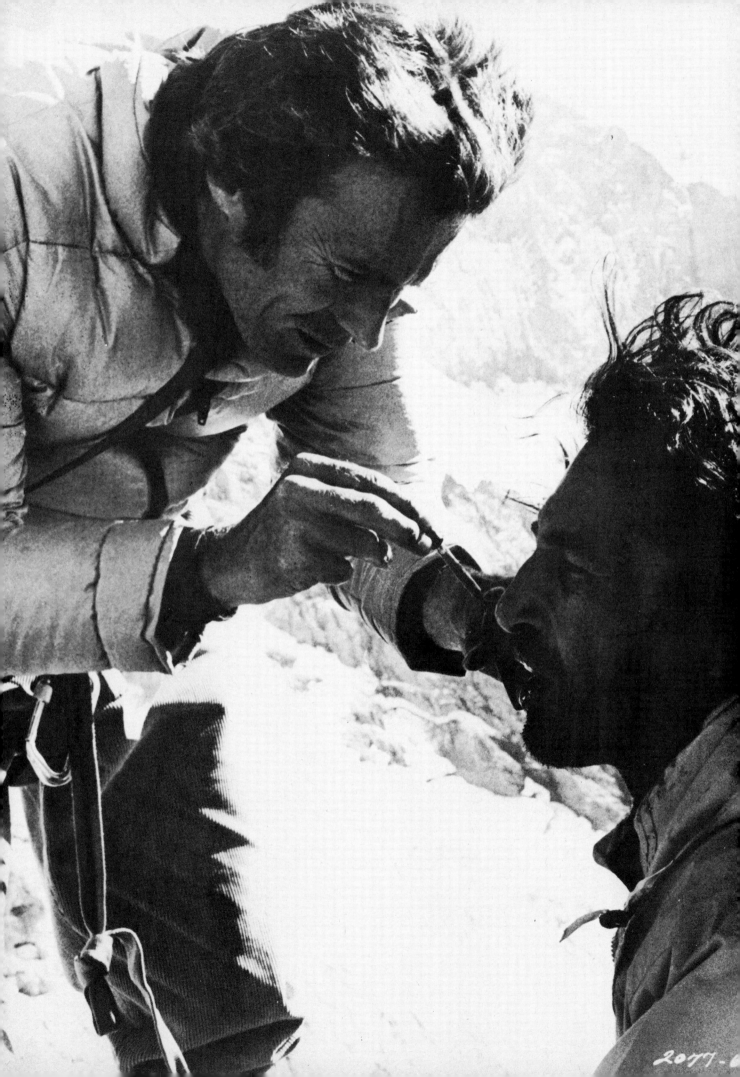

A New Maturity

The Outlaw Josey Wales
The Gauntlet

10

The Word of Life

Both John 'Thunderbolt' Doherty and Jonathon Hemlock had brought Eastwood financial benefits but artistically they had taken him nowhere; neither represented any significant development on Harry Callahan in terms of screen persona. At face value his next project seems an even more retrograde step. He chose to do a Western, the genre that had first brought him success, but at a time when fewer Westerns than ever were being made, mainly because the public no longer appeared to be interested. Even major stars like Jack Nicholson, Marlon Brando, Paul Newman and John Wayne, who all starred in Westerns at this time, were unable to attract large audiences.

Paradoxically the Westerns they made were among the most striking and original ever filmed. Films like Nicholson and Brando's *The Missouri Breaks*, Newman's *Buffalo Bill and the Indians* and Don Siegel's *The Shootist* with John Wayne put the myth of the Old West under a new and searching light which took into account the shocks to America's national conscious-

ness caused by the defeat in Vietnam and the revelations of Watergate.

But, fine though those films were, they registered that national disillusionment and uncertainty rather than offered a solution. Unlike the disillusionment portrayed in Sergio Leone's Western – made in happier times – it was not a liberating force that overturned outdated conventions for the sheer hell of it; rather it was another reminder of the country's painful internal divisions and its loss of political innocence – and all expressed in a genre which had traditionally housed America's most self-confident and optimistic impulses. No wonder people stayed away.

Eastwood's film career had so far only touched on the relatively superficial and dramatic aspects of America's problems in the late sixties and early seventies. The violence that Harry Callahan faced on the streets of San Francisco was a mirror of America's ever-increasing and ever more violent involvement in South-East Asia; all of Dirty Harry's deadliest opponents are Vietnam veterans – the vigilante cops,

175

Bobby Maxwell and even Scorpio who wears black parachute boots laced in military style and displays a soldier's familiarity with a variety of firearms. Eastwood had offered no solutions, either – except in instant, emotional terms. Callahan's victories leave him no less embittered or frustrated with his situation; the mysterious stranger of *High Plains Drifter* is a kind of auto-destructive robot programmed for a single and unrepeatable task; and No Name's uninhibited mayhem, in the light of current events, began to seem almost playful.

It was appropriate, then, that Eastwood, who had first championed disillusionment in the Western, should be the man to show a way out of it. And in doing so he made a major step forward as a director and in terms of his screen persona. The opportunity came in a book called *Gone to Texas* by Forrest Carter which the author sent to Malpaso. Carter, according to an interview Eastwood gave in 1976, was a 46-year-old half-Cherokee Indian, without formal education but with great skill at oral poetry and story-telling. He had been persuaded to write down one of his tales and so written his first book, which was eventually published in Arkansas in a limited hardback edition of seventy-five copies. Iain Johnstone's biography of Eastwood, *The Man With No Name*, suggests Carter's background may actually have been more prosaic; there is evidence that he was in fact a speechwriter for Alabama's controversial Governor George Wallace.

What is important, however, is that Robert Daley read the book and was immediately impressed. He showed it to Eastwood who liked it too. It was an epic story, in the traditional sense of celebrating the deeds of a heroic figure over a span of years and in a well-known historical epoch – in this case, the American Civil War. Eastwood had, he said later, been searching for such a story for some time. Malpaso acquired the film rights and hired Philip Kaufman to write the screenplay.

Kaufman was a writer and director whose 1971 Western *The Great Northfield Minnesota Raid* had impressed Eastwood with its witty, bizarre and grittily authentic view of the Old West. Still mentally and physically weary after his exertions on *The Eiger Sanction*, Eastwood was happy to have him direct the picture too, but in the first week of shooting it became obvious that Kaufman's conception of the story was different from his own and Eastwood took over. It proved to be a happy decision.

The Outlaw Josey Wales opens at another period in American history when the country was deeply divided – the eve of the Civil War – and in a location where the issues at hand first gave rise to violence, of a particularly vicious and bloody kind. This is the Kansas and Missouri border. Kansas is about to enter the Union as a fully fledged state and the debate is whether or not it will allow slavery. A majority of its inhabitants oppose the practice, while the opposite is the case in Missouri.

Previous page: *Eastwood starred in and directed* The Outlaw Josey Wales, *1976.* Right: *Two scenes from* The Outlaw Josey Wales

176

The struggle for Kansas began with ballot-rigging and intimidation by pro-slavery groups but swiftly escalated into widescale violence along the line of the border. Vigilante groups of either political persuasion carried out a series of reprisal and counter-reprisal raids, aimed at dissuading or simply slaughtering settlers who didn't happen to agree with them. When the Civil War broke out in 1861 a savage guerilla war was waged in the same area, resulting in some of the worst atrocities of the conflict.

It's an anarchic environment with which Leone's Man With No Name would be totally familiar, but there is little suggestion of what is to come when we are first introduced to Josey Wales, a hard-working farmer busy clearing the wilderness with a horse and a plough and his young son at his side. The scene is sylvan and idyllic and Eastwood, unarmed and wearing a floppy hat, resembles the Pardner of *Paint Your Wagon*. The distant figure of his wife recalls the boy to the house and there comes the first hint of impending danger, a faint roll of thunder. The thunder fades into the thudding of horses' hooves. Smoke curls above the treeline. There are shots. And Wales is running home.

Pro-Unionist vigilantees – 'Kansas Red Legs', so called because of their distinctively coloured boots – are raiding his house. They burn it to the ground, raping and killing Wales' wife and slaughtering his son. Wales is knocked unconscious by a sabre blow from the vigilante leader, Terrill (Bill McKinney) and left for dead.

Eastwood portrayed a post-Civil War westerner seeking revenge in The Outlaw Josey Wales

179

When he wakes he buries his family, uttering his first coherent words of dialogue: 'Lord gives . . . Lord takes away . . .' Then he finds his pistol in the ruins of his home and begins to practice. A group of pro-slavery vigilantes, led by a 'Bloody Bill' Anderson, appear and tell him who was responsible. They are now going up to Kansas to 'set things aright'. 'I'll be coming with you,' says Wales.

Dramatically and economically, he's been given the motive and the emotional justification of the *High Plains Drifter* stranger. As martial drums roll, against a counterpoint of pistol shots, the woodland colours fade to a dull and lifeless grey; a montage of Civil War confrontations, punctuated by repeated face-on charges by Wales and his vigilantes, passes behind the credits. When they, and the War are over, Wales has acquired the lethal skills of the High Plains drifter and of No Name. He is a renowned 'Missouri pistoleer' with a fearsome reputation.

Anderson's vigilantes end their war on a dreary hillside, huddling by a poorly made fire. They are 'the last of the hold-outs', listening to a plea by a now ex-Confederate officer, Fletcher (John Vernon), who offers them the chance to surrender at a nearby Union camp. All they have to do is give an oath of loyalty and then each man 'can take up his horse and go home'. The offer proves irresistible to all but Wales; his home no longer exists and he has still not revenged himself on the man who took it from him. Despite a well-intended warning from Fletcher that he will not be allowed to remain free, Wales decides to fight on.

The vigilantes surrender their weapons at the Union camp where they are alarmed to see Terrill – now sporting the uniform of a Union army captain. As they take their oath of allegiance the flap of a wagon is thrown back and a Gatling gun, concealed inside, mows them down. Wales, who has been watching from a distance, makes a single-handed attack, captures the Gatling temporarily and turns it on the Union soldiers. He escapes with the only survivor, a young vigilante called Jamie (Sam Bottoms), whom Terrill wounds.

Wales resolves to take refuge in Indian territory before returning to deal with Terrill. Terrill and Fletcher, with the remainder of the 'Red Legs', are ordered to hunt down Wales.

So begins an epic journey in which the outlaw reluctantly re-acquires a new 'family' composed of misfits and outcasts, fellow victims of war and injustice, and finally a new home, another sylvan retreat but this time on the border between the United States and Mexico.

Wales and Jamie escape from Terrill across the Missouri River but Jamie's wound grows worse. This does not prevent him from saving Wales's life when he is captured by two backwoodsmen intent on claiming the reward of $5000 now offered for his head. When Jamie dies, Wales mourns him. As he says later, 'When I get to liking someone they ain't around long.'

He reaches Indian territory alone and meets an elderly Cherokee Indian, Lone Watie (Chief Dan George) who lost a war with the white man and was transported to this area. On the 'trail of tears' that brought him there his wife and two sons died, and he is no more enamoured of the Union than Wales.

He tells the outlaw that he has heard of other vigilantes who did not surrender and are now operating in Mexico. Wales decides to go in search of them and finds he has acquired the Indian as a travelling companion.

At a trading post he acquires another, Little Moonlight (Geraldine Keams), a Navajo squaw who has been rejected by her tribe for not resisting fiercely enough when she was captured and raped by Arapahos. An ownerless dog also adopts the group.

After a gunbattle with four Union soldiers in a frontier town, they come upon a party of commancheros who have captured a wagonload of settlers. When Lone Watie accidentally reveals his presence and is captured too. Wales rescues him and the two settlers who remain alive, Grandma Sarah (Paula Trueman), a native of Kansas whose son fought and died with the Red Legs, and her fey granddaughter, Laura Lee (Sondra Locke).

The enlarged group travel to the border town of Santa Rio, near which Grandma Sarah's son has a farm. Here they decide to set up home together, with the help of a middle-aged Mexican and a cowboy from the town. Santa Rio is virtually a ghost town since the local silver mine has run out and the few people that remain – as much misfits as the rest of Wales's group – are eager to help the newcomers. Even so, Wales has to deal with a bounty hunter who has tracked him this far.

Further trouble arises with the local Commanche chief, Ten Bears (Will Sampson), when the group move into the farm house. Ten Bears, like Wales, has been chased by the authorities as far as he will go and will allow no further intrusion on his territory. Wales rides out to meet him, offering him the choice of immediate battle, which Wales clearly cannot win, or mutual co-existence, 'my word of life'. Ten Bears has heard of Wales's reputation and

knows they share a common hatred of the Union army; Wales's conviction and obvious willingness to die if it cannot be helped impress the Commanche chief, who opts for peace.

Wales, however, cannot forget his desire for revenge, despite a developing romance with Laura Lee and the obvious attractions of the 'regular Paradise', as Grandma calls it, which they have found. He decides to return to Missouri, but as he leaves Terrill and his Red Legs appear outside the farm. Wales confronts them and the inhabitants of the farm join in the battle. Together they account for all the Red Legs except Terrill whom Wales pursues and kills with the sabre Terrill once used against him.

Wounded, Wales rides into town, only to find Fletcher waiting in the saloon with two Texas Rangers. The townspeople pretend Wales is a 'Mr Wilson' and one of them claims to have heard of Josey Wales' death in Mexico, where he has allegedly been shot down by 'five pistoleros'.

Fletcher clearly recognises the outlaw but does not disclose the fact. He refuses to believe that only five pistoleros could dispose of a man like Wales. He insists that he must still be alive and that he will follow him to Mexico. 'I think I'll try to tell him the war is over,' he says, looking at Wales. Blood drips conspicuously onto the outlaw's boot from the wound he has attempted to conceal.

'What do you say, Mr Wilson?' Fletcher adds pointedly. 'I reckon so,' Wales breathes in reply – his catchphrase throughout the film. He adds: 'I guess we all died a little in that damn war.'

Fletcher leaves and Wales rides back to his newfound home, and family.

To the film critic Philip French, author

181

of *Westerns*, the film's use of the Civil War was 'clearly a substitute for Vietnam, and the shaping into a community of the disparate outcasts who join the fugitive Wales on his travels is a binding up of the wounds caused by the Indo-Chinese War and the social divisions of the Sixties'.

There is plenty of evidence to support this argument. When the Anderson vigilantes surrender, the senator who commands the Kansas Red Legs talks in the 'hearts and minds' jargon that characterised American discussion of Vietnam among politicians and the military: 'War's over,' he tells Fletcher. 'Our side won the war. Now we must busy ourselves winning the peace.'

Moments later he demonstrates what these words actually mean by having unarmed prisoners machine-gunned to death. 'They were decently fed,' he tells an appalled Fletcher, 'and then they were decently shot!'

Lone Watie also suffers the effects of the linguistic dishonesty of an ostensibly benevolent colonial power. 'Here in the nation,' he tells Wales, 'they call us the civilised tribe. They call us civilised because we're easy to sneak up on. White men have been sneaking up on us for years.'

The Indian wears a frock coat when Wales first encounters him. He first put it on for a visit to Washington before the war as one of the representatives of the five civilised tribes; they had all wanted to look like Abraham Lincoln. The secretary of the interior was so impressed he gave them all a medal 'for looking *so* civilised'. But when they told him how their lands had been stolen from them and their people were dying, 'he shook our hands and said, "Endeavour to persevere!" ... We thought about it for a long time – "Endeavour to persevere!" And when we had thought about it long enough we declared war on the Union.'

Lone Watie's rambling and bizarrely appropriate speeches, as performed by seventy-six-year-old Chief Dan George, are one of the chief joys of the film and justly earned him an Oscar nomination. Like Wales, Lone Watie did not surrender when his war was over. 'But they took my horse,' he says, 'and made him surrender. They have him pulling a wagon up in Kansas, I'll bet.' Words are meaningless unless men's hearts are engaged.

The same theme is reiterated in Wales's speech to Ten Bears, the key statement of the film and the longest continuous piece of dialogue, or monologue, Eastwood had yet allowed himself on film.

'Governments don't live together,' he says. 'People live together. With governments you don't always get a fair word or a fair fight. Well, I've come here to give you either one, or to get either one from you. I came here like this so you know my word of death is true and that my word of life is then true.'

His 'word of life' consists of an offer to take no more from the land they share than they need to survive and to provide the Commanche with cattle for their journey north every spring. His 'word of death'

Previous page: The Outlaw Josey Wales *was filmed in Arizona, Utah and northern California – a harsh and awesome terrain*

Right: *As detective Ben Shockley in* The Gauntlet, *1977*

lies in his pistols and the rifles of Ten Bears' tribe. 'I ain't promising you nothing extra,' Wales adds. 'I'm just giving you life and you're giving me life. And I'm saying that men can live together without butchering one another.'

Ten Bears replies: 'It's sad that governments are chiefed by the double tongues. There is iron in your words of death for all Commanche to see, and so there is iron in your words of life. No signed paper can hold the iron. It must come from men. The words of Ten Bears carry the same iron of life and death. It is good that warriors such as we meet in the struggle of life and death.' And he decides: 'It shall be life.'

That affirmation represents a major advance in the development of Eastwood's screen persona. It's a commitment – of a kind that Harry Callahan was incapable of making – to the value of common humanity between free individuals, and the value of the community those individuals can create when they work together freely and willingly. Neither Callahan nor No Name belonged in any real sense to a community; Callahan claimed to protect innocent fellow citizens but they were almost always anonymous figures, faceless victims of far more interesting villains whom Dirty Harry despatched for reasons of personal principle rather than the selfless reasons of public duty.

Wales's similarly ruthless behaviour arises from deep, personal commitment to others; unlike Callahan or No Name, he has both a past and a future which explain and condition his present aims. Having taken the decision to go it alone, he still rides to the rescue of his fellow vigilantes. He cares for Jamie and grieves for him when he dies in communal as well as personal terms:

'This boy was brought up in a time of blood and dying. He never turned his back on his folks or his kind. I rode with him. I got no complaints.'

He acquires new companions by acts of reluctant generosity – which become the film's running joke. When the dog joins the company, Wales sighs; 'Might as well ride along with us. Hell, everybody else is.'

Yet each of the newcomers repays that generosity amply – in terms of providing a new destination, new hope or simply a helping hand in a gunbattle.

Each, too, is sharply and originally delineated in human terms. Lone Watie is forever seeking to gain an 'edge' and constantly failing; Little Moonlight talks incessantly in a tongue Wales doesn't understand (providing him with a rather lame excuse to rescue Lone Watie and the settlers from the commancheros: 'I'd have been halfway to Mexico by now except for that crazy squaw,' he complains. 'I can't understand a word she says!') Grandma Sarah distrusts everyone who doesn't come from Kansas; Laura Lee entrances Wales with observations such as 'Clouds are dreams floating across the sky of your mind', reminding him of a tenderness torn from him years before.

Wales and Lone Watie watch Little Moonlight washing in a pool at a camp site. Later the same night Wales, obviously aroused, creeps across to where she is sleeping, only to find her already curled up with Lone Watie. 'Is something wrong?' he asks the astonished outlaw, adding thoughtfully, 'I guess you were right. I ain't that old after all.'

Wales even explains the psychology of his fighting methods. When the farmhouse is expecting a raid from Ten Bears he tells his companions: 'Now remember, when

186

things look bad and it looks like you're not going to make it then you've got to get mean. I mean plum, mad dog mean, 'cos if you lose your head and you give up then you neither live nor win. That's just the way it is.'

Self-explanation, however, doesn't undermine the prowess of Wales as a fighter or the mythic qualities of Eastwood's screen persona at its most impressive. Like the Siegel version of Harry Callahan, he's pictured in almost elemental terms, an incarnation of demonaic wrath. 'Hell is where he's headed,' promises the senator commanding the Red Legs after Wales has made his escape. 'He'll be waiting there for us,' adds Fletcher. At the trading post where Wales meets Little Moonlight he is recognised by two rascally trappers. 'Mister Chained-blue-lightning himself!' gasps one. And Wales proves it by performing a 'border roll' – magically reversing the two guns he carries, butts forward – and shooting the trappers dead.

When he approaches the commancheros to rescue Lone Watie, he rears against the skyline, haloed by the sun, as much an avenging angel as ever the High Plains Drifter was. Seeing him, Lone Watie warns his fellow prisoner, Grandma Sarah: 'Get ready, little lady. Hell is coming to breakfast.' And so it does as Wales drops his flag of truce – the 'flagpole' is a shotgun – blasts four commancheros from their mounts and swoops and weaves among the startled remainder, dealing death from his twin Navy Colts.

He displays a familiar sardonic humour too. Crossing the Missouri River, he's assailed by a glib, white-suited salesman who extols the apparently unlimited number of uses to which the elixir he is peddling can be put. Wales's response is to spit

a stream of tobacco juice – a practice he follows throughout the film and which took him months to perfect – down the front of the man's suit. 'How's it with stains?' he enquires.

Moments later the ferry which has deposited Wales, Jamie and the salesman on the riverbank is returning with Terrill's Red Legs who have been in hot pursuit. Jamie is all for making a swift escape but Wales – using an intelligence reminiscent of No Name – retrieves a buffalo gun from his saddle pack. There is no way he will be able to shoot all the men on the ferry before they shoot him, scoffs the salesman who adds, self-importantly: 'There is such a thing in this country called justice.' 'Well, Mr Carpetbagger,' Wales replies, 'we've got something in this territory called the Missouri boat ride.' And with a single shot he severs the rope along which the ferry is being hauled, and sends the ferry and its occupants swirling helplessly away downstream.

Eastwood's directorial triumph was in deftly combining all these disparate elements of humour and mythology, tragedy and self-satire, violence and sentimentality into a cohesive and dramatically satisfying whole. His shooting style is as assured as it was in *High Plains Drifter*, though perhaps slightly more self-effacing, with only lingering traces of Sergio Leone's influence – the rapid cross-cutting between Wales at practice with his pistols and brief views of the farm which he is mentally abandoning, along with the way of life it represents; a shot during his climatic battle with the Red Legs when Wales's two pistols rise into the frame from below its bottom edge to shoot down riders approaching the camera.

But its economy in scenes of high tension had never been more effective – both in terms of dramatic effect and in a wider suggestibility. A fine example is when Wales finally corners Terrill after the battle at the farm. Appropriately it's in the ruins of another abandoned dwelling. Out of ammunition, Terrill cowers against a wall as Wales advances on him, pistols in hand. He pulls the triggers over and over again on empty cylinders, exchanging the guns for another pair in the process.

In one sense this Western form of Russian roulette is Wales's vengeful torture on the man who ruined his life. In another it's a highly dramatic mime of the outlaw's bloody progress over the past years, a progress that was actually a rehearsal for this single moment; without Terrill there would have been no Outlaw Josey Wales, and Wales wants him to know that. Yet when the moment comes for Wales to despatch his tormentor it's not done cleanly, at a distance, as No Name and Harry Callahan dispose of their enemies. Wales has no more bullets than Terrill, a fact the Red Leg leader only realises when his opponent is within grappling distance. And grapple they do, man to man, a tactile, human confrontation as Terrill tries to draw the sabre that once physically, and spiritually scarred Wales. He succeeds, but Wales's greater strength and determination turn it back on himself and he dies, quite literally, by the sword he also lived by.

The Outlaw Josey Wales was deservedly a commercial and critical success. Critics like Dilys Powell of *The Sunday Times* acknowledged and warmly praised the advance it represented for Eastwood. 'It's a very different image and very promising,' she said. 'I think it's a very, very good Western.'

Time magazine rated it among the year's ten best films and recognised that in this movie Eastwood had moved beyond his bloodier and more controversial manifestations. 'Rather,' wrote Richard Schickel, 'he reminds us of a traditional American style of screen heroism – a moral man, slow to rile but wonderfully skilled when he must finally enforce his concepts of right and wrong. In these moments he links us pleasingly, satisfyingly with our movie pasts, rekindles briefly a dying glow.'

Even Pauline Kael admitted that *Josey Wales* was 'perhaps an improvement'.

But since *Dirty Harry* Eastwood's career had consisted of two successful strands – the lone gunman of the Old West, and the equally isolated modern city cop. *Josey Wales* had brought his Western image to maturity with an unprecedented depth and resonance. The next obvious move would do the same for his modern image, and in *The Gauntlet* that was precisely what he attempted.

Dented Invulnerability

Though *The Enforcer* was Eastwood's next film and, as it turned out a highly astute choice financially, there is evidence that he made it largely at the prompting of Warner Brothers who were anxious to capitalise on Harry Callahan's previous success. Malpaso had now moved to Warner's Burbank Studios and Eastwood owed them a film.

Eastwood's reluctantly egalitarian relationship with Tyne Daly in the last of the Dirty Harry series might be seen as some indication of the new maturity shown in *Josey Wales*, though the relationship ends in

188

Inspector Moore's death, after a baptism of fire, and despair for Callahan. In *The Gauntlet*, however, a similar relationship survives *its* baptism, which turns out to be even more fiery and spectacular.

Eastwood again plays a detective, a Ben Shockley, but a very different cop from Inspector Harry Callahan. Callahan gets results; Shockley doesn't. He's a shambling, semi-alcoholic who has long ago given up hope of 'breaking that big case' and earning his captain's bars. Now he is only 'a faded number on a rusty badge' with only retirement to look forward to. Yet his principles are as firmly held as Callahan's, though more simply expressed and practised with much less violence: 'If you break the law you get busted and booked. That's about all there is to it.' He joined the police because he 'began to realise that the only people I knew who stood for something were cops.'

Like Josey Wales, Shockley is a simple man who only wants to do his job and raise a family – though Shockley hasn't yet met the right girl. Like Wales, too, the extraordinary events in which he is forced to take part transform him into a hero.

An accident of history provides the stimulus for Wales's transformation. In Shockley's case, more interestingly, it's the policeman's own personality that qualifies him for the task in hand. The new police commissioner of Phoenix, Arizona chooses Shockley to extradite a trial witness from Las Vegas because 'he's a man who gets the job done'. The description is ironical; Shockley has been chosen for precisely the opposite reason and there's a hint of it when Commissioner Blakelock (William Price) adds: 'It's a nothing witness for a nothing trial.'

We first meet Shockley as he drives through early morning Phoenix after an all-night poker game, stumbling from his car outside police headquarters and letting a whisky bottle shatter in the gutter. He's unkempt and unshaven – no indication of disapproval for an Eastwood hero – and the film toys with the audience's expectations as we come to realise that in this case a shabby appearance suggests not a self-sufficient super-competence but actually, and more realistically, a character who doesn't have that much going for him.

Shockley has even lost his partner of many years, Josephson (Pat Hingle) who has recently been promoted to a desk job. Somewhat smartened up, Shockley arrives in Las Vegas to pick up Gus Mally, the trial witness, and receives the first of a series of shocks that will justify his name.

'Gus' is short for Augusta; Mally (Sondra Locke) is a tough-minded, abusive young prostitute who insists that her life is in danger; odds have even been placed on her chances of surviving the day. Shockley is unimpressed by both her story and her looks: 'On a scale of ten,' he tells her guard, 'I'd have to give her a two, and that's only because I've never seen a one before.'

As he waits for her papers to be cleared, however, he notices a horse called Mally No-Show quoted at fifty to one on a restaurant betting board. The odds rise to seventy to one as he enquires about it. Suspicious, Shockley arranges for a rental car to be parked halfway to the airport and smuggles a protesting Gus out of the police station in an ambulance.

'If – and I say if – what you're saying is true, somebody's betting I can't do my job,' he tells her. 'Well, they're full of shit.' A statement that impresses her not at all.

They reach the waiting car but when the

ambulance driver goes to start it up it explodes. Shockley drives away immediately, giving Gus his gun and telling her to shoot anyone who comes up close behind. A car does and its occupants open fire. Awkwardly Gus returns the fire and the car slews off the road. When she realises Shockley is still headed for the airport she struggles with him; eventually he agrees to drive to her home.

There he rings Blakelock and asks for two police cars to be sent to escort them to the airport. In a bid to escape Gus attempts to seduce Shockley. 'Somehow,' he tells her as they lie down together, 'I get the feeling your heart is not in your work.' She stomps away to the bedroom while outside dozens of armed police surround the house, and call out for them to surrender. Astonished, Shockley goes to fetch Gus but her bedroom door is locked. He shoots open the lock, and the police take the shot as their cue to open fire.

In a remarkable display of firepower the house is literally shredded with bullets and finally collapses into itself. Cowering on the floor, Shockley finds an entrance to a cellar which in turn leads to the outlet of a large storm drain. Outside Gus is waiting.

Now thoroughly confused, Shockley takes her down the street to a police car which he hijacks. The driver (Bill McKinney) informs him that the Las Vegas police were told Gus's house contained three or four armed and dangerous men; he also discloses that the mob are after Gus. Shockley stops and calls Blakelock again, demanding an escort of Arizona police cars who can meet him at the state border.

As they travel, Gus reveals that she has a college degree and skilfully and sharply puts a stop to a bout of sexual taunting by the driver. She also suggests to Shockley that it might be wise to take precautions with this next rendezvous. Eventually, to the Las Vegas policeman's disgust, he agrees. The driver drops them just before he greets the occupants of five cars waiting at the border. His car is riddled with bullets.

Shockley and Gus spend the night in a desert cave where they argue hotly. By the morning Shockley has worked out that there must be a connection between the mob and the Phoenix police department. Gus derides his powers of deduction but eventually admits that the trial taking place in Phoenix is of a mob member who hired Gus to pleasure someone from the police department. She describes Blakelock.

A large crowd of Hell's Angels appear outside. In a virtuoso display of bluff, Shockley sends them all packing and steals one of their motorbikes. He and Gus ride to a roadside phone booth where Shockley calls Josephson. He is about to reveal what he has discovered about Blakelock when a helicopter appears overhead and someone inside opens fire at him.

A spectacular chase ensues, only ending when the helicopter flies into some high-tension cables and explodes. The motorbike is also damaged by a bullet. Abandoning it, Shockley and Gus leap aboard a passing freight train – and find they are sharing a boxcar with the Hell's Angels whose bike Shockley stole. They beat him up savagely, almost killing him before Gus distracts them by offering them her body. As they start to rape her, Shockley regains consciousness, recovers his gun and throws all three Angels from the train.

Shockley and Gus leave the train at Wickenburg where they wait in a motel for

With 'Gus' Mally (Sondra Locke) in a scene from The Gauntlet

the bus to Phoenix. From there Shockley rings Josephson again, says he and Gus are coming into Phoenix's city hall in a coach and describes his exact route. Blakelock, he argues, will know as soon as he leaves Wickenburg and will prepare an ambush; Shockley wants the streets cleared so that innocent people aren't hurt.

Gus tries to persuade him to run away with her, or give himself up somewhere less conspicuous. Shockley refuses because he wants to prove Blakelock was wrong in choosing him, that he can do the job, even if he dies in the process. Gus promptly rings her mother and announces that she has met the man she wants to marry.

When the Phoenix bus arrives they hijack it and Shockley constructs a makeshift iron shield to surround the driving position. Meanwhile Blakelock organises a gauntlet of police along Shockley's intended route. His partner in crime, the Assistant District Attorney, Feyderspiel (Michael Cavanaugh), suggests a secondary plan to stop Shockley, using Josephson.

Shockley's coach reaches Phoenix and is

flagged down by Josephson who tells Shockley of Feyderspiel's plan to sneak him into city hall by the back door. But, unknown to Josephson, it is simply a ruse to get Shockley out of the coach and into the sights of a police marksman. The marksman shoots and kills Josephson. Shockley is wounded in the leg but with Gus's aid gets the coach moving again.

Crouching behind their shield, they survive two corridors of continuously shooting police who riddle the coach. It finally expires on the steps of city hall. Inside the trial for which Gus is the key witness is in progress.

Shockley emerges from the wreck to deliver his prisoner as an enraged Blakelock runs from the building, ordering the vast crowd of policeman to shoot the detective dead. Feyderspiel tries vainly to restrain him. Instead Shockley grabs a revolver and presses it to Feyderspiel's head, forcing him to admit his and Blakelock's mob connections. Blakelock, too, grabs a gun and shoots both Feyderspiel and Shockley. Gus snatches Shockley's gun and kills Blakelock. She clutches Shockley and his eyes flicker open; he is only wounded.

The plot was unashamedly fantastic – a fact that annoyed many critics, since Eastwood the director played that element to the full ; he spent a million dollars on special effects to disarm his audience's incredulity with extraordinary detail and he directed with a visual panache and an eye for colour that fully exploited the story's potential for spectacle. Eastwood the actor sprang dusty but alive from predicaments that would have made James Bond blanch; logically Shockley cannot survive in a house that is literally shredded by seven thousand bullets (the number of special effects squibs that were used), he cannot survive the eight thousand bullets that turn his fortified coach into a motorised sieve, no more than he can avoid the bullets from a helicopter as he drives a motorbike in a dead straight line across a desert landscape which has no hint of cover. The fact that he does both reinforces the superhuman and mythic aspects of his image and deflates them at the same time, because Shockley's miraculous escapes are effected largely by blind accident; dogged determination, at best, is the only personal quality that contributes to his success; he doesn't employ the devious intelligence of No Name or the street cunning of Harry Callahan. He literally stumbles over Gus's escape route from her home, he ignores the safety of convenient road tunnels in the helicopter pursuit and he drives into the climactic gun barrage reconciled to the fact that he will not survive.

This is a step beyond *Josey Wales* in terms of screen persona. All of Wales's newly acquired companions are constantly subverting his professed desire to remain emotionally self-sufficient – even his dog, constantly besmirched by a stream of accurately directed tobacco juice, runs back for more – but none of them deny his deadly prowess as a killer. Poor Ben Shockley is undermined on every front – as a resourceful hero, intellectually and emotionally; Gus Mally's attack on his macho sensibility and on his limited powers of deduction is accurate and devastating.

Shockley's triumph is that he overcomes these inadequacies by transforming them into virtues; he comes to see the truth behind Gus's relentless baiting and learns from it; he comes to recognise that Gus's shrewish attitude and superior intelligence mask a loneliness and disappointment with life as profound as his own. No wonder the woman falls in love with him.

Shockley's self-transformation is the real story of *The Gauntlet* and the special effects and feats of derring-do are – though highly entertaining – so much window dressing and, as such, tend to unbalance the film. In his faltering way Shockley arrives at the kind of transfiguration that Josey Wales enjoyed in mid-career, riding out of the sun as the avenging, all-conquering hero. But Shockley's transfiguration, however fantastically arranged, is of a much more mundane and recognisably human kind. In bringing Gus in to Phoenix, he finally breaks 'that big case' and, more importantly, justifies those principles he has almost lost through the grind and disappointment of his career.

That in itself is a more familiar and sympathetic achievement for most members of Eastwood's audience – few of whom were likely to have had their loved ones butchered by vigilantes or shot down by maniac blackmailers. The ultimate object of Shockley's heroism is not the short-term emotional satisfaction of a Harry Callahan pulling the trigger on Scorpio or Bobby Maxwell; it's another 'word of life' – he wants simply to do his job, uphold the law and raise a family. In this way Eastwood at last found a means to fuse the mythical and the human aspects of his persona – a human aspect which had previously only expressed itself fully as self-defeating wrath or sardonic humour.

In doing so the romantic dilemma of *Two Mules for Sister Sara* is finally resolved. The invulnerability of the superhero can at last risk being dented by emotional commitment because a deeper, more human form of heroism has been unearthed. The macho image can be discarded because it has become redundant.

The film is a remarkably acute dissection of machismo, beginning with Gus's taunting of Shockley as he tries to restrain her in the ambulance en route to Las Vegas airport. 'You really get off roughing up girls, don't you, big man?' she accuses. 'Big forty-five calibre fruit!' 'That's me,' grunts Shockley, unimpressed. 'Macho mentality . . .' Gus grumbles on. 'Tough guys. Big tin star egomaniacs,' she continues as Shockley handcuffs her to the hijacked Las Vegas police car to make his second call to Blakelock. The scene that follows is one of the most extraordinary and most highly charged in the film.

The kidnapped policeman is a 'country boy', a red neck male chauvinist who displays equal amounts of contempt and prurient interest in Gus. To Shockley's annoyance, he demands to know the details of Gus's professional life, swiftly developing his own masturbatory fantasies about imagined lesbian experiences. 'I bet it don't take much to get you all wet and hot to truck, does it?' he breathes. 'Come on, talk to me, I want to know what it's like being a whore.' To him Gus is literally the embodiment of a sexual fantasy, to be despised in public and relished in private; she has no other dimension.

Her reply is to compare being a whore to being a cop. After a detailed and acute summary of corrupt police practices, she concludes: 'The only difference between you and me is that when I quit work I take a long hot bath and I'm as clean as the day I was born. But a cop, especially a flunky like you, the sheriff whistles – you squat – and what he does to you rots your brain. No amount of water on earth can get you clean again . . . I know you don't like women like me. We're a bit aggressive, we're frightening. But that's only because you've got filth in your brain . . . Oh, does your wife know you masturbate?'

The policeman's response is to lose control, of himself and of the car.

Significantly the sexual experience between Blakelock and Gus which sets the whole plot in motion is a masturbatory one. She is required to sprawl naked face-down on a bed while Blakelock holds a gun barrel between her legs. 'Didn't take much imagination to know what he was doing with his other hand,' she tells Shockley. Not only is this a teasing commentary on Eastwood's earlier screen persona, with the phallic associations of Callahan's forty-four magnum, but it links the macho view of women as masturbatory objects to violence and death. Gus finally repays Blakelock for his dehumanising act in an appropriate manner – she shoots him dead.

Shockley is able to accept Gus's initial insults and consequent advice in a way that No Name or Callahan, Deputy Sheriff Coogan or Sister Sara's Hogan could never do because he lacks those characters' self-esteem from the very beginning; he gives himself no more importance than he gives to Gus. Within minutes of first meeting her, he tells her: 'No one gives a damn about a dumb-arse cop and a two-bit hooker on Air West.'

His decision to take her advice at the Arizona border is a crucial one, not simply because it saves their lives but because Shockley is forced to reject the one stable element of his life, the structure which upholds his principles – the basic honesty of his fellow cops. 'You chose sides!' the kidnapped policeman tells him with especial venom. 'Got yourself a little nookie and chose sides!' 'Shit . . .' sighs Shockley with genuine regret and even more uncertainty. In the light of Gus's previous remarks about police corruption that particular expletive has an ambiguity which characterises much of the superficially foul language of the film.

Gus and Shockley's verbal sparring match in the desert cave further establishes the couple's common ground; both have been set up, both are losers – 'Welcome to the ranks of the disenchanted!' Gus crows – and both, ultimately, are fighters: 'I'm a counter-puncher, Shockley,' Gus announces. 'If you can't last twelve rounds then stay out of the ring.' After a night's cogitation, he pleads for her help in solving the crime in which they're both involved – the first time any Eastwood hero has said 'Please' to a woman, and meant it.

From that point on Shockley begins to contribute to the relationship and it starts to turn into a genuine and equal partnership. His action in frightening away the Hell's Angels, which at first seems reckless stupidity to Gus, earns her praise by its courage and audacity. Shockley begins to become a hero – but a vulnerable one, acutely aware of his limitations When Gus asks him if he can ride the stolen motorcycle, he replies: 'It's been a few years but . . . we'll fake it.'

Soon he is whisking her to safety from the bullets of the helicopter marksman and she is saving his life by means of the skill she practices best – her own sexuality. They have become a team. Eastwood's direction of *The Gauntlet* demonstrated not only an enhanced visual flair – only the pictorial delights of *High Plains Drifter* can really match it – but a new subtlety as well. He had long ago absorbed Don

Siegel's pace and economy; now he began to display his old mentor's gift for thematic allusiveness.

The process of Shockley's transfiguration is underlined gently and ironically by recurring religious imagery. When the Las Vegas police demolish Gus's home the camera picks out a sign in the background: 'God Makes House Calls.' There's a similar sign to hand when the kidnapped policeman's car is riddled. 'God Gives Eternal Life,' it blinks out of the darkness. And when Shockley tries to bluff the Hell's Angels he announces that 'reasonable suspicion' that a crime is being committed allows him to go anywhere ''cos I got this badge, I got this gun and I got the love of Jesus right here in my pretty green eyes'.

Gus's remark that she can wash herself clean at the end of every day while a cop can't is ironically prefigured by the elaborate ornamental fountains outside the Las Vegas police headquarters. Shockley is photographed in such a way as to suggest he is wading through them, waist-deep.

And Shockley's catchphrase throughout the film – like Josey Wales's 'I reckon so' and Callahan's 'a man's got to know his limitations' in *Magnum Force* surfaces first in his conversations with Josephson at the beginning of the film. 'Nag, nag, nag . . .' sighs Shockley as his former partner fusses round him like a mother hen, insisting he tidy himself up for his first meeting with Blakelock; he even wishes he had time to shave Shockley himself. The ex-partners' relationship is plainly the only emotional relationship Shockley then enjoys. 'Nag, nag, nag . . .' Shockley repeats to Gus as they hop aboard the freight train; she's afraid they won't make it. And those words are the last in the film, spoken by the detective as he opens his eyes on the steps of city hall and shows that his new life with Gus will be possible after all.

Flawed as it was, *The Gauntlet* marked an extraordinary development in Eastwood's established screen persona. The hero whose prowess depended on superhuman abilities had been transformed into a hero no less admirable but as imperfect as the rest of us. A common humanity had been acknowledged, while the mythic overtones remained relatively untouched. Eastwood's capacity for this kind of dynamic change within the limitations of superstardom is, more than any other single factor, the reason why he had managed to dominate the world's cinema box offices for over a decade. With *The Gauntlet* and *Josey Wales* he carved out a new and fruitful path in his career, though its immediate destination was to startle everybody.

The Super But Human Hero

Every Which Way But Loose
Escape from Alcatraz
Bronco Billy
Any Which Way You Can

Firefox
Honkytonk Man

11

Just Monkeying Around

From the initial 'bad step' of taking up Sergio Leone's offer to work in Italy to choosing an obscure novel as the basis of *Josey Wales*, Eastwood's career has shown a distinct, yet invariably correct, tendency to go out on a limb, to find gold dust in the most intractable and unlikely material. But the film that followed *The Gauntlet* seemed to be his most eccentric choice yet. Eastwood was to play a truck driver and part-time bareknuckle prize fighter whose closest companion was a fully grown orang-utan called Clyde.

The subtle irony of *The Gauntlet* went out the window, and in came unabashed burlesque. The film was not only Eastwood's first straightforward comedy it was a story rooted in the red neck culture of California's semi-industrialised San Fernando Valley, adopting its broad belly-laugh humour and its characteristic country and western music.

All of Eastwood's business associates advised against the project, but then his agent and then business manager had done the same with *A Fistful of Dollars*.

Eastwood's instincts again proved to be the right ones. *Every Which Way But Loose* – a film the critics regarded with almost universal distaste, if not disbelief – became the star's most commercially successful film ever, grossing nearly $52 million which put it among the top thirty money-earning films of all time. When it was released just before Christmas 1978 only *Superman* with its spectacular array of special effects – Eastwood's film had none – could attract larger audiences.

In retrospect Eastwood's reasoning was less bizarre. His friend and rival in the Hollywood macho stakes, Burt Reynolds, had taken a similar kind of red neck role in *Smokey and the Bandit* which, to his surprise, had outgrossed Eastwood's previous huge success *The Enforcer* and become the third most profitable film of 1977. Eastwood also knew that some of his most ardent and loyal fans were in the Mid-West, America's conservative heartland, people he described himself, not disparagingly, as 'the straight, hardhat crowd'. By employing a soundtrack that included

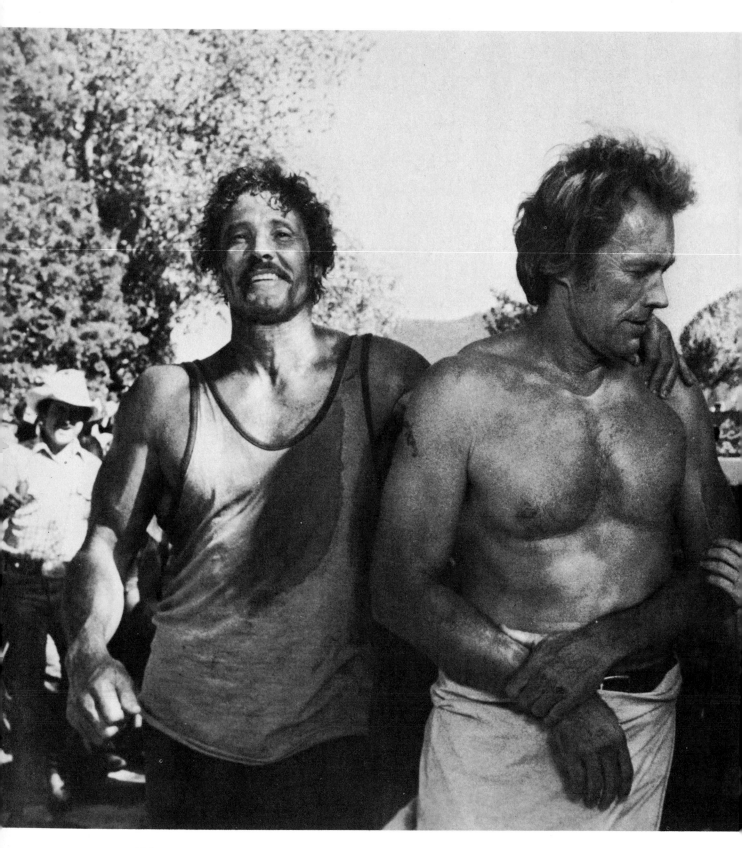

198

songs by Country and Western stars like Charlie Rich, Eddie Rabbitt and Mel Tillis, he expanded the film's appeal, as he did by including Clyde – a risky move for any actor, to whom animals, like children, are traditionally anathema, but an astute method of attracting a younger audience excluded by Eastwood's normal 'X' rating.

He prepared for the role in his characteristically thorough fashion, taking professional boxing training from Al Silvani who had coached Sylvester Stallone to success in his 1976 hit *Rocky*, and learning to work with Manis, an eleven-year-old, twelve stone orang-utan who played Clyde.

This time, however, he delegated the direction once more to James Fargo. Clearly he had enough on his hands controlling 'Clyde' but the decision reveals a more relaxed attitude to film-making. *The Gauntlet* had shown Eastwood he could drop his guard with safety; he now felt able to treat his craft with as much professionalism as before but a much lighter touch. And *Every Which Way But Loose* is very light indeed.

Eastwood played Philo Beddoe, a kind of working class Ben Shockley who is no brighter than the detective and shares his uncomplicated, and occasionally simplistic, moral values. He lives with a truncated version of Josey Wales's unusual 'family' – a sidekick, Orville Boggs (Geoffrey Lewis), an amiable mechanic and salvager of car wrecks who acts as Philo's prize-fighting

Previous page: Eastwood with his pal Clyde the orang utan in Any Which Way You Can, *1980.*
Left: William Smith, Clint Eastwood and Sondra Locke in a scene from Any Which Way You Can

manager; Clyde, whom Phil won in a fight and rescued from a desert zoo and who now acts as his rather unorthodox sparring partner; and Ma Boggs (Ruth Gordon), Orville's eccentric and crotchety mother – a comic version of Grandma Sarah, who is forever complaining about Clyde's anti-social behaviour (his toilet habits are unconventional) and the orang-utan's penchant for her Oreo biscuits.

The loose and episodic plot revolves around Philo's abortive wooing of a young Country and Western singer, Lynne Halsey-Taylor (Sondra Locke), whom he sees performing in the Palomino Supper Club, San Fernando Valley's premier C & W night spot. Philo has little trouble in becoming acquainted but when he drives the girl home to the trailer where she lives he discovers that she shares it with a boy-friend, Schyler. Lynne's blithe assertion that he won't object to her liaison with Philo fails to impress the trucker. 'Slightly advanced,' he murmurs, bidding her good-night.

The relationship, however, appears to flourish and they see a lot of each other. Lynne is saving up $7000 to open her own Country and Western bar, she tells Philo, and Schyler is helping to do it. Philo, consequently, gives her $2000 of his own to help her break with the boyfriend. Immediately after he has done so, Lynne leaves for her home town of Denver, with only the briefest of farewell notes. Puzzled but undeterred, Philo sets off in pursuit with Orville and Clyde. They in turn are pursued by two sets of people whom Philo has angered in several of his numerous brawls – the first is a gang of ageing, incompetent Hell's Angels known as the Black Widows; and the second, two off-duty policemen, Herb and Putnam.

En route Orville picks up a girlfriend of his own at a roadside fruit stall – Echo (Beverly D'Angelo).

By chance Philo spots Lynne on the road and they spend the night together, but the following night she fails to turn up at an agreed rendezvous. Philo's enemies now catch up with him. He outwits Herb and Putnam when they ambush him while he is fishing, and fights his way out of another ambush by the Black Widows in Georgetown – helped out by Orville who flattens their motorcycles with a waste dis-posal truck.

Eventually Philo reaches Denver and tracks Lynne down to a Country and Western bar. He interrupts her in the process of picking up another man and she rounds on him angrily, admitting that she has been trying to get rid of him since their first date; she has simply been using her charms to dupe Philo, among many others, out of his money to benefit herself and her boyfriend. Philo's declaration of love only angers her more and in a fit of hatred, directed as much at herself as at him, she attacks him. Philo makes no move to defend himself and then leaves.

Orville, meanwhile, has arranged a fight with the local prize-fighting champion, a legendary figure called Tank Murdoch whose prowess has been alluded to throughout the film. He turns out to be middle-aged and overweight, an obvious has-been. Philo is set for an easy victory when he realises that a defeat will destroy the man in front of his home crowd. He deliberately throws the fight and returns home with Orville, Echo and Clyde, pas-sing the dejected Black Widows and Herb and Putnam en route.

Like Ben Shockley, Philo's own person-ality leads him into trouble. As an enraged

200

Lynne shrieks at him: 'You're just not too smart, are you? Why couldn't you just quit like everybody else? Why did you have to come chasing after me and spoil it all?' ''Cos I'm just not too smart, that's all,' Philo concedes. ''Cos up to now I'm the only one dumb enough to want to take you further than your bed.'

It's an expression of simple human faith, all the more annoying to the girl for the accuracy of its observation. In Philo Eastwood follows on the thread of common humanity that he began with Wales's 'word of life' speech and continued with Ben Shockley's confession of principles in the Wickenburg motel room. Appropriately, in view of the story's outcome, Eastwood's equivalent speech here is given to Clyde, over a lonely campfire at night and beside a bubbling stream. 'I suppose you think I'm crazy traipsing across the country after a girl I hardly even know,' he says. 'Hell, I'm not like Orville. Takes me a long time to get to know a girl, even longer to let her know me . . . I'm not afraid of any man, but when it comes to sharing my feelings with a woman my stomach just turns to Royal gelatin.'

The film cuts to Lynne making a successful pick-up at a bowling alley – 'pickup' in the sense of knocking over three remaining pins on her alley, and also in the sense of meeting a handsome onlooker. Her emotional toughness shatters relationships with ease, but when she and Philo meet on the road and make love in a motel room rain trickles down the windowpane, the sound of running water linking the scene with Philo's 'confession' to Clyde and suggesting that, for a brief time, the couple share Philo's emotional honesty and trust.

Significantly the only fight in which Philo shows obvious signs of physical hurt is when Lynne attacks him.

But their relationship is only a pale echo of the Shockley–Gus Mally pairing and finally introduces a sour note that seems at odds with the broad humour of the rest of the film.

Eastwood retains his mythic stature – suitably scaled down – in his fist fights, all of which he wins. They are staged convincingly, allowing Philo to display apparently authentic competence and his opponents are portrayed as genuine threats; one even snatches up a meat hook in a vain attempt to stave off defeat. Only his comic opponents are dealt with in a burlesque manner; after defeating Herb and Putnam, a bare-chested Philo celebrates with a Tarzan call – 'I think he's spending too much time with Clyde,' comments Orville; and his final confrontation with all twelve Black Widows is presaged by a few bars from Morricone's *The Good, the Bad and the Ugly* score.

All the incidental brawls are staged Tom and Jerry fashion with the maximum of destruction and the minimum of actual bodily hurt. Invariably they involve the Black Widows in their constant but doomed attempt to prove their toughness – they are demolished by Philo, by a café full of belligerent truck drivers and even by Ma Boggs; she complains bitterly about being left behind by Orville and Philo, 'a vulnerable old lady alone', but when the Widows arrive in search of Philo and playfully begin to tear down her porch her instant reaction is to lift a gigantic, repeating shotgun from her rocking chair and open fire with catastrophic effect.

The plot boasts some useful but unforced parallels. Philo's dogged pursuit of Lynne is matched by Ma Boggs' equally dogged attempt to pass her driving test, at which she finally succeeds – chiefly because an elderly examiner takes a shine to her. Orville's relationship with his girlfriend plainly 'Echo's' Philo with Lynne and provides a telling contrast in the use of firearms: when Philo wins a match and the local crowd refuse to pay him his winnings, Echo persuades them by producing a revolver and demonstrating her skill at marksmanship – she's clearly an asset to the team. Lynne, on the other hand, persuades Schyler to pretend to threaten Philo with a shotgun in an early attempt to scotch their growing relationship, thereby demonstrating her deviousness, her capacity for using other people and her potential for danger – the gun goes off, close enough to put her in peril.

The red neck background is the source of the humour but not its butt, and any suggestion that it may be is squashed early in the film: Philo attempts to pick up a girl at the Palomino who turns out to be a sociology student doing a paper on 'the country–western mentality'. Asked what that is, she replies: 'Well, if the lyrics of the song are any indication, it's somewhere between moron and dull normal.'

Philo's revenge is to slip a set of false teeth – supplied by Orville – into the girl's clam chowdah. Naturally they appear in her next spoonful and she exits, shrieking. 'This wild clam got out of control,' Philo comments, returning the teeth.

The irony is hardly on the subtle and subversive level of *The Gauntlet* but it makes no pretence to be. Eastwood was deliberately trying to expand his audience and he succeeded brilliantly and without lowering his standards as an actor. He had now increased the range of his screen persona to such an extent that he could express more than ever before while appearing to do even less than usual. His next film would push that increased range to the limits.

Mythical Acting

The lights of San Francisco glow in the twilight. Streams of car headlamps flicker across the Golden Gate bridge. The camera pans leftward, through the bars of the bridge's support cables, out across San Francisco bay. As rain starts to fall and a muted drum roll sounds, it picks out a bleak and isolated rock a mile offshore. Alcatraz. For nearly thirty years America's supposedly escape-proof maximum security prison – 'supposedly' because on 11 June 1962 three convicted bank robbers, Frank Morris and the brothers John and Clarence Anglin, escaped from their cells and vanished into the freezing water and fierce currents that surround the rock. Nothing has been heard of them since.

So begins *Escape from Alcatraz*, Eastwood's twenty-second starring role and his fifth film under the direction of Don Siegel. Siegel had bought the film rights from a book on the only successful escape from Alcatraz by J. Campbell Bruce. The character of Frank Morris had an especial appeal for him. In reality the son of an unmarried chorus girl who had abandoned him at the age of three but with an exceptionally high IQ, Morris displayed many of the qualities of the typical Siegel hero: a flawed loner, a gifted individualist at odds

As Frank Morris in Escape from Alcatraz, *1979*

202

with society, operating in an environment where the codes of criminal and authoritarian society come into direct and continuous conflict.

Siegel's B-movie classic *Riot in Cell Block 11* had dealt with a similar subject in 1954, though the emphasis there was on penal reform, the attitude of outside society to prison life. *Escape from Alcatraz* took a more interior view – literally; the opening shot of the film directs the audience away from the bright lights of the outside world into a closed society which the film leaves only briefly at the very end. As the Warden (Patrick McGoohan) tells the newly arrived Morris: 'From this day on your world will be everything that happens in this building.'

The film is about the effects of imprisonment on individuals and the attitudes of the prison staff, the reasons for the convicts' being in gaol are all 'given', and only criticised by implication. We never learn what crimes first brought Morris to gaol, only that he disobeyed the rules of prison. Morris's past life is seen only in penal terms – 'Where did they transfer you from?' asked a fellow prisoner. 'Atlanta,' replies Morris. 'Nice town, Atlanta.' 'I never saw it.' When he's asked what kind of childhood he had, he replies, 'Short.'

There are no riots, no hysterical breakdowns, no shootings and only minimal displays of violence. The film's emphasis is on the state of mind of its hero and his fellow prisoners and the physical details of the hero's ingenious escape method, reproduced with such authenticity – so far as they are known – that Siegel insisted on shooting most of the picture in Alcatraz itself. Half a million dollars were spent in restoring the crumbling cell blocks and many of the improvements are still there

as permanent displays for tourists, the only visitors the rock enjoys these days.

Choosing the right actor to play Morris was vital. He would be on screen for almost the entire two hours of the film yet his dialogue would be minimal. Suggestion – mere screen 'presence' – would be all. Eastwood leapt at the chance. The result was the most muted yet eloquent performance of his career.

There are only the faintest touches of those characteristic 'Eastwood' moments: a scene of violence in the showers when Wolf (Bruce M. Fischer), a brutal psychopath, attempts to make Morris his new homosexual 'punk' – Morris's response is pretended compliance, followed by a knee in the belly and a bar of soap thrust into the prisoner's mouth, literally washing it out with soap and water for making the obscene suggestion.

There are echoes of Eastwood's familiar laconic put-downs as he encounters English (Paul Benjamin), a negro convicted in Alabama for killing two white racists who attacked him. After hearing the tale, Morris asks: 'Are you through killing white guys?' 'Why?' asks English. 'I don't know,' replies Morris, turning away. 'I figured next time I wouldn't turn my back on you.'

Later he joins English on the highest of a series of steps in the prison yard, only to be told that the steps mark an internal hierarchy: the higher you sit, the higher your prestige – the privilege of the top step is the ability to see a narrow line of the bay over the prison wall. Morris grunts his understanding and takes the step below English. 'Now I figure there's two reasons why you didn't sit down on my step,' concludes the negro. 'Either you're too scared, or you just hate niggers. Now which is it, boy? You too scared, eh?' 'No,' replies Morris after a suitable pause. 'I just hate niggers.' He is the only white man on the steps.

For the remainder of the film Eastwood suggests an utterly convincing blend of controlled apprehension and granite-like stoicism, innate pride and well-tempered caution, loyalty to those who deserve it and an unstated threat to those who don't. He is as self-sufficient as No Name or Harry Callahan but he doesn't maintain that attitude with the help of a suitably favourable arrangement of the plot. He builds that state of mind carefully and patiently in spite of exterior forces; self-containment is in fact his only means of survival and Eastwood makes us see and appreciate that.

Like Ben Shockley he triumphs over horrific and impossible odds – far worse odds than the inept detective faced, since he could only be physically extinguished; Morris is threatened with mental and spiritual death. Despite the emphasis on the details of the escape, the film is really about his inner triumph over the state of mind engendered by imprisonment.

The magnitude of his task is clear from the beginning of the film. Led down to the prison ferry through darkness and lashing rain, he is chained hand and foot inside its cage-like cabin. Cramped camera angles, dim lighting, the silence of the guards and a musical score by Jerry Fielding that drones and rumbles like some vast industrial machine build a disorientating atmosphere. Morris's first view of the rock is a blinding searchlight which stabs out of the darkness.

Inside the cell block, barred doors slide open and crash shut under electronic control. Morris is ordered to strip, examined impersonally by a doctor and marched naked down a dimly lit and apparently endless corridor of cells. As his cell door slams shut on him a guard utters the first line of dialogue that is not an order or a necessary statement of fact: 'Welcome to Alcatraz.' A crash of thunder underlines his words.

The dehumanising aspect of the place is further emphasised in Morris's first meeting with the Warden. 'We don't make good citizens,' he is told, 'but we make good prisoners . . . Alcatraz was built to keep all the rotten eggs in one basket. I was specially chosen to make sure the stink from the basket does not escape . . . No one has ever escaped from Alcatraz, and no one ever will.'

But as Morris meets his fellow prisoners he finds out that humanity is managing to flourish in these bleak surroundings. Negatively in the case of Wolf who eyes him speculatively over the breakfast table, but positively in the cases of Litmus (Frank Ronzio), a middle-aged man who sniffs glue and secretly keeps a pet mouse, and Doc (Roberts Blossom), an older inmate who has been here for twenty years and only lives to paint. His urge to survive is symbolised by the chrysanthemums he grows and includes in a self portrait; 'that's something inside me they can't lock up with their bars and walls,' he tells Morris. After tackling Wolf in the showers, Morris is attacked by the psychopath with a knife in the yard. Both are sent to D Block as punishment: solitary confinement in a bare, silent, windowless cell.

On his return Morris becomes friendly with a new arrival, Charley Butts (Larry Hankin), a man only guilty of car theft but who annoyed a guard at a previous prison. On a random search of the cells, the War-

FA-5078-23

den discovers a portrait of himself concealed in Doc's cell. It captures the megalomaniac aspect of his nature perfectly and the man is clearly flattered, but he punishes what he regards as Doc's insolence by withdrawing his painting privileges. 'It's not a suspension,' he tells a guard. 'It's an elimination.'

This proves to be more accurate than intended when Doc responds by chopping off the fingers of his painting hand publicly in the carpenter's shop. Outraged Morris presents the guard with Doc's severed fingers, and when he reaches into his overall pocket he finds a single crushed chrysanthemum which Doc has previously placed there.

Doc's self-mutilation seems to represent the Warden's most complete victory to date; the elderly prisoner has been killed spiritually; imprisonment has wreaked its worst. But it's at this low point that a brooding Morris first notices the key to his escape. As imprisonment has largely failed to crush the humanity of the prisoners, so the fabric of the prison itself is failing too. The action of the salt air has worked a gradual corrosion of the cement and the steel of the cell block. Morris discovers that the wall surrounding the ventilation grill in his cell has started to crumble and that he can accelerate the process relatively easily.

On the arrival of the Anglin brothers, John (Fred Ward) and Clarence (Jack Thibeau), whom Morris knows from an earlier prison, he reveals his plan of escape. If they can remove the ventilation

Morris (Eastwood) is attacked by a fellow prisoner in a scene from Escape from Alcatraz

207

grilles in their cells they will be able to climb the ventilation shaft beyond and reach the roof of the cell block. From there they can drop to ground level, scale a wire fence and reach the sea. They will use raincoats treated with contact cement as makeshift life jackets and swim not for the city but for the more distant Angel Island on the opposite side of the bay.

In order to delay the discovery of the escape they will make dummy heads to place in their beds and papier-mâché replacement grilles to disguise their work in progress.

The brothers agree to the plan and include Charley Butts. Numerous problems are solved ingeniously though at great risk. Meanwhile the prisoners' confrontation with the Warden rises to a new pitch when he removes one of Doc's chrysanthemums from the dining table claiming it is against regulations. Enraged, Litmus objects violently and drops dead from a heart attack. 'Some men are destined never to leave Alcatraz alive,' the Warden comments. Morris decides to make the escape bid on Tuesday night.

The Warden, however, decides Morris and Butts should be separated, picking Tuesday morning as the time to move them to new cells. But Wolf is released from D Block and makes an abortive attempt on Morris's life. Morris decides to go on the Monday night instead. The escape takes place without problems, though Butts loses his nerve at the last moment and stays. Morris and the Anglins swim off into the night.

The next morning the Warden lands by helicopter on Angel Island where Clarence Anglin's wallet has been found. A massive search is in operation. On the shore the Warden finds a single chrysanthemum flower resting on a rock. Chrysanthemums, he is told, do not grow on Angel Island.

'They drowned,' he insists as he is recalled to Washington.

Despite the brilliance of Eastwood's performance and Siegel's direction, the film is not without flaws. There is a disappointing lack of tension in the final break-out. It might be argued that this is unimportant in thematic terms because Morris has won his victory simply by proving the possibility of escape and the escape itself is an almost unnecessary rounding off of the achievement, a form of coda. But the script is not structured in that way; a great deal of screen time is lavished on every step of the escapers' progress, which is unimpeded, and in purely dramatic terms it is unsatisfying.

While only the Warden is portrayed as a truly repressive and even sadistic representative of the authorities – the 'bulls' or guards are seen to act decently on the whole – the prisoners receive very much the benefit of the scriptwriter's doubt; their past crimes are either excusable, in the case of English, ludicrously petty in comparison with the punishment, as in Charley Butts' case, or simply never revealed.

That kind of moral anonymity reinforces the theme of the film – the fact that the characters are prisoners is clearly more important than *why* they are. But in a context that is otherwise intensely realistic it smacks of deliberate manipulation of the audience's sympathies, especially when Doc explains the presence of a chrysanthemum in his self-portrait in somewhat clichéd terms. Alcatraz was built to house three hundred of America's arch criminals, but there never were that many in custody at one time; as a result the ultimate gaol came to hold prisoners, like Charley Butts, who had done little to deserve such a harsh regime. That, in itself, bolsters the argument of the film, but the film does not mention it.

Cliché, too, haunts the portrayal of the Warden who has little to do but mouth the tough sentiments of the regime. It's to Patrick McGoohan's credit that he is able to invest such one-dimensional dialogue with suggestions of incipient megalomania and genuine moral doubt as well as grim determination. The most telling touch of all is that he likes Doc's portrait of him, mirroring its slightly twisted expression as he looks at it, yet he still punishes the man.

But in lending the character this kind of substance, McGoohan gives a consciously 'star' performance that is out of tune with the muted nature of the film and of Eastwood's performance. That said, *Escape from Alcatraz* was deservedly an enormous success. Commercially it topped the gross earnings of Eastwood and Siegel's previous hit *Dirty Harry* by almost $4 million in America and Canada alone. Critically, too, both Eastwood and Siegel received rave reviews. '*Alcatraz's* cool, cinematic grace meshes ideally with the strengths of its star,' wrote *Time's* Frank Rich. 'At a time when Hollywood entertainments are more overblown than ever, Eastwood proves that less really can be more.'

But perhaps the finest accolade came from Vincent Canby in *The New York Times* in a review that acknowledged the mythic and ultimately unanalysable centre of Eastwood's talent. 'Mr Eastwood fulfills the demands of the role and of the film as probably no other actor could. Is it acting? I don't know, but he's the towering figure in the landscape.'

Eastwood's new maturity had enabled him to expand his screen persona to encompass broad comedy and high, critically acclaimed drama. His next move was to attempt to draw both these strands together, choosing another comedy as his vehicle but a comedy that had more to do with the subtle ironies of *The Gauntlet* and *The Outlaw Josey Wales* than with the belly laughs of *Every Which Way*.

Cowboys and Clowns

Eastwood chose to direct himself in his new project, *Bronco Billy*, and the film represented a return to familiar and tested ground. It was a Western, though a modern one set in the Mid-West states of Oregon and Idaho where Eastwood's appeal had always been high. And he surrounded himself with familiar faces – Sondra Locke, Geoffrey Lewis, Bill McKinney and Sam Bottoms.

Eastwood starred as Bronco Billy himself, the owner of a travelling Wild West show whose performers form a 'family' as bizarre as Josey Wales's, and equally misfitted to society. There is Two Gun Left Le Bow (Bill McKinney), a one-armed former bank teller gaoled for taking his work home with him; Doc Lynch (Scatman Crothers), the ringmaster, once gaoled for practising medicine without a licence; Chief Big Eagle (Dan Vadis), a former armed robber, now secretly a writer, whose 'legendary rattlesnake dance that no white man has ever seen before' invariably ends with his being bitten by his snakes; his wife Running Water (Sierra Pecheur) who is not an Indian; and Lasso Leonard James (Sam Bottoms) who is a Vietnam draft dodger.

Bronco himself is an ex-shoe salesman from New Jersey who only left the city at the age of thirty-one, though he has always wanted to be a cowboy. He, too, is an ex-convict, having served seven years for the attempted murder of his adulterous wife. He shares Philo Beddoe's uncomplicated morality, expressing himself almost exclusively in the clichéd language of the Old West. 'Get out of my truck, you yellow-bellied sidewinders,' he growls when his employees venture to point out that they have not been paid in six months. 'I thought I had the best bunch but I guess I've been dealt a crooked hand.' 'Don't you love the wide open spaces where the deer and the antelope roam,' he comments on a particularly featureless area of the Mid-West. He has a special fondness for children, his 'little pards' or 'buckaroos', to whom he gives solemn warnings about the dangers of 'hard liquor and cigarettes'. A gentle but devastating irony under-mines almost every aspect of his character. Surprising a group of children who are admiring Billy's large red convertible with its pistol-shaped door handles and moose head on the bonnet, he looms out of the sun like a stetsoned parody of Josey Wales. 'Stick 'em up or I'll plug ya!' he demands. The children's alarm turns to awe as they realise who it is.

'Now look,' Billy explains, 'I don't take kindly to kids playing hookey from school. I think every kid in America ought to go to school, at least up to the eighth grade.' The children exchange embarrassed glances. 'We don't go to school today, Bronco Billy,' one replies. 'It's Saturday.' Billy backtracks awkwardly. 'Well, I've been riding late last night. A man's brain gets kind of fuzzy when he's been on the range.'

Billy's own stage act is bedevilled by his inability to find a suitable female assistant, willing to be strapped to a revolving target while Billy bursts the balloons that sur-round her, first using a handgun and finally a throwing knife.

At the beginning of the film Big Eagle's snake dance goes wrong yet again, announced by an off-screen howl – 'I don't know why he can't just do the Great Apache Flaming Arrow Act,' sighs Billy – and an air of comic doom overshadows our first view of the Wild West show in action.

Billy drags his latest, and quaking assis-tant into the tented arena for his 'death-defying Wheel of Fortune Shoot-out'. 'Are those bullets?' she enquires. 'Special buck-shot, doesn't go too far,' Billy explains. 'But don't worry. I never miss.'

The assistant is strapped in place and Billy begins his spiel. 'Miss Mitzi,' he announces, 'would you like a blindfold?' 'No, Bronco Billy,' she replies nervously. 'You're the best shot in the Old West.' 'Very well,' Billy declaims, 'but *I* will wear one.'

Disaster naturally strikes as Billy's knife grazes the assistant's leg, drawing blood. Swift close-ups – of the audience, the show people and Billy's horse – match a gasp, and a whinny, of horror. But, as with Ben Shockley and Philo Beddoe, Billy's appa-rent simplicity has a deeper basis than pure comedy, and this is brought out in his

Eastwood as Bronco Billy McCoy and Sondra Locke as Antoinette Lily (top) *in two scenes from* Bronco Billy, *1980*

relationship with Antoinette Lily (Sondra Locke), a New York heiress whose cynical and sophisticated urban manners are in direct opposition to his own.

Antoinette's path crosses Billy's when she reluctantly marries John Arlington (Geoffrey Lewis) at a small Mid-West town where the show is playing. The marriage is one of convenience since Antoinette has to be married by her thirtieth birthday in order to fulfil the conditions of her inheritance. Spoiled and dictatorial, she makes no bones of her loathing for her inept, fortune-seeking husband – to such an extent that he abandons her at their honeymoon motel.

Left without money, clothes or identification, she is discovered on a garage forecourt by Billy who offers to help in return for her acting as his assistant until he can find a replacement. Their personalities clash immediately. Antoinette refuses Billy's invitation to join him in a duet of 'Bar-room buddies', shoots as accurately as he does, sends up his stage act mercilessly and publicly and dismisses him as 'nothing but an illiterate cowboy'.

She leaves the show as soon as she can only to find that John Arlington has been accused of her murder and is now in gaol. Antoinette's stepmother, Irene (Beverlee McKinsey), who will inherit the family wealth on her stepdaughter's death, has been in no hurry to investigate Antoinette's apparent disappearance. Instead she despatches the family lawyer, Edgar Lipton (William Prince) to offer Arlington half a million dollars if he will plead guilty on the grounds of temporary insanity. Arlington accepts, on the promise that his sentence will not last longer than three years.

Antoinette rejoins the show, pretending

greater compliance to Billy's wishes. As a result she begins to understand that Billy is more than an illiterate cowboy. 'Are you for real?' she asks him, after he has admitted his actual background. 'I'm who I want to be,' he says simply. Later Running Water explains Billy's philosophy more fully. 'Don't you understand what Bronco Billy and the Wild West show are all about?' she asks. 'You can be anything you want. All you've got to do is go out and become it . . . Until you know who you want to be you're never going to get very far.'

But Antoinette's presence seems to bring bad luck. Lasso Leonard is arrested on a drunk and disorderly charge and his desertion is discovered; Billy successfully bribes a corrupt sheriff to obtain his release and suffers intense humiliation in the process. The show tent burns down during a performance and, with no funds left to buy a replacement, the company stage a ludicrously inept attempt at a train robbery; the only occupant of the train to notice them is an excited child who cries 'Cowboys and Indians!' to its slumbering mother who doesn't even open her eyes. Rather appropriately the show's next port of call is a home for the criminally insane – one of numerous institutions where Billy performs his show for free.

Part of the patients' therapy is making American flags and Billy persuades the home's director, Dr Canterbury (Woodrow Parfrey), to stitch together a new tent in return for lessons on the quick draw.

The home makes Lefty nervous. 'Some of these people are just the same as you and I,' chides Doc. 'That ain't saying much,' replies Lefty. But Doc's words prove more accurate than he realises. One of the inmates is John Arlington, sent-

212

enced to life imprisonment despite Edgar Lipton's promises.

Recognising Antoinette, he tells his story to Dr Canterbury who takes him to Billy and Antoinette. 'Whenever a patient of mine has a hallucination,' the doctor explains, 'I try to confront him with the facts of life.' To his surprise Antoinette confirms Arlington's story immediately. Billy is equally surprised; he and Antoinette have just become lovers.

The media descend on the home and Antoinette is whisked back to her penthouse apartment in New York. Lonely and unhappy, she attempts suicide while Billy and his company go into hiding, afraid of a kidnapping charge. At the last minute Running Water telephones Antoinette to tell her Billy needs her desperately. She spits out a mouthful of sleeping tablets and leaves at once.

Meanwhile Billy is staging the Wild West show again. As he goes into his Wheel of Fortune Shoot-Out, Antoinette appears in the new tent, which is made up entirely of hundreds of American flags. Reunited amid thunderous applause, they proceed with Billy's act which concludes with an address by Billy straight on to the camera: 'I've got a special message for you little pardners out there. I want you to finish your oatmeal at breakfast and do as your Ma and Pa tell you because they know best. Don't ever tell a lie and say your prayers at night before you go to bed. And so, as our friends south of the border say, *adios amigos*!'

Bronco Billy is Eastwood's gentlest and funniest film, an updated fairy tale rendered palatable by its total lack of pretension and its style of continuous deflation. Superficially it appears to be a final demolition job on his own screen persona,

but there is solid bedrock beneath the fun. Dreams, its suggests, may be insubstantial and unreliable but they are also part of the great American Dream – the dream that populated the landscape Billy crosses and which his Wild West show celebrates, however ineptly. Billy and his cronies may be naïve and not too bright but their virtues are unquestionable: determination, courage, faith and loyalty.

Billy shocks Antoinette when he describes how he found his former wife in bed with his best friend. 'What did you do to him?' she breathes. 'I shot her,' he replies. '*What?*' she gasps. 'What about him?' 'He was my best friend,' Billy says. Loving someone 'with all my heart . . . sometimes . . . just isn't enough'. But the love that binds Billy's unlikely 'family' together is; it's a unit of survival, not romance. Isolated in her New York penthouse and surrounded by human sharks who mouth as many pious clichés as Billy but who would not dream of being taken seriously, Antoinette finds it easy to choose Billy's wise simplicity.

Bronco Billy delighted the critics who relished its geniality and its subtle humour. Philip French in the *Observer*, keen as ever to make a political allusion, saw it as 'a fable about the troubled America of Carter's Presidency, the need for community, the restoration of self-confidence and affirmative values'.

David Robinson in *The Times* suggested that the gap between Billy's and his young audience's image of himself and the less than glamorous reality was a metaphor for Eastwood's own stardom. And it could well have been. Hollywood stardom in itself is a prime example of the America Dream in action.

At the box office, however, the film's

reception was less than enthusiastic. To an audience expecting the broad humour of *Every Which Way*, *Bronco Billy* was an obvious disappointment.

Superficially Bronco is an idiot and his dimness isn't compensated for by any obvious prowess, like Philo Beddoe's pugilistic skill. When Billy does demonstrate his shooting ability in a situation of genuine danger – two armed robbers walk into the bank where he is cashing a three dollar cheque – the danger is instantly undermined: Billy only draws and fires – to devastating effect – when one of the robbers dashes a young boy's piggy bank to the floor and smashes it; as Billy's bullets send the robber's pistol cartwheeling into the air, the boy mouths a silent 'Wow!'

Eastwood may have intended the film as a reworking of relatively safe material but in the context of his career it bears a closer resemblance to some of his bolder and more creditable experiments. For his next film he really did pick safe ground, or ground that is as safe as any can be in the uncertain world of commercial cinema; it was a sequel to *Every Which Way*, entitled *Any Which Way You Can*.

Plain Values

Eastwood entrusted the direction of his second Philo Beddoe adventure to Buddy Van Horn, another new hand who had nevertheless worked with the star as a second unit director and a stunt coordinator for over fifteen years. The result was a slicker, faster moving film with a lot more emphasis on spectacular stunts, mechanical, human and animal. Stanford Sherman's script broadened the comedy of the original, filled out the characterisation and the background and provided a tighter and more relevant plot. Otherwise the formula was unchanged: burlesque, bouts of action and backing by leading musical talents, like Ray Charles, Fats Domino and Glen Campbell.

The Philo Beddoe of *Any Which Way* is a more sober individual than the rather simple-minded purveyor of comic violence seen in the original. He still purveys violence, and in a comical manner, but it's done with ingenuity and style rather than sheer musclepower, often employing other agencies than his fists. Again the Black Widows are the main recipients. Drawing up next to his truck at a traffic light, in a straight line of bikes that stretches the width of the road, they taunt Philo and Clyde. Philo's response is to order 'Right turn, Clyde', a command, it has been established early on, that results in the orang-utan's bunched fist flying out the right window of the truck. It connects with the chin of the nearest Widow who tumbles sideways into his companion, eventually tumbling every bike like a pack of cards.

Later, rather less credibly, Philo leads the pursuing Widows under the spray arm of a tar-laying truck. When he reaches a dead-end, he turns to find the bikers frozen in threatening attitudes, caked from head to foot in cooling tar. One by one, hissing threats of dire retribution, they topple into the dust. Philo's pugilistic violence is treated more seriously now. He is not just a local bruiser who happens to win all of his fights, but one of the leading lights of an alternative sporting world, whose equally illegal activities include bouts between a rattlesnake and a mongoose. Philo's fame has spread nationwide and the main thrust of the plot concerns a

214

championship to decide the country's fore-most bareknuckle brawler. This boosts the mythic aspect of Eastwood's screen persona. Philo Beddoe is now a sporting anti-hero, a folk hero, like No Name or Josey Wales, who breaks all the rules but still earns the cheers. When the two would-be champions meet in battle it's a contest between equals who respect and like each other, who fully realise the dangers of the sport – Philo's opponent, Jack Wilson (William Smith) has already maimed one opponent and killed another – but who fight out of an almost abstract respect for excellence and the values of their craft, which has nothing to do with monetary reward: the fight, in fact, takes place when all betting is off.

Even the mechanics of boxing are delved into: we see Philo undergoing an appropriately arduous training prog-ramme and gaining some insight into the masochistic dangers of the sport. At the beginning of the film Philo discovers he is beginning to enjoy the pain and decides to give it all up, though, fortunately for the plot, not for long.

All this adds to the weight of Philo's character, without detracting from the comedy, and gives Eastwood rather more to bite on in dramatic terms. After the sour romantic note of *Every Which Way*, of course, he is entitled to be more cautious, but there are no such downbeat notes in the sequel.

After a preliminary bout and Philo's decision to quit, he is reunited with a con-trite Lynne Halsey-Taylor. The reconcilia-tion is effected by Clyde whose role is greatly expanded from the original. Apart from his direction indicator trick, he takes a quiet beer at the Palomino's bar, deters an obstreperous cowboy by casually bend-ing a brass bar rail in half, demolishes two cars, dresses in drag and outflashes a shocked flasher and takes a shower in a bath hat shortly before noisily seducing a female of his species. He also blows expressive raspberries, shares Philo's – and Lynne's – bed, and is saddled with an unexplained and embarrassing penchant for defecating in the front seats of police patrol cars. It's no wonder when the orang-utan fails to carry out a fairly com-plex instruction that an exasperated Philo sighs, 'Clyde, sometimes I think you're not too tightly wrapped.' Compared to the original Clyde, whose performance in retrospect seems almost subdued and smacking of gimicry, this great ape fully justifies Philo's description of him as 'a free person'.

The romance here is not only trans-formed into sweetness and light but merges with the general tone of burlesque by becoming bawdy. In the film's most extraordinary and most grotesque scene, four seductions take place simultaneously at a motel where Philo has taken Lynne. Next door Clyde and his temporary mate, Bonnie – whom Philo has just borrowed from a nearby zoo – engage in energetic loveplay. This is overheard by Philo who imitates Clyde's courtship display by hanging from a light fitting. A middle-aged couple, Luther and Loretta Quince (Logan and Anne Ramsey), who are staying on the other side of Clyde's room also overhear his activities; mistaking them for uninhibited human passion, Luther is inspired to regain some of his marriage's neglected magic, and promptly cricks his back. Meanwhile, an elderly and voyeuristic motel clerk is trying unsuccess-fully to spy on Clyde and Bonnie only to be surprised by an indignant Ma Boggs who is searching for Philo to warn him of impending danger from a group of gangsters. Romance blossoms instantly, shown by the clerk superimposing Ma's face on a swim-suited Bo Derek jogging down the beach in slow motion in *10*. As Clyde somersaults inelegantly across the motel bed into the arms of a demure Bonnie, it is difficult to know who is apeing who.

Romance, however, soon takes on a subsidiary role, as does Sondra Locke, when Lynne is kidnapped by gangsters. Two New York gamblers James Beekman (Harry Guardino) and Patrick Scarfe (Michael Cavanaugh) want Philo to fight Jack Wilson for $25,000 in prize money. At first Philo agrees but after being reunited with Lynne, he is persuaded by her to turn down the fight because of Wilson's violent reputation. The gamblers' response is to have Lynne hidden away until Philo arrives at the fight's venue, the ski resort of Jackson Hole in Wyoming.

Philo, Orville and Clyde head for Wyoming, pursued yet again by the Black Widows who are keen to see their old enemy suffer a defeat. In Jackson, Philo is contacted by Wilson who expresses his dismay that Philo has been blackmailed into fighting. The two brawlers join forces and, with the aid of Clyde and Orville – who suffers a bullet wound in the process – succeed in discovering where Lynne is being held and release her. As a result the fight is off and the gambling and sporting enthusiasts who now crowd the town prepare to go home. But Philo and Wilson decide they must know who is the better fighter for their own satisfaction. They start to fight and their battle takes them the length of the town, drawing huge crowds. En route Philo is saved, unwittingly, by the Black Widows who spot Beekman's gang-

ster friends about to shoot him. Beddoe, they have decided, is the better fighter and they have sold their bikes in order to bet on his victory. As their leader, Cholla (John Quade) says, 'War is war, but *business is business*.'

For a moment it seems that Philo is defeated when Wilson breaks his arm. But Philo refuses to give in and in a last burst of energy concludes the fight single-fistedly by knocking his opponent momentarily unconscious. This final scene takes place in a public park and its entrance appears to be an archway of cattle horns, twisted together to resemble a crown of thorns; appropriately the bloody and half-crippled Philo stumbles through it in pursuit of his climactic victory. Incidental humour from the onlookers surrounds the battle but the battle itself has an epic quality that is pure Eastwood. With his title of bareknuckle champion secure, Philo leaves for home, retirement and domesticity with Lynne and Clyde. Orville – newly promoted to 'hero' by his bullet wound – decides to stay and convalesce in the arms of an admiring nurse, and jubilant Black Widows, newly enriched by their winnings, make peace with their former enemy.

Released in time for Christmas 1980, *Any Which Way You Can* swiftly followed in its predecessor's commercial footsteps, grossing close to $40 million from the USA and Canada alone. By the end of 1981 it had become the year's sixth most successful film, and is currently Eastwood's second highest money earner.

True to his career pattern Eastwood now followed commercial success with experimentation – but experimentation of a new and curious kind. It had two strands, and the first was largely administrative. With *Bronco Billy* Malpaso had

spawned a new company, Robert Daley Productions, which allowed Eastwood's associate to work on projects that did not involve the star. Daley, however, remained as executive producer on *Bronco Billy* and *Any Which Way*, with Fritz Manes promoted from associate to producer proper.

With Eastwood's new project, *Firefox*, scheduled for release in 1982, Daley stepped out, Manes became executive producer and Eastwood himself took on the role of producer for the first time, as well as both directing and starring in the picture. Involved as he always had been in every aspect of commercial film making, the move was a logical one for the star, but it was to place additional burdens of

As American fighter pilot Mitchell Grant in Firefox, *1982*

responsibility on him, the effects of which were to be discernible in the film.

The second strand of experimentation was the *Firefox* story itself. It involved the theft, by an American agent, of a new and secret Soviet warplane, the MIG-31 – codenamed 'Firefox' – which can fly at six times the speed of sound, is invisible to radar and is armed with a comprehensive weapons system controlled by the thought impulses of the pilot. For all its basis on the theft of the real-life Soviet 'Foxbat'

217

warplane and current developments in direct thought control by electronic means, the idea is a science fictional one. Eastwood was well aware that the cinema blockbusters of the last quarter of the seventies – *Star Wars, Close Encounters of the Third Kind, Superman* – were science fiction epics, built around a dazzling array of unprecedented special effects. Throughout his career he had always dabbled with the most successful current genres – 'rogue cop', 'buddy' movie, 'red neck' comedy. There seemed no reason not to do the same again.

But in making that decision he finally tore up one of his cardinal rules, made at the foundation of Malpaso a decade earlier – that no film should cost more than $4 million. Inflation had inevitably undermined that dictum, though *Every Which Way But Loose* had been budgeted at $4 million and *Bronco Billy* at only one million more. The special effects demanded by *Firefox*, however – which included an aerial battle at the climax of the film – rocketed the budget to $18 million, $3 million more than the gross American earnings of *Bronco Billy*. The film had to be a big commercial success simply to cover its costs.

Eastwood also reverted to a pattern which had previously resulted in relatively moderate success – at least in his own terms. *Firefox*, like *The Eiger Sanction*, was based on a best-selling novel of the same name, by British author Craig Thomas. It was a fast-moving and efficient thriller, given substance more by the technical details of the imaginary warplane than its main characters or the authenticity of its Russian setting. But its hero, Mitchell Gant, had a number of correspondences with Eastwood's developing screen per-

sona. He is a brilliant ex-Vietnam fighter pilot who has suffered a severe breakdown as a result of his wartime experiences. Though he has been highly trained both in Russian speaking and in what facts are known of the mysterious Firefox, he is prone to sudden temporary relapses, particularly in moments of tension. He is as deficient mentally as Josey Wales was emotionally and Ben Shockley intellectually. But, like all of them, the privations he undergoes rebuild his character and enable him to carry out heroic deeds.

Eastwood's film version made Gant's traumatic past more specific, and pictorial; recurrent flashbacks establish that he was captured by the Viet Cong and witnessed a napalm attack by helicopter gunship on a young Vietnamese girl. This is a nightmare that comes to him at the beginning of the film when a military helicopter lands near his remote log cabin in Alaska. A quaking Gant is told of the Firefox mission with a gentle reminder that his present retreat is on government land, implying he may lose it if he does not cooperate.

In London he mets Kenneth Aubrey (Freddie Jones), a British intelligence head, who informs him that he will enter Russia disguised as Leon Sprague, an international businessman known by the Russians as a drug smuggler. In Moscow he will be contacted by agents who will take him to the Firefox's secret base. He will be helped inside by key members of the design team – Jewish dissidents who have been supplying the West with details of the new aircraft.

Suitably disguised with spectacles, moustache and greying hair, Gant flies to Moscow. The night of his arrival he takes a stroll along a quiet section of the Moskva

River, fully aware that he is under constant surveillance by the KGB. Three men approach him, Paval Upenskoy (Warren Clarke), the real Sprague and another Russian. To Gant's astonishment, Upenskoy and his companion promptly beat Sprague to death, put Gant's identification papers on the body and toss it into the river.

When the KGB arrive they believe that the Sprague newly arrived in Moscow has been killed by his drug smuggling associates. Meanwhile Upenskoy and Gant escape into the Moscow Metro. Gant learns that he has now taken on the real Sprague's false identity – that of Michael Grant, an American tourist. Accordingly, he sheds his glasses and moustache, but the Metro is now sealed off by police and KGB searching for Sprague's murderers. After a number of close calls, Gant's nerve breaks when he is questioned by a KGB man in a public lavatory. In a blind panic he attacks and strangles the man with a roller towel.

An appalled Upenskoy berates him but the two men succeed in reaching a warehouse where they spend the night. In the morning they leave for the Firefox base in a van driven by Upenskoy. Gant, now dressed as a driver's mate, replaces a man called Glazunov – another associate of Upenskoy's – who spends the day at home.

All Russian security matters concerning the Firefox, meanwhile, are being monitored by Colonel Kontarsky (Kenneth Colley) of the KGB. He knows of the dissidents' espionage and will tolerate it only until the aircraft's first official test flight, due to be witnessed by the Russian premier in the near future. He has also arranged for Upenskoy's van to be followed. When Glazunov is seen to be absent from

it, he has the man arrested at home. Glazunov refuses, or is unable, to reveal the identity of his replacement and dies under torture. Kontarsky decides simply to observe Upenskoy's new companion for the time being.

As night falls, Gant and Upenskoy approach Bilyarsk, the site of the Firefox base, and Gant leaves the van without being detected by the trailing KGB. He is met by Semelovsky (Ronald Lacey), one of the Firefox dissidents who smuggles him into the base. Disguised as a captain in military intelligence, Gant enters the Firefox hanger and waits in the crew quarters for the test pilot, Voskov (Kai Wulff). When Voskov arrives, Gant knocks him unconscious, dons his flying suit and helmet and walks to the plane. Simultaneously, Semelovsky and the dissidents stage a violent diversion, designed to destroy a second and incomplete model of the Firefox. They are shot dead in the process, but Gant reaches the cockpit of the first Firefox and takes off as the Russian premier lands to witness its test flight.

First he flies south to rendezvous with a Russian airliner and thus give the impression that he is heading in that direction. But, once out of sight, he turns north again and aims for the Arctic Circle. After skilfully avoiding the Russian air defence system which is now directed against him, he successfully lands on an ice floe in the Barents Sea where an American nuclear submarine surfaces and refuels him. In the meantime Voskov has recovered and the second Firefox is found to be serviceable. Voskov takes off in pursuit and a dogfight takes place over the Arctic. Gant wins and heads for home.

The formula of a genuinely rather than ironically flawed hero combined with spectacular special effects must have seemed a potent one to Eastwood but in practice it failed to gell. Gant's flaws are all we learn about him, with the occasional exception of his insistence on his flying skill, which is only proven towards the end of the film. Eastwood broke another of his own rules in dispensing with any quintessentially 'Eastwood' moments. Gant is quaking jelly, ferried about helplessly from Alaska to London to Russia, and his sudden transformation into superhero at the controls of a superplane carries neither credibility nor conviction.

This is partly due to the script – Gant's defeat of Voskov is accomplished with such glib expertise that all the violent exertions of the dogfight seem to have been unnecessary. It is partly the difficulty of giving even an understated dramatic performance when encased from head to foot in a flying suit and helmet and sitting in a cramped cockpit. Ironically *Firefox* completes a full circle in Eastwood's film career, right back to his bit part in *Tarantula* when he was a similarly anonymous fighter pilot.

But what is less forgivable is that the simplified outline of Gant's character extends to the rest of the film. No one doubts for a moment that the West is justified in stealing the Firefox. Colonel Kontarsky and his KGB companions are portrayed as stock Nazi-style thugs who could have stepped straight from any clichéd World War Two epic with barely a change of uniform. As the First Secretary (Stefan Schnabel) follows the progress of the stolen Firefox, his mood fluctuates between profound self-satisfaction with the might of the Soviet air defence system to equally intense blame when Gant outsmarts it yet again, with such astonishing rapidity that the scene goes beyond credibility and deliberate comedy.

Only the Bilyarsk dissidents, played by Ronald Lacey and Nigel Hawthorne, give a hint of genuine human tragedy behind the disguises and the feats of derring-do. And Eastwood, too, provides the same glimpses of his old magic, but all too infrequently. Eastwood the producer is apparently a lot less sympathetic to his leading actor than Eastwood the director. The film might be 'only' a thriller, but Eastwood's films have rarely been 'only' one thing; within the limitations of his screen persona he has explored a remarkable range of issues. It seems unlikely that the black-and-white simplicity of *Firefox* – its good Allies versus bad Russians morality – is deliberate, a kind of *Bronco Billy* minus the irony. The very fuzziness of its expression suggests that the actor in his new triple role may simply have overstretched himself.

Even the special effects fail to rescue the end of the film; the Firefox may look sensational on the ground but flying, it begins to resemble a refugee from *Thunderbirds*. While its movements appear authentic against backgrounds of clouds, ocean and ice, actually seeing an advanced jet fighter in continuous action is alien to most audiences and the scenes take on an air of fantasy. It was Eastwood's ill fortune, perhaps, that the British release of the film coincided with the first showing of news film from the Falklands campaign; there jet fighters fought either invisibly or as relatively slow moving dots swooping low across the landscape. The elegant aerobatics of the duelling Firefoxes seem to belong to a different world.

But Eastwood in an action film – however subdued his performance – has a built-in audience appeal. *Firefox* was released in June 1982 and by January had grossed $24 million in the United States and Canada, making it America's eleventh most profitable film of 1982. The high production costs were recovered confortably, if with a comparatively minor net profitability, but Eastwood had kept faith with his fans. He was fifty-two now, still the world's most popular movie star and with a personal fortune so large even he may not be able to calculate it – and despite a divorce settlement with Maggie rumoured to be in the region of £10 million.

Yet with *Firefox* completed, he moved straight onto a new production for release in Christmas 1982. In *Honkytonk Man* he again produced, directed and starred himself. It's a tale appropriate to the times, set in Depression America where Eastwood plays Red Stovall, a drunken, consumptive country and western singer. Given a once in a lifetime opportunity to appear at Nashville's Grand Ole Opry, he sets out on a meandering odyssey, accompanied by his fourteen-year-old nephew, Whit, (actually Eastwood's own son, Kyle), who acts as his driver.

The formula matches several of the films of Eastwood's maturity: the rambling journey in the company of an unconventional partner or family unit, the hero who may not be too aware – intellectually or emotionally – yet who emerges battered but victorious from a period of testing. But there are important variations. *Bronco Billy* and the Beddoe movies were essentially dramatic comedies; *Honkytonk Man* is first and foremost a drama with comic overtones, yet a drama rooted in a tragic reality rather than the overblown fantasy of *The Gauntlet*. It may prove to be East-

wood's boldest experiment yet, not least because it is the first film since *The Beguiled* in which Eastwood actually dies, literally singing his heart out at a first and final recording session.

So far the critical response has been mixed. 'A meandering and downbeat tale where the actor seldom gets to exhibit much of the bravura his fans will long for,' wrote *Variety*. 'A folksy, boring movie that will be a real test of the loyalty of Eastwood's fans,' added the *Motion Picture Product Digest*. *Time*, however – one of the most accurate arbiters of American popular taste – had a very different view. 'Clint Eastwood has fashioned a marvellously unfashionable movie, as quietly insinuating as one of Red's honky-tonk melodies. It is a guileless tribute not only to plain values of plain people in Depression America, but also to the sweet spirit of country-and-western music . . . As both actor and director, Eastwood has never been more laconic than he is in this film . . . It is persistence rather than big talent or bold stroke heroism that *Honkytonk Man* wants to celebrate.'

That persistence and those plain values are what Eastwood has been celebrating with growing vigour from *Josey Wales* onwards. His attempts to mythologise them may lack the violent catharsis of a No Name or a Harry Callahan in explosive action, but they work at a deeper level which is ultimately more relevant and more meaningful to his audience. Such values may indeed be 'marvellously unfashionable' but in a time of confusion and uncertainty they need to be reiterated, and with the kind of dynamism Eastwood uniquely can project.

Where does he go from here? At the age of fifty-three, having achieved an unpre-

cedented degree of commercial and artistic success, he has no obvious need to go anywhere. His niche in cinema history is assured. But Eastwood shows no sign of slackening off or losing any of his enthusiasm for film-making.

For some years now he has hinted that he may give up acting in favour of directing, but his sound commercial instincts have prevented him from denying himself starring roles in his own pictures. His next experiment could well be a film he directs but does not act in; it could equally well be something utterly unexpected. Unpredictability has long been Eastwood's forte. 'Every once in a while,' he has said, 'you've got to just lose your mind, and do something different. Take chances.' He has been taking chances ever since he first climbed on board the plane to Rome, chances few other 'superstars' would contemplate, let alone bring to a successful conclusion. That has been Eastwood's greatest strength in the past, and there is no reason why it should not be so in the future. It seems not at all unlikely that the best of Clinton Eastwood – actor, director, producer – is yet to come.

Eastwood as Red Stovall posing for a family shot in Honkytonk Man, *1983*

223

ACKNOWLEDGEMENTS

To the City and County of San Francisco/Bureau of Records and Statistics.

To CBS-TV, NBC-TV, Associazione Nazionale Industrie Cinematografiche Ed Affini (ANICA), Cinema International Corporation (Netherlands) B.V., City Film Distribution B.V., Metro-Goldwyn-Mayer Inc., Nova Film B.V., Paramount Pictures Corp., Produzioni Europee Associate (PEA), RKO General Pictures, Twentieth Century-Fox Film Corp., United Artists Corp., Universal Pictures, Warner Bros. Inc./Warner Bros. (Holland) B.V., also to Cinema City, Free-lance, Larry Edmunds Bookshop Inc., the Laufer Company, LIFE Magazine, Redwood Empire Association and Vitaprint.

Colour section:

1st page: *Coogan's Bluff* (The Kobal Collection)
2nd page: Off-set during the filming of *Beguiled* (The Kobal Collection)
3rd page: *For a Few Dollars More* (Aquarius)
4th page: *Top:* With Jessica Walter in *Play 'Misty' For Me*. *Bottom:* With Sondra Locke in *Any Which Way You Can*. (Both pictures The Kobal Collection)

To the following individuals:

Susan E. Albrecht
R. B. Bakker
C. G. M. Berendsen
P. C. Boland-van Rhijn
Jack Curtis
Gino De Dominicis
M. Di Gianfrancesco
Florence DiNapoli
Bill Eppridge
Gwen Feldman
Richard O. Fowkes
Nancy Gilliland
Karin Gratz
F. P. Hoogwerf

Bernadette van Hoorn
Saul Jaffe
Harry Klooster
Ida Kolodny
Lee Lankford
Marna Libbey
Git Luboviski
Verna Mitchell
Tom Rathmann
Sheldon H. Sroloff
Julie Stowe
Cheryl Tiegs
Rein van Willigen
Ruth Zitter

224